D1610431

THE ALCHEMIST

Arden Early Modern Drama Guides

Series Editors:
Andrew Hiscock
University of Wales, Bangor, UK and Lisa Hopkins,
Sheffield Hallam University, UK

Arden Early Modern Drama Guides offers practical and accessible introductions to the critical and performative contexts of key Elizabethan and Jacobean plays. Each guide not only introduces the text's critical and performance history but also provides students with an invaluable insight into the landscape of current scholarly research through a keynote essay on the state of the art and newly commissioned essays of fresh research from different critical perspectives.

1 Henry IV edited by Stephen Longstaffe
The Alchemist edited by Erin Julian and Helen Ostovich
Doctor Faustus edited by Sarah Munson Deats
The Duchess of Malfi edited by Christina Luckyj
'Tis Pity She's a Whore edited by Lisa Hopkins
The Jew of Malta edited by Robert A Logan
King Lear edited by Andrew Hiscock and Lisa Hopkins
A Midsummer Nights' Dream edited by Regina Buccola
Richard III edited by Annalise Connolly
Women Beware Women edited by Andrew Hiscock
Volpone edited by Matthew Steggle

THE ALCHEMIST

A Critical Reader

Edited by
Erin Julian and
Helen Ostovich

The Arden Shakespeare

1 3 5 7 9 10 8 6 4 2

First published in 2013 by The Arden Shakespeare

Copyright © Erin Julian, Helen Ostovich and contributors 2013

The Arden Shakespeare is an imprint of Bloomsbury Publishing Plc

The Arden Shakespeare
Bloomsbury publishing Plc
49–51 Bed ford Square
London WC1B 3DP

www.ardenshakespeare.com

Hardback ISBN: 9781441154156
Paperback ISBN: 9781780938295
EPUB ISBN: 9781441176257
EPDF ISBN: 9781441180599

Available in the USA from Bloomsbury Academic & Professional,
175 Fifth Avenue/3rd Floor, New York, NY 10010.

A CIP catalogue record for this book is available from the British Library

This book is produced using paper that is made from wood grown in
managed, sustainable forests. It is natural, renewable and recyclable.
The logging and manufacturing processes conform to the environmental
regulations of the country of origin.

Printed and bound in India

CONTENTS

SERIES INTRODUCTION

The drama of Shakespeare and his contemporaries has remained at the very heart of English curricula internationally and the pedagogic needs surrounding this body of literature have grown increasingly complex as more sophisticated resources become available to scholars, tutors and students. This series aims to offer a clear picture of the critical and performative contexts of a range of chosen texts. In addition, each volume furnishes readers with invaluable insights into the landscape of current scholarly research as well as including new pieces of research by leading critics.

This series is designed to respond to the clearly identified needs of scholars, tutors and students for volumes which will bridge the gap between accounts of previous critical developments and performance history and an acquaintance with new research initiatives related to the chosen plays. Thus, our ambition is to offer innovative and challenging Guides which will provide practical, accessible and thought-provoking analyses of Early Modern Drama. Each volume is organized according to a progressive reading strategy involving introductory discussion, critical review and cutting-edge scholarly debate. It has been an enormous pleasure to work with so many dedicated scholars of Early Modern Drama and we are sure that this series will encourage you to read 400-year-old playtexts with fresh eyes.

Andrew Hiscock and Lisa Hopkins

NOTES ON CONTRIBUTORS

David Bevington is the Phyllis Fay Horton Distinguished Service Professor Emeritus in the Humanities at the University of Chicago. His books include *From 'Mankind' to Marlowe* (1962), *Tudor Drama and Politics* (1968), *Action Is Eloquence* (1985), *Shakespeare: The Seven Ages of Human Experience* (2005), *This Wide and Universal Theater: Shakespeare in Performance, Then and Now* (2007), *Shakespeare's Ideas* (2008) and *Shakespeare and Biography* (2010). *Murder Most Foul: Hamlet through the Ages* (2012). He is the editor of *Medieval Drama* (1975), *The Bantam Shakespeare* and *The Complete Works of Shakespeare*, 6th edition (2008). He is Senior Editor of the Revels Student Editions, the Revels Plays, *The Norton Anthology of Renaissance Drama* and *The Cambridge Edition of the Works of Ben Jonson*.

Bruce Boehrer, Bertram H. Davis Professor of English and Frances Cushing Ervin Professor of English, teaches at Florida State University and has published five single-author books including *The Fury of Men's Gullets: Ben Jonson and the Digestive Canal* (University of Pennsylvania, 1997). His recent scholarship has investigated animals: *Animal Characters: Nonhuman Beings in Early Modern Literature* (University of Pennsylvania Press, 2010), *Parrot Culture* (University of Pennsylvania Press, 2004) and *Shakespeare Among the Animals: Nature and Society in the Drama of Early Modern England* (Palgrave/St. Martins Press, 2002).

Emma Cox is a Lecturer in Drama and Theatre at Royal Holloway, University of London. She has published a number of scholarly essays in two main research areas: Australian and New Zealand performances of Shakespeare's plays, particularly Aboriginal and Maori productions on stage and film; and the representation and participation of asylum seekers in contemporary theatre, film, writing and activism. She is the author of *Theatre & Migration*, forthcoming with Palgrave Macmillan in 2013, and *Across the Borderlines: Cultural Responses to Asylum Seekers in Twenty-First Century Australia*, forthcoming with Anthem Press in 2013. At Royal Holloway she is the Co-ordinator of the Performance and Asylum Transnational Research Network, and the Associate Editor of the British journal *Australian Studies*.

Mark Houlahan is Senior Lecturer in English at the University of Waikato, Hamilton, New Zealand, where he teaches Renaissance literature and critical theory. He has published many essays on Renaissance playwrights, prophets and polemicists, including his chapter deconstructing John Ford in the 2009 Continuum volume on *'Tis Pity She's a Whore* (ed. Lisa Hopkins). He is currently editing, with David Carnegie, an edition of *Twelfth Night* for Broadview and the *Internet Shakespeare Editions* series (www.ise.uvic.ca).

Erin Julian is a doctoral candidate at McMaster University. Her MA thesis was 'Dangerous Boys and City Pleasures: Subversions of Gender and Desire in the Boy Actor's Theatre', McMaster University, 2010. She is now writing her Ph.D. dissertation, 'Laughing Matters: Representations of Sexual Violence in Jacobean and Caroline Comedy'. She has co-written a review essay, 'Seduction and Salvation: Chester 2010 in Review', for *Research Opportunities in Medieval and Renaissance Drama* 49 (2010): 110–27.

Ian McAdam is Professor of English at the University of Lethbridge, and the author of *The Irony of Identity: Self and Imagination in the Drama of Christopher Marlowe* (1999) and *Magic and Masculinity in Early Modern English Drama* (2009). He is currently working on a project titled 'Marlowe, Shakespeare, and the Secular Christ'.

Mathew Martin is Professor of English Language and Literature at Brock University, Canada. Author of *Between Theatre and*

Philosophy: Skepticism in the Major City Comedies of Ben Jonson and Thomas Middleton (2001), he has edited Christopher Marlowe's *Edward the Second* and *The Jew of Malta* for Broadview Press. His current projects include editions of *Doctor Faustus* for Broadview Press and *The Famous Victories of Henry the Fifth* for *Queen's Men Editions*, and a book on psychoanalysis and textual criticism.

Helen Ostovich is Professor of English at McMaster University and Editor of *Early Theatre: A Journal associated with REED*; a Senior Editor for the Revels Plays; General Editor of *Queen's Men's Editions*; and play-editor of six plays by Jonson including *Every Man Out of His Humour* (2001) for the Revels Plays; and *The Magnetic Lady* for *The Cambridge Works of Ben Jonson* (2012). She completed digital editions of *The Late Lancaster Witches* and *A Jovial Crew* for *Richard Brome Online* (2010), and is currently editing *The Ball* for the Oxford Works of James Shirley, as well as *The Merry Wives of Windsor*, Q and F, for *Norton Shakespeare 3*. She has co-edited several volumes of essays, most recently with Holger Syme and Andrew Griffin, *Locating the Queen's Men, 1583–1603: Material Practices and Conditions of Playing* (2009), and with David Klausner and Jessica Dell, *The Chester Cycle in Context, 1555–1575: Religion, Drama, and the Impact of Change* (2012), both for Ashgate.

Julie Sanders is Professor of English Literature and Drama at the University of Nottingham. She has published widely on seventeenth-century literature including Shakespeare, Jonson and Caroline Drama. Her collection of essays, *Ben Jonson in Context* was published by Cambridge University Press in 2010. She has edited Jonson's *The New Inn* for the *Cambridge Works of Ben Jonson* and Brome's *The Northern Lass* and *The Sparagus Garden* for *Richard Brome Online* (2010). Her monograph, *The Cultural Geography of Early Modern Drama, 1620–1650*, was published by Cambridge in 2011. She is currently working with James Loxley on a project around Jonson's 1618 walk to Scotland.

Elizabeth Schafer is Professor of Drama and Theatre Studies at Royal Holloway, University of London. Her publications include *MsDirecting Shakespeare: Women Direct Shakespeare*; the Shakespeare in Production volumes on *The Taming of the Shrew* and *Twelfth Night*; and (co-author) *Ben Jonson and Theatre*. Her *Lilian Baylis: A Biography* was short-listed for the Theatre Book Prize 2006. She edited *The City Wit* for *Richard Brome Online* (2010), and co-edited the anthology *Australian Women's Drama*. She has edited three collections of essays on Australian drama and theatre, and published widely in Australian studies. She is currently writing the Shakespeare in Performance volume on *The Merry Wives of Windsor* for Manchester University Press.

Matthew Steggle is Professor of English at Sheffield Hallam University. His publications include *Wars of the Theatres* (1998), *Richard Brome: Place and Politics on the Caroline Stage* (2004) and *Laughing and Weeping in Early Modern Theatres* (2007). He has edited *The English Moor* for *Richard Brome Online* (2010), and together with Eric Rasmussen, he has co-edited *Cynthia's Revels* for the forthcoming *Cambridge Works of Ben Jonson*. He is editor of the e-journal *Early Modern Literary Studies*, and his current project is a text of *Measure for Measure* for *Norton Shakespeare 3* (Stephen Greenblatt et al., eds).

TIMELINE

423 BC   *The Clouds* by Aristophanes was performed at the Athens Dionysia Theatre, but only came third in competition. Its satire on trendy learning in natural philosophy and other arts inspired Jonson's similar plot in *The Alchemist*, which attacks John Dee and Edward Kelley as models similar to Aristophanes' Socrates.

1294   Death of Roger Bacon, experimental scientist, alchemist, Oxford professor and Franciscan friar: a model for Subtle.

1541   Death of Paracelsus (Philip von Hohenheim), physician and alchemist whose major work, *On the Miners' Sickness and Other Diseases of Miners*, documented the job-related dangers of metalworking. He is a model for Subtle.

1572   Jonson was born on 11 June, sometimes argued as 1573, posthumous son of a Scottish gentleman who lost his estate during Mary I's reign, and became a minister. His mother subsequently married a bricklayer.

1582–9   John Dee, mathematician, astrologer and alchemist, worked with Edward Kelley, alchemist and scryer, with whom he recorded conversations with angels, in their attempts to locate and produce the philosopher's stone. Dee and Kelley are models for Subtle and Face.

1588   Robert Greene's *Friar Bacon and Friar Bungay* was probably performed early in the year sometime before Richard Tarlton died on 3 September; the role of Miles was written for him.

1589   After leaving Westminster School, where he had studied under William Camden, who remained a scholarly influence and friend, Jonson was apprenticed to a bricklayer.

| 1591–2 | Jonson served as a soldier in the Netherlands, where he killed an enemy in single combat. |

1593   Jonson sought work in the theatre as actor and as writer.

1594   On 14 November, Jonson married Anne Lewis, whom he described later as 'a shrew yet honest'.

1597   Jonson's earliest surviving play, *The Case Is Altered*, was performed by Pembroke's Men.

Jonson collaborated with Thomas Nashe on *The Isle of Dogs*, also for Pembroke's Men, at the Swan Theatre. But the play caused an outcry and was destroyed. Nashe fled to Great Yarmouth; Jonson was arrested with two actors, charged 15 August in Greenwich, and released from prison 2 October. Pembroke's Men never recovered from this incident.

1597/8 Edward Kelley, alchemist, died as a result of injuries when he tried to escape from Emperor Rodolph's castle outside of Prague, where he had been imprisoned for failing to produce gold from base metals.

1597–9 Jonson worked on plays (no longer extant) for Henslowe, often in collaboration with Dekker, Chettle, Marston, or others.

1598   Autumn saw Jonson's first success: *Every Man in His Humour* was performed by the Lord Chamberlain's Men at the Curtain Theatre in Shoreditch.

On 22 September, Jonson was charged with manslaughter, after killing a fellow-actor Gabriel Spencer in a duel, but escaped hanging and was released on his plea of benefit of clergy. His goods were confiscated, and his thumb branded with T (for Tyburn). While in prison, he converted to Roman Catholicism under the auspices of Father Thomas Wright, and remained in that faith until 1610.

1599   In November, *Every Man Out of His Humour*, performed by the Lord Chamberlain's Men at the new Globe Theatre, started the trend for comical satire and city comedy, modes which dominated the stage for the next century.

1600 *Every Man Out of His Humour* became a best-seller, selling
      out three printings within approximately eight months.

  Cynthia's Revels was performed by the Children of the Queen's
Revels at Blackfriars.

1601 The Children of the Queen's Chapel performed *Poetaster* at
      Blackfriars. This play satirizes John Marston and Thomas
      Dekker inspiring what was called 'the war of the theatres'.

  Jonson's daughter Mary died, probably of plague.

1603 *Sejanus His Fall* was another Lord Chamberlain's play at
      the Globe, probably performed in May. Jonson was charged
      with popery and treason, and questioned by the Privy
      Council. His collaborator may have been George Chapman,
      but Jonson rewrote the play on his own before printing it in
      1605.

  Jonson's son Benjamin died of plague.

  The Entertainment at Althorpe (June) began Jonson's long career
at court writing entertainments and masques.

1604 Christopher Marlowe's play, *The Tragicall History of the
      Life and Death of Doctor Faustus*, was first published after at
      least a dozen years of stage success. Faustus is a dark model
      for Subtle, and Mephistopheles for Face.

1605 *The Masque of Blackness* (6 January) began Jonson's asso-
      ciation with Queen Anne, who commissioned two more
      masques for her ladies (*Masque of Beauty*, 10 January 1608,
      and *Masque of Queens*, 2 February 1609). It also began his
      acrimonious working relationship with the designer Inigo
      Jones.

  Eastward Ho!, the seamless collaboration by Jonson, Marston
and Chapman, was performed in the summer by the Children of
the Queen's Revels at Blackfriars. The play names its characters
after the components in the process of alchemical purification
described in *The Alchemist*. Jonson and Chapman were imprisoned for anti-Scots satire (Marston fled), but were released without further punishment in early October.

  Jonson may have been involved in spying related to the
Gunpowder Plot (5 November).

1606   *Volpone* was performed by the King's Men at the Globe,
          and at Oxford and Cambridge within the year.
1608/9   John Dee died without having his day in court to disprove
          charges that he was a magician who talked to spirits.
1609   *Epicene* was performed by the Children of the Queen's
          Revels at Whitefriars in December. Jonson was again
          questioned owing to a complaint by the King's cousin,
          Lady Arbella Stuart.
1610   *The Alchemist* was intended for performance by the King's
          Men at Blackfriars, probably in late spring, but it may have
          been staged first in Oxford by late summer instead, when
          London theatres were closed because of plague.

On 14 May, Henri IV of France was assassinated in Paris, arous-
ing fears of extremist anti-Catholic action in England. Jonson
returned to the Church of England.

1611   *Cataline His Conspiracy*, performed by the King's Men
          at the Globe, failed on stage, but was praised later as a
          printed text.

Shakespeare's *The Tempest* was first performed on 1 November
at Whitehall for King James and his court. Prospero is loosely
based on Bacon and other natural philosophers, and is possibly a
response to Subtle.

1612   *The Alchemist* was published in quarto.
1612–13   Jonson travelled in France as tutor for Sir Walter
          Ralegh's son.
1614   *Bartholomew Fair* opened at the Hope Theatre, also a
          bear-baiting pit, performed by the combined company,
          Lady Elizabeth's Men.
1615   *Mercury Vindicated from the Alchemists at Court* (6 and
          8 January) pleased the court, perhaps recalling the suc-
          cess of *The Alchemist*.
1616   Jonson's first folio of his *Works* coincided with
          Shakespeare's death that same year, printing nine plays
          (including *The Alchemist*) and two collections of poetry,
          Epigrams and *The Forest*. Because plays were consid-
          ered ephemeral trifles, Jonson had to endure some

chaffing on turning 'plays' into 'works', which seemed like a contradiction in terms. Jonson received a royal pension as de facto laureate.

The Devil Is an Ass was performed by the King's Men at the Globe.

1618 Jonson walked to Scotland, where he was given the freedom of the city of Edinburgh, and visited poet William Drummond of Hawthornden, who recorded their conversations.

1619 Jonson was officially inducted as MA of Oxford.

1621 *The Gypsies Metamorphosed* (3 and 5 August; early September), arguably Jonson's most popular, certainly his most satirical, masque, depended on fast talk, fancy footwork and sleight of hand, like *The Alchemist*.

1623 A fire in Jonson's lodgings destroyed his library and current work. He wrote 'An Execration upon Vulcan' to mark his losses. He also formalized 'the Tribe of Ben' that met regularly at the Apollo Room in the Devil and St Dunstan Tavern near Temple Bar.

1626 *The Staple of News* was performed by the King's Men.

1628 George Villiers, Duke of Buckingham, Charles I's closest adviser, was assassinated on 23 August. Jonson was again questioned by the Privy Council about remarks he was alleged to have made in support of the assassin. Buckingham and family were the satirical targets of *Gypsies*.

1629 Jonson was paralyzed by a stroke.

The New Inn was performed by the King's Men, and was not well received. Jonson wrote 'An Ode to Himself' about the audience's insensitivity.

1631 Final bitter breakdown of the artistic relationship between Jonson and Inigo Jones over masque presentation at court, occasioned by Jonson's last two court masques, *Love's Triumph through Callipolis* (9 January) and *Chloridia* (22 February). Both masques suggest guidance from Henrietta Maria (as had been the case with her mother-in-law's Jacobean masques).

1632	*The Magnetic Lady* was performed by the King's Men. It was heckled by some of Jonson's enemies, including Nathaniel Butter, Alexander Gill and Inigo Jones.
1633	*The Tale of a Tub*, performed by Queen Henrietta's Men, included a satire on Inigo Jones.
1634	*Love's Welcome at Bolsover* (30 July), written for William Cavendish, Duke of Newcastle, Jonson's last and arguably most loyal patron, whose own plays show him to be a 'son of Ben'.
1637	Jonson died in Westminster, 6 August, and was buried in Westminster Abbey. His incomplete works included *The Sad Shepherd* and *Mortimer His Fall*.
1640	The second folio of Jonson's *Works* was published in two volumes by Sir Kenelm Digby.
1667	John Dryden published his *Essay upon Dramatic Poesy*, in which he argues that Shakespeare (the poet of 'Nature') is superior, although Jonson (the poet of 'Art and Judgement') wrote two perfect plays, *Epicene* (a play much imitated by Restoration playwrights) and *The Alchemist*.
1668–82	John Dryden and Thomas Shadwell have their own war of the theatres, debating the relative merits of Shakespeare and Jonson, and then moved on to personal squabbles. Dryden won the debate with *MacFlecknoe* (1682), itself a Jonsonian satire, by placing Shadwell not as a son of Ben, but as a son of Richard Flecknoe, the King of Dullness.
1676	Shadwell's *The Virtuoso* (Dorset Garden Theatre) attacks popular enthusiasm for the new 'science', in the humours style of Jonson, very loosely picking up on dupes and ideas in *The Alchemist*.
1692	The third folio of Jonson's *Works* was published, including a third volume containing previously omitted works.
1710	For the revival of *The Alchemist* at the Queen's Theatre, London, on 14 January, an anonymous composer

pirated and adapted George Frideric Handel's overture to *Roderigo* to create the incidental music (now listed in *Händel-Werke-Verzeichnis* as HWV 43).

1743   David Garrick revived interest in Ben Jonson with his production of *The Alchemist*, in which Garrick played Drugger (as Colley Cibber had done earlier in the century). He first played the role in Dublin, but repeated it frequently in London.

1756   Peter Whalley edited *The Works of Ben Jonson* in seven volumes, including annotations and commentary.

1770   Samuel Foote wrote a farce, *Drugger's Jubilee*, inspired by Garrick's stage practice. Francis Gentleman's *The Tobacconist* similarly follows Garrick.

1777   David Garrick published his adaptation, *The Alchymist*.

1816   William Gifford published a new edition of *The Works of Ben Jonson*, 9 volumes, along with the biographical essay 'Memoirs of Ben Jonson', defending Jonson from his eighteenth-century detractors.

1899   William Poel revived *The Alchemist* in an Elizabethan Stage Society production.

1932   Ralph Richardson plays Face in Malvern, Worcestershire.

1947   The Old Vic production had Ralph Richardson as Face and Alec Guinness as Drugger.

1962   The Old Vic mounted another production starring Leo McKern as Subtle.

1969   *The Alchemist*, directed by Jean Gascon, was performed at the Stratford Ontario Shakespeare Festival.

1977   Trevor Nunn directed the RSC production with Ian McKellen as Face, using a script modernized by Peter Barnes.

1987   Gregory Hersov produced *The Alchemist* for the Manchester Royal Exchange.

1991   Sam Mendes directed *The Alchemist* for the Royal Shakespeare Company, Stratford-upon-Avon.

1996   Neil Armfield directed *The Alchemist* for Belvoir St Theatre, Sydney.

1997   *Shooting Fish*, a film loosely based on *The Alchemist*,
        directed by Stefan Schwartz, starring Dan Futterman,
        Stuart Townsend and Kate Beckinsale, was a con-man
        romance whose best scam involved an all-knowing com-
        puter named Jonson.

1999   *The Alchemist* was revived and collapsed under the poor
        direction of Douglas Campbell at the Stratford Ontario
        Shakespeare Festival.

2000   Barry Edelstein directed a modernized *Alchemist* in New York.

2009   John Bell toured *The Alchemist* across Australia.

Introduction

ERIN JULIAN AND HELEN OSTOVICH

He can set horoscopes, but trusts not in them. He, with the consent of a friend, cozened a lady with whom he had made an appointment to meet an old astrologer in the suburbs, which she kept; and it was himself disguised in a long gown and a white beard at the light of dim-burning candle, up in a little cabinet reached unto by a ladder.[1]

Jonson's prank, a story he told on himself when visiting William Drummond of Hawthornden in 1618, indicates his scepticism about some branches of early modern science and his enjoyment of its concepts as the basis for comedy, especially the kind of 'comedy of affliction' he wrote about in *Epicene* and subsequently in *The Alchemist*. All the elements of Jonsonian comedy are here: the joke of the disguise, shared tricksterism with a collaborating 'friend', the dupe 'a lady', the place secret, dark, and hard to approach, and the mirth reserved for backstage, offstage or subsequent extratheatrical retelling. The 'old astrologer' tale resonates not only with all the visitors to the house in Blackfriars, seduced and deceived by Subtle, Face and Doll, but also with similar dupes that congregate in Jonson's plays. Truewit, for example, tells a story in *Epicene* of the lady, trapped in her boudoir, forced by politeness to receive the morning visit of Truewit and another 'rude fellow' before she was properly dressed:

TRUEWIT	. . . the poor madam, for haste, and troubled, snatched at her peruke to cover her baldness and put it on the wrong way.
CLERIMONT	Oh, prodigy!

TRUEWIT	And the unconscionable knave held her in compliment an hour, with that reversed face, when I still looked when she should talk from the tother side.
CLERIMONT	Why, thou shouldst ha' relieved her.
TRUEWIT	No, faith, I let her alone, as we'll let this argument, if you please.

$$(1.1.105–10)^2$$

Although Truewit enjoys this lady's distress, he does not particularly enjoy being 'lurched . . . of the garland' (5.4.182–3) when he finds out that Dauphine has tricked his friends as well as his victims. If the gullible cannot see through the entrapment, or read the situation accurately, Jonson insists, they have to suffer the consequences. In *Epicene*, the joke is about the constructedness of social and personal display, about gender, about abused hospitality, about the refusal to end extreme discomfort or discomfiture for fear of gossip, more humiliation, more confusion – losing the game, whatever that game is, even when the dupes do not know they are playing in the first place. And the laughter the game provokes is the malicious pleasure of observing the downfall of another, the pleasure of being the audience to a ludicrous situation, and not the victim. Perhaps it is the laughter of the lucky escape – like Face's smirk at the end of *The Alchemist*.

For Jonson, alchemy is an elaborate joke that works on several levels, from the simple superstitious belief in astrology to far more complex systems of faith in religion or science. He worked out a system of applying the alchemical formula to character when he was writing *Eastward Ho!* with Marston and Chapman. In that play, Touchstone is both a bully and a dupe, but he is also the only way to test for purity in the career progress of Golding, the successful apprentice who marries the boss's daughter and becomes an alderman of the city, and Quicksilver, the mercurial ex-apprentice who finds a way out of what might have been a desperate situation. In *The Alchemist*, the elements in the alchemical process intertwine with the 'venter tripartite' – sulphurous Subtle, salty Face and mercurial Doll – with delusions of false gold, criminal business like coining or counterfeiting, political aspirations of rebellious power overthrowing the state, and duplicitous rhetoric in commercial, religious and alchemical cant. All ideas, hopes and dreams are open to prostitution, reducing the potential for perfection – Subtle points out that 'lead and other metals, | . . . would be gold if they had time' (2.3.135–6) – to the base mettle that is humanity.

Jonson's fascination with alchemy spans most of his career. He frequently refers to alchemists and astrologers like Paracelsus, Robert Fludd and John Dee (see the 'mystic character' of Drugger's sign in *The Alchemist*, 2.6.15–25), and their goal of achieving the quintessence of life, the *magnum opus*, 'great work', or philosopher's stone. Volpone woos Celia by claiming she has transformed him with her metaphorical/sexual elixir:

> Why art thou mazed to see me thus revived?
> Rather applaud thy beauty's miracle;
> 'Tis thy great work, that hath, not now alone
> But sundry times, raised me in several shapes.
>
> (3.7.145–8)[3]

The sexual is never far from the scientific in Jonson's usage; the 'stone' may empower a wealth of understanding and achievement, but it is also slang for 'testicle', and being 'raised' puns on penile erection. The alchemical tricks in con-games echo as farts in the reduction of the metaphysical to the physical, particularly in 'On the Famous Voyage' in which 'Poor Mercury', once a god, now operates only as a cure for syphilis:

>   crying out on Paracelsus,
> And all his followers, that had so abused him:
> And in so shitten sort so long had used him:
> For (where he was the god of eloquence

And subtlety of metals) they dispense
His spirits now in pills, and eke in potions,
Suppositories, cataplasms, and lotions.

(96–102)[4]

Similarly, in *Mercury Vindicated from the Alchemists at Court*, a masque recalling the success of *The Alchemist*, Mercury complains of the torture of laboratory experiments in which

I am their crude and their sublimate, their precipitate and their unctuous, their male and their female, sometimes their hermaphrodite; what they list to style me.

(39–40)[5]

He also cites many of the 'vexations' of metals Face recites after 2.5.20 as part of his catechism of alchemical procedures. The flasks used in these experiments illustrate the male and the female in the marriage of ingredients: copulating figures representing Sol [Sun] and Luna [Moon], the male and female principles, sulphur and mercury, as they heat and cool, ultimately producing that desired fifth element of the perfect profit. So, in *The Alchemist*, alongside the laboratory, Doll runs her brothel, heating and cooling her customers to produce gold, and demonstrates the dangers of alchemical study with her mad rabbinical lady, spouting zealous puritan polemic as the verbal equivalent to the act 4 explosion of potions. As Jonson wrote later in 'An Execration upon Vulcan', one of the dangers of playing with fire and mercury is insanity – on occasion suspiciously Subtle's involuntary state as the mad scientist:

Some alchemist there may be yet, or odd
Squire of the squibs, against the pageant day,
May to thy name a *Vulcanale* say,
And for it lose his eyes with gunpowder,
As th'other may his brains with quicksilver.

(43.118–22)[6]

Doll's mad act certainly impressed the audience of her day, enough that in 1617 Sir Edward Coke accused his estranged wife, the former Lady Hatton, of being a lady alchemist who transformed his gold and silver household items, in a kind of reverse alchemy, into base metal replacements. Coke's charge (of theft, not of science) redefines the 'venture tripartite' as a criminal scheme devised by his wife, her lawyer and her friends. She wrote to the lords of the council in July 1617:

> May it please your lordships to excuse these lines to which I am compelled by the unworthy defamation Sir Edward Coke hath cast upon me publicly at the board, for I am informed he hath accused me to have embezzled all his gilt and silver plate and vessels (he having little in any house of mine, but that his marriage with me brought him), and instead thereof I have foisted in alchemy of the same suit, fashion, and arms, with this illusion to have cheated him of the other. Hereupon he threatens Master Attorney and other my friends who have covenanted (by order from this honourable board) to in [i.e. sequester] all such goods, as he wanting, by the inventory annexed to that deed by late Sir William Hatton, or Chancellor Hatton deceased, to sue them and thereby recover many thousands from them, if the covenant by them undertaken be not observed.[7]

Unlike the lady in Jonson's tale of the 'old astrologer' with which this introduction began, Lady Hatton refused to be trapped by her predicament, rejected the disguise of the lady alchemist and the accusation of illicit partnerships in crime, calling on the law to support her evidence of victimization and intimidation. But the anecdote illustrates the community's alertness to alchemy games, just as the wise were equally alert to 'Fairy Queen' games, such as we see in *The Alchemist* 3.5 and 5.4. This scam had real-life equivalents in the tricksterism of Judith Philips, as reported in *The Brideling, Sadling and Ryding, of a Rich Churle in Hampshire, by the Subtill Practise of One Judeth Philips, a Professed Cunning*

Woman, or Fortune Teller (London, 1595);[8] later in the similar case of Sir Anthony Ashley and his brother, sued in Chancery in 1609 for fleecing Thomas Rogers, who believed he was betrothed to the Fairy Queen; and subsequently in the case of Alice and John West, convicted in 1613 for posing as the King and Queen of Fairies in order to dupe clients who paid for access to fairy gold. Although the final scene of *The Merry Wives of Windsor* might seem to have provoked another Fairy Queen display by the Lord Chamberlain's Men, the company that performed both plays, in fact the law courts were the better source. Since many of Jonson's friends were members of the Inns of Court, that source is entirely reasonable.

Why a new book on *The Alchemist*?

The chapters in this collection attempt to guide readers through the reception history of Jonson's play, both critically and theatrically. In our rapidly changing world, the drama that still entices us or makes us laugh, no matter what its age, deserves new approaches to understanding why it still works. For that reason, we rely on the new *Cambridge Works of Ben Jonson* as our primary source for up-to-date modern texts.

In the first chapter, assessing the critical backstory of Jonson criticism from the seventeenth century to the year 2000, David Bevington points out how this play, despite its structural perfection, worried, even alarmed, audiences who could not come to grips with its apparent cynicism regarding the immorality to which even the best of us will sink. Why does Lovewit profit from his servant's crimes? Why does Dame Pliant reject marriage with Surly, her rescuer? And why does Surly want to be a truth-teller in a world that punishes him for not lying? Even Jonson's admirers, aside from the sons of Ben, tend to be detractors, dismissing his wit as 'art', uncomfortable with his learning and squeamish about his judgements. Fear of Jonson's challenges, despite his supremacy as the most influential playwright of the seventeenth century, probably led to the 'polarity' Bevington discusses, a relieved preference by the eighteenth century for Shakespeare's emotionally driven drama, as though sentiment, sensation or passionate feeling were the critical benchmark for a writer. Such a rationale does little for the stature of either poet. By the end of the eighteenth century, especially after the death of Garrick, the last of the great actors (including Richard Burbage, Joseph Taylor and Robert Armin) who made *The Alchemist* a memorable and hilarious experience, the play stayed off the boards until 1899. Bevington's narrative of the success, failure and new modern success of the play covers early theatre history, adaptations, editions (Herford, Simpson, Greg, Bowers and many other editors rethinking bibliography) and critical changes, whether based on character, structure, satire, historicism, cultural materialism, source studies (including alchemy and its practitioners), poetics, psychoanalytical and biographical readings, principles of Greek and Roman comedy or medieval moralities, imagery of all varieties. As a result, Jonson emerges as, in Bevington's words, 'a profoundly ambivalent figure' (31).

The last 30 years of critical approaches have moved closer to restoring Jonson to his primary place in the history of drama, although still not according him bard-like status. Bevington singles out Jonas Barish on prose comedy, Thomas Greene on the 'centered self', Michael Flachmann and Alvin Kernan on satire and alchemical experiment governing the play, Richard Levin on irony, Donald Gertmanian and Ian Donaldson on redefinitions of comedy, Anne Barton on rejection of moralistic readings, and finally Leah Marcus and Katharine Eisaman Maus on revisionist editorial and post-modern theories. New interpretations of Jonson's women, whether from feminist, historicist, geographical, cultural or pedagogical theories, have been blasting away at his so-called misogyny and preparing the way for more thoughtful treatments of gender in recent evaluations.

Our second chapter gives insight into the theatre history of *The Alchemist*. Elizabeth Schafer and Emma Cox follow up Bevington's brief comments on early staging with very specific discussion of performances that changed the way we read the play. Schafer and Cox describe this 'farce-based comedy' (43) as a 'dazzling showcase for theatrical virtuosity' (43), including stage business based on 'voice, accent, pacing and energy' (44). Beginning with the theatre history written by Robert Noyes in 1935, with his detail on eighteenth-century productions and spin-offs, Schafer and Cox move forward to Ejner Jensen's work on productions between 1899 and 1972, and Lois Potter's discussion of the RSC and the Swan Theatre in Stratford-upon-Avon as allowing for more actorly close focus on Jonson's original stage directions in the 1612 quarto and 1616 folio printings. The actual printing style, with its copious use of dashes for pauses and interruptions, or parentheses for asides and digressions, offers tools to support readers and actors who work out the action and delivery for the stage. Jonson's stage directions themselves, in the quarto and more densely in the folio, suggest the playwright's attempt to control 'the play's theatrical afterlives' for future readers, performers and audiences. Schafer and Cox selected six runs in the play's theatre history that illustrate *The Alchemist*'s individuality as a city comedy, its characters as original takes on comic types and its particular challenges as metatheatre. They begin with David Garrick's adaptation in the mid-eighteenth century, with Drugger as the star turn, and then leap into 40 years of productions in Stratford, Ontario (Jean Gascon, 1969), Manchester (Gregory Hersov, 1987), Stratford-upon-Avon (Sam Mendes, 1991), Sydney (Neil Armfield, 1996) and the more recent Australian touring production (John Bell, 2009).

Gascon's production was notable for its speed of delivery and smoky visual gags, including a well-endowed Doll, with perhaps too much Molière for a Jonson play. Hersov's, on the other hand, began in Manchester and toured in the North, and the attempt to stage London in the round took on different, even negative, resonances for the audiences. If Gascon's production seemed on the verge of FLQ violence amid the flimflam,[9] Herzov's seemed to demonstrate the egotistic, offensively yuppie lust and greed of Thatcherism, even though the costuming was Elizabethan. Mendes's RSC production celebrated Doll's 'threatening presence' (58) by giving her stage space to eavesdrop and oversee, even when she had no lines, empowered as much by transhistorical costumes, set and props. Like Mendes's cultivation of timelessness, Neil Armfield's Sydney production played with a double sense of space and place, but unlike either Mendes or Hersov in dealing with location, Armfield allowed Sydney to upstage London as the Australian idea of the big crime-laden city. Indeed, the Australianization of Jonson's play embraced the convict origins of the 'Walzing Matilda' nation: Subtle, Doll and Face were recognizable second-class citizens in a way that Jonson did not envision but that captured the energy of the play. Finally, John Bell's 2009 *Alchemist* began in Brisbane, before touring to Sydney, Canberra and Perth, a coast-to-coast theatrical adventure that did not allow for a single city to stand in for London. Instead, the target was globalized world crime dependent on e-mail and patterns of the modern culture of consumption. Schafer and Cox present all of these productions with copious detail and an eye not just on major innovations that import meaning for local audiences, but also on the little bits of staging that can make clear to any reader–observer–interpreter just how flexible and inclusive Jonson's script can be.

Questions about Jonson's moral ambivalence and *The Alchemist*'s status as a metatheatrical city comedy also emerge among the principal topics of discussion that the authors of the 'New Directions' chapters take up, in ways that are both innovative and yet historically rooted, as Chapters 1 and 2 suggest, in a long tradition of critical and performance studies on *The Alchemist*. The centrality of the space and place of the city in Jonson's ouevre, the theatre's position within this developing urban space, the roguery that results when unscrupulous individuals take advantage of the desperate victims of urban overcrowding (and those particularly susceptible to theatre), and the possibilities that theatre and roguery open up for women in a highly regulated patriarchal space – as well as the status of alchemy in early modern England – are the questions that continue to preoccupy recent (2000–present) criticism of Jonson's play, as Matthew Steggle outlines in his chapter on 'The State of the Art' (Chapter 3). Steggle's discussion of the past 12 years of work on *The Alchemist* encompasses recent editorial interventions in the play (culminating in Peter Holland and

William Sherman's edition in the *Cambridge Works of Ben Jonson*), as well as data examining the effects of internet publication on the recirculation of public domain editions of the play. His chapter also begins a dialogue between recent critical articles discussing space and place, time, the historical status of the Blackfriars theatre in 1610, early modern debates on gender, histories of science and economics, the play's take on performance, and other approaches. Steggle suggests paired readings and useful connections between critics, focusing particularly on articles published recently and simultaneously and which consequently have not yet had the chance to be read together; among these pairings are Melissa Aaron's 2006 work on the ownership of the Blackfriars theatre in 1610 and Anthony Ouellette's 2005 work on the movement of the King's Men into the Blackfriars district and the city of London proper, and their attempts to repackage theatre for elite audiences and 'honoured "guests"' rather than 'consumers' (85).

Both of these articles indicate that theatre was becoming an increasingly permanent institution in early modern London and (despite attempts to style itself as elite entertainment) was vital in shaping the consumer habits of London's residents. Mathew Martin's chapter, 'Space, Plague and Satire in *The Alchemist*' (Chapter 4), compellingly examines theatre's ability to permanently indoctrinate its audiences in disruptive plague-time practices. Martin argues that the play's ending attempts to regulate wild and apocalyptic desires, insisting that 'a house in Blackfriars is a house in Blackfriars (and all the places it is not are to vanish like smoke at the play's end)' (105); in the real London outside the play, however, the destablizing forces of recurring plague continually imposed a carnival rule upon the city that – along with spatial structures designed to regulate and contain disorder: the '[p]oor houses, playhouses, bawdy-houses, madhouses, hospitals and houses of correction' within the city (107), and the liberties without – become a more or less permanent feature. And the play registers these permanencies. Not only rogues and dupes, but also regulatory and disruptive anti-patriarchal forces compete in *The Alchemist*. Whereas regulatory forces constantly threaten all characters (including the rogues), all characters (especially the rogues) are able to retaliate by subverting these forces to unscrupulous ends. Lovewit's marriage may restore patriarchal regulation, but ultimately, 'The rogues' alchemical con-game . . . disciplines the clients' bodies and their desires to function within the anti-patriarchal, consumer economy incubated in the plague-time space of the house in Blackfriars' (124): Drugger's rearranged shop continues to operate, and Mammon, Kastril and Dapper continue to harbour fantasies of excessive consumption.

Martin registers a number of critical problems which Ian McAdam and Julie Sanders, Bruce Boehrer, and Mark Houlahan also take up in their chapters following (Chapters 5–7), including the idea that London's inhabitants struggled to come to grips with new ways of perceiving and regulating an urban space with a steadily increasing population, theatre's position in this space, the way Jonson's theatre mirrors, encourages or condemns the consumption and waste that go along with living in an overcrowded space, and the ways that London's inhabitants could take advantage of overcrowding and new consumer practices in order to thwart patriarchal regulation.

In their co-written chapter on 'Staging Gender' (Chapter 5), Ian McAdam and Julie Sanders take on the old argument about Jonson's misogyny. McAdam takes up the argument by appraising the men's attitudes towards women in the play; he observes that the male characters divide along the lines of those who reduce Doll and other women to sexual objects (Face, Lovewit) and those who can 'imagine greater (social) possibilities' (132) for Doll – and for themselves! Men like Subtle and even Mammon are revolutionary fighters against a more conservative masculinity. But Subtle is truly radical, teaming up with the female Doll (another possessor of a sophisticated interiority) in order to realize his own social potential. McAdam ultimately argues that the play forecloses its radical gender possibilities in the conservative marriage of Lovewit and Pliant in the final act, but the beginning of a challenge in gender relationships has emerged, and later drama will take this challenge further. Julie Sanders continues the discussion with a direct look at female roles in the play. Sanders begins 'Performing Women in *The Alchemist*' by citing actresses' complaints about the dearth of lines Jonson assigns his female characters. But line distribution 'can . . . be misleading' (141), and Sanders provides a careful reading of the sixth neighbour's words in 5.1 to note that, even when absent, women's authority haunts Jonson's play. Sanders focuses most of her argument on the role of Doll Common, however, suggesting that it may be more even-handed to read her as 'a feminized version of the Plautine witty servant' (146) and a key member of the acting troupe that is the venture tripartite – rather than a potential sexual prize for the play's men. As McAdam admits that the play put limits on its challenges to conservative gender relationships, Sanders concludes that the play restrains its full appreciation for Doll's wit as a theatrical performer; Doll's cleverness nonetheless suggests a challenge to the idea that Jonson wrote flat and limited female characters, and also reveals that Jonson himself may have had 'considerable empathy for the female condition' (149) and the ways that women's potential was limited by social roles and regulations.

Bruce Boehrer's 'The Alchemist and the Lower Bodily Stratum', like Martin's and McAdam and Sanders's chapters (Chapters 4 and 5), argues that Jonson's London is a city at the crux of change. *The Alchemist* exhibits for us a city whose inhabitants might substantially reshape their practices and their relationships both with the city and with one another. London, however, may not be developing into a healthy space. After considering the 'merits and demerits' of critical explanations for Jonson's fascination with 'excrementality' (160), Boehrer posits that 'we might credit him with a mode of proto-ecological awareness' (170) – a consequence of living, and writing in and about a city that was both 'rich in shit, but also . . . rich, pure and simple' (165). London's rapid population growth and development were the causes for both fortunes: a city with economic and population resources is one that can develop and improve in infrastructural and social ways, but always at an environmental and a human cost. In Boehrer's words, 'the filth we produce in service of our dreams generally endures longer than the dreams themselves' (170). Jonson's rogues might make a hilarious living from selling shit for gold (and even Mammon thinks he can change the world with his gold made out of the base materials of the world), but ultimately none can escape the stench of excrement that pervades the house in Blackfriars and London in general.

In the preceding 'New Directions' chapters, alchemy functions symbolically, as an example of subversive anti-patriarchal consumption, as a pattern of extremist (Anabaptist) thinking, and as a metaphor for urban development. Mark Houlahan's chapter, 'Waiting for the End? Alchemy and Apocalypse in *The Alchemist*' (Chapter 7), connects these metaphoric impulses firmly to the sincere desire to achieve a metaphysical change in the world (a desire perhaps given strength by the destructive threats of plague, serious poverty, and other social and medical illnesses in London in 1610). If alchemy involves rearranging base elements into a more perfect formation, then it participates in the same processes that Millenarian Christians believed were going on in the world as it prepared itself for the Second Coming – rearranging its elements, and its 'great male and female capacities' (178), in a perfectly harmonious arrangement. While the play exposes alchemy as fraudulent, it does not, Houlahan points out, completely mock the desire to change the world for the better. Ananias and Tribulation's attempts to prepare the world for its mystical transformation with the products of financial investment might be misguided, and Mammon might grotesquely mistake the rewards of the second kingdom with a 'lavishly material golden age' in his own lifetime (184) – indeed all the alchemical and apocalyptic projects might fail spectacularly in the play – but the remote hope that transformation might be possible, even if only in the form of the audience's moral transformation, remains, as does Jonson's fascination with alchemy itself, and the theatrical fun to be had with it.

We have tried to foreground Jonson's love of theatre and of alchemy (despite the potential for both to be parasitic) in Chapter 8's summary of teaching resources. Jonson's affection for both theatre and alchemy, we argue, provides a sturdy foundation on

which students can build their appreciation of *The Alchemist*.
We also suggest primary, critical and web resources which, when
paired with the play, will help students make sense of the (bustling, productive, overcrowded, dirty and often criminal) urban
environment in which the play takes place, and the subgenre of
city comedy in general. These resources, like this volume, aim to
present *The Alchemist* as a play with both a rich critical backstory
and a myriad of exciting new directions to explore.

CHAPTER ONE

The Critical Backstory

DAVID BEVINGTON

'Upon my word', declared Coleridge in 1834, 'I think the *Oedipus Tyrannus*, *The Alchemist*, and *Tom Jones* the three most perfect plots ever planned.'[1] This is not to say that Coleridge was perfectly satisfied with *The Alchemist*. He held to the common view that, although Jonson has a remarkable gift for creating 'humorous' characters, those characters tend to be abstractly generic and for that reason are not persons 'in whom you are morally interested'.[2] Jonson's intellect is arrestingly original, for Coleridge, but fails to rise to the level of genius. Jonson thereby suffers by comparison with Shakespeare, even if he excels in gifts that are peculiarly his own, and nowhere better, in Coleridge's view, than in his construction of *The Alchemist*.

By 1834, the comparison of Jonson and Shakespeare had become a commonplace. Milton, in his brief survey of 'the well-trod stage' in *L'Allegro* (c.1631–2), contrasts 'Jonson's learned sock' with 'sweetest Shakespeare, Fancy's child', who is so beautifully able to 'Warble his native wood-notes wild'.[3] In 1667, John Dryden, while grouping Jonson with Shakespeare and Fletcher as the old 'poets . . . whose excellencies I can never enough admire',[4] distinguishes among the three by giving Fletcher Wit, Shakespeare Nature, and Jonson Art and Judgement.[5] Samuel Butler, pursuing the same comparison of Art and Nature in the contest of Shakespeare and Jonson in the late 1660s, gives Jonson the edge, since 'he that is able to think long and judge well will be sure to find out better things than another man can hit upon suddenly'.[6] Thomas Fuller, conversely, compares Jonson to a Spanish great galleon and Shakespeare to an English man-of-war, the one 'built far higher in

learning, solid but slow in his performances', the other built lighter
and thus able to 'turn with all tides, tack about and take advantage
of all winds, by the quickness of his wit and invention'.[7] To Aphra
Behn, Shakespeare's plays have 'better pleased the world', while
Jonson inspires his auditors 'to admire him most confoundedly',
as in the case of one spectator who has been observed to 'sit with
his hat removed less than a hair's breath from one sullen posture
for almost three hours at *The Alchemist*'.[8] Samuel Johnson, in 1747,
juxtaposes 'Jonson's art' with 'Shakespeare's flame'.[9]

Critical praise of Jonson and *The Alchemist* throughout the
seventeenth century focuses on brilliance of plot construction
and on characterization. Dryden singles out *The Alchemist* for the
design and architectonic beauty of its plot: 'If then the parts are
managed as regularly that the beauty of the whole be kept entire,
and that the variety become not a perplexed and confused mass
of accidents, you will find it infinitely pleasing to be led in a laby-
rinth of design, where you see some of your ways before you, yet
discern not the end till you arrive at it.'[10] No less impressively, *The
Alchemist*, along with *Epicene* and *Volpone*, is for Dryden Jonson's
supreme achievement in the creation of character in the genre of
comedy devoted to observing the town and studying the court.
Wherever 'various characters resort', writes Dryden, Jonson in his
art has 'borne away the crown'. Jonson's refusal to debase his plays
with 'low farce' or to adulterate his sublime wit with 'dull buffoon-
ery' is at its best in *The Alchemist*, even more so than in *Volpone*;
'When in *The Fox* I see the tortoise hissed', writes Dryden, 'I lose
the author of *The Alchemist*.'[11]

Often the praise is broadly stated in terms of superlatives. For
James Shirley, *The Alchemist* is 'a play for strength of wit | And
true art made to shame what hath been writ | In former ages', not
excepting what 'Greeks or Latins have brought forth'.[12] Sir John
Suckling praises Jonson, albeit sardonically, for his presumptuous
boast of having 'purged the stage | Of errors' and for having laid
out his claim that '*The Silent Woman*, | *The Fox*, and *The Alchemist*'
were 'outdone by no man'.[13] James Howell writes to Jonson in a
letter dated c.1632 that 'you were mad when you writ your *Fox*,

and madder when you writ your *Alchemist*', going on to explain that 'The madness I mean is that divine fury, that heating and heightening spirit which Ovid writes of.'[14] An anonymous broadside penned in 1660, 'Prologue to the Reviv'd Alchemist', proudly announces a revival of that play, brought to Oxford on the wings of Pegasus, 'our winged sumpter', 'Who from Parnassus never brought to Greece | Nor Roman stage so rare a masterpiece'.[15]

During the Restoration period, when the play enjoyed great popularity, Samuel Pepys saw it twice at the Vere Street Theatre, on 22 June and on 14 August 1661, on the first of which occasions Pepys pronounced it 'a most incomparable play', and again on 2 and 4 August 1664, when he praised Walter Clun of the King's Company for his performance of Subtle as 'one of his best parts that he acts'.[16] On 17 April 1669, Pepys saw the play yet again, judging it 'still a good play', though suffering this time from the absence of Clun.[17] Edward Phillips declares, in 1675, that Jonson, for his authorship of his three main comedies, 'may be compared, in the judgment of learned men, for decorum, language, and well humouring of the parts, as well with the chief of the ancient Greek and Latin comedians as the prime of modern Italians'.[18] Examples multiply in the pages of G. E. Bentley's *Shakespeare and Jonson*, and in *The Jonson Allusion-Book* assembled by Jesse Franklin Bradley and Joseph Quincy Adams, still further expanded in C. B. Graham's 'Jonson Allusions in Restoration Comedy'.[19]

Throughout most of the seventeenth century, in fact, as Bentley has shown, Jonson was the more acclaimed writer of the two by a considerable margin, in sheer numbers of allusions and as measured by standards of literary greatness. Even though Aphra Behn judged Shakespeare's writings to have 'better pleased the world than Jonson's works',[20] Jonson turns up more often on lists of major English writers. He is more often quoted. Performances of his plays are noted twice as often as are those of Shakespeare's plays. *The Alchemist* remained actively a part of the repertory of the King's Men until the closing of the theatres in 1642, with Richard Burbage as Face until his death in 1619 and with Joseph Taylor in the part thereafter. Robert Armin excelled in the role of Abel Drugger. *The Alchemist* was apparently the only Jonson play to provide materials for the 'drolls' or farcical sketches that persisted in a marginal status during the Interregnum. Allusions to Jonson outnumber those to Shakespeare by a factor of three to one throughout most of the century, especially in the first fifty years. Only in the creation of vital dramatic characters like Falstaff and Cleopatra and Hamlet does Shakespeare surpass Jonson. From such numbers begins to emerge a durable polarity: Jonson is more widely imitated and discussed, but Shakespeare is seen as the more endearing and inspired writer. To admire Jonson and love Shakespeare becomes the rallying cry of criticism for centuries to come.

Nowhere in the Jonson canon are the criteria of admiration and imitation more at work than in critical commentary on *The Alchemist*. Characters like Subtle, Face and Doll become household names. In Richard Brome's *The Asparagus Garden*, 1640, a man greets his friend with as much friendliness and closeness 'as ever Subtle and his Lungs [i.e. Face] did'.[21] The verbal pyrotechnics in Jonson's play offer a vivid metaphor for emotional excess in William Cavendish's *The Country Captain*, 1649, when one character exclaims to another: 'Is thy head to be filled with proclamations, rejoinders, and hard words beyond *The Alchemist*?'[22] An allusion to 'mad Bess Broughton' by Henry Tubbe in 1655 makes its humorous point by asking the audience to recall Jonson's depiction of Broughton's works as the ravings of a zealous Puritan divine.[23] The actor John Lowin of the King's Men was celebrated for his portrayal of Sir Epicure Mammon, along with Morose in *Epicene*, Volpone and Falstaff. Even negative comments testify to the English nation's continued absorption in the antics of Jonson's rogues; as Margaret Cavendish, Duchess of Newcastle, writes, 'Can any rational person think that *The Alchemist* could be the action of one day, as that so many several cozenings could be acted in one day by Captain Face and Doll Common? And could the Alchemist make any believe they could make gold in one day?'[24] The famous jibe at Jonson for presuming to write *Works* 'where others were but plays' aims its satirical venom at Jonson's self-importance even while acknowledging his supremacy in the field of English literature.[25]

At the same time, *The Alchemist* was also perceived by early critics to represent the summit of Jonson's achievement from which he soon descended. 'Thy comic muse from the exalted line | Touched by *The Alchemist* doth since decline | From that her zenith', cautioned Thomas Carew.[26] This implicit consignment of Jonson's later plays, including *The Staple of News* (1626) and *The Magnetic Lady* (1632), to the category of Jonson's 'dotages' is thus of early date.

The critical method of assessing the literary greatness of *The Alchemist* by measuring its extraordinary skill in characterization and plot construction persists, by and large, throughout most of the eighteenth century. William Burnaby, in 1701, opines that 'Our famous Ben Jonson's *Silent Woman*, *The Fox*, and the *Alchemist*, and most of Molière's plays, are the surest standards to judge of comedy.'[27] For Richard Steele, *The Alchemist*, as performed on 11 May 1709, 'is an example of Ben's extensive genius and penetration into the passions and follies of mankind'.[28] John Dennis agrees, writing in 1702: '*The Fox*, *The Alchemist*, the *Silent Women* of Ben Jonson are incomparably the best of our comedies.'[29] Charles Gildon, in *The Laws of Poetry*, 1721, focuses on *The Alchemist*'s remarkable cleverness in 'letting the audience into the knowledge of all that was necessary for them to be informed in, in relation to what was antecedent to the opening of the play, by that comical quarrel between Face and Subtle, in which the sage Doll Common is the prudent moderator'.[30] Theophilus Cibber and Robert Shiells note in 1753 that '*The Alchemist*, *The Fox*, and *The Silent Woman* have been oftener acted than the rest of Ben Jonson's plays put together', having been 'performed to many crowded audiences in several separate seasons, with universal applause'.[31] Richard Hurd (1753–7) praises *Volpone* and *The Alchemist* as most worthy of serious criticism among English comedies, even though *The Alchemist* falls short of Molière's *The Misanthrope* and *Tartuffe* in achieving the 'genuine unmixed manner' of those French comedies, by which Hurd means comedy without the 'impure mixture' of farce.[32] David Erskine Baker, in 1764, hails *The Alchemist*, along with *Volpone* and *Epicene*, 'as the Chef d'Oeuvres of this celebrated poet'.[33] David Garrick's portrayal of Abel Drugger, extending over many years until shortly before his death in 1776, was such a phenomenal success as to make *The Alchemist* a favourite play of that era, able to make us 'shake our sides with joy', as one rapt spectator put it, and to demonstrate vividly the combined skill of the dramatist and the actor in portraying 'humorous' character.[34] Horace Walpole does not hesitate to aver that '*The Alchemist* is his [Jonson's] best play.'[35]

Yet by 1776, George Colman could complain that 'The subtle *Alchemist* grows obsolete, | And Drugger's humour scarcely keeps him sweet.'[36] Some critics indeed were inclined to assign the credit for Garrick's success in playing Abel Drugger more to the actor than to the dramatist. After Garrick's death in 1776, *The Alchemist* went into a rapid decline on the London stage. Apart from a few heavily adapted productions, one of them with Edmund Kean as Drugger in 1814–15, the play was dropped from the repertory until William Poel's 1899 revival for the Elizabethan Stage Society. Apart from Coleridge's great praise of *The Alchemist*, Charles Lamb's assessment that 'If there be no one image which rises to the height of the sublime, yet the confluence and assemblage of them all produces an effect equal to the grandest poetry', and William Hazlitt's fervent wish that Jonson could create more sympathetic characters, the play fared poorly in the nineteenth century.[37]

Belatedly in the century, Algernon Charles Swinburne, in *A Study of Ben Jonson* in 1899, does present at last a serious study of *Volpone* and *The Alchemist* in order to show how the two plays come to stand as 'the consummate and crowning result' of Jonson's genius.[38] Yet, Swinburne does so at the expense of *The Alchemist*; although it is 'perhaps more wonderful in the perfection and combination of cumulative detail, in triumphant simplicity of process and impeccable felicity of result' (thus essentially agreeing up to this point with Coleridge's analysis), *The Alchemist* must yield precedence, in Swinburne's view, to *Volpone* as the more graced with 'imagination' and 'romance'. Swinburne's chief objection to

The Alchemist is 'the absolutely unqualified and unrelieved rascality' of its various manipulators and schemers. The dupes are, to Swinburne, 'viler if less villainous figures than the rapacious victims of *Volpone*'. The 'imperturbable skill' of villainy in Face and Subtle cannot sufficiently compensate for the 'immoral sympathy' that draws us as audience unwillingly into a conspiratorial collaboration with the rogues. The 'incomparable skill' and 'indefatigable craftsmanship' of the villains cannot satisfy audiences with what is ultimately no better than 'intellectual or aesthetic satisfaction'. Coleridge is wrong, in Swinburne's view, if only because he has had the temerity to pair *Oedipus Tyrannus* with Fielding's *Tom Jones*! Perhaps, we can see in this essay by Swinburne a profound reason why *The Alchemist* fell out of favour in the age of Queen Victoria and even shortly before: the play seems to endorse a sort of anarchic amorality that the play's ending merely confirms rather than (as, arguably, in *Volpone*) endorsing some sort of moral standard.

John Addington Symonds, on the other hand, is more tolerant of Jonson's satirical purpose. Symonds celebrates the play's ending as one that is truly 'comic' in the Jonsonian sense of castigating not crimes but follies. Mammon is, for Symonds, 'the twin-brother of Tamburlaine in his extravagant conceits'. The play, for all its local colour, 'remains true to the permanent facts of human roguery and weakness'.[39] Perhaps the end of the nineteenth century and its pointed ignoring of Jonson are about to end.

With the advent of the twentieth century, scholarly and critical discussion of *The Alchemist* and of other of Jonson's works (as also in Shakespeare criticism) turns its attention away from character study and broadly generalized neoclassical appreciation for the play's structural beauties to historical research. One important result of this new emphasis is to be found in the editing of Jonson, and particularly, for our present purposes, of *The Alchemist*. Of special note here are the editions of Herford and Simpson, spanning a 27-year publication period, presenting *The Alchemist* in volume 5 in 1937, and F. H. Mares's 1967 edition for the Revels Plays.[40]

Prior to Herford and Simpson, the play had of course its own history of publishing. *The Alchemist* was registered to Walter Burre on 3 October 1610[41] and appeared in quarto in 1612 as printed (rather carelessly) by Thomas Snodham, with John Stepneth as Burre's partner in the enterprise, at the sign of the Crane in St Paul's Churchyard. Folio publication followed in 1616, as printed by William Stansby, with fairly minor textual changes other than the correcting of some printing errors and a toning down of phrases that might seem to violate prohibitions against profanity. Burre, as one who controlled seven of the nine plays included in the 1616 Folio, ultimately came to an agreement with Stansby over the rights to those seven plays, one of them *The Alchemist*. By the time Jonson died in August of 1637, most of the original owners were dead. Subsequent folios appeared: a second folio in 1640–1 with as many of Jonson's writings as were then available, and a third folio in 1692 adding a few new Jonson texts but generally a reprise of its predecessor.

Peter Whalley's edition of the *Works* in 1756 provided, for the first time, annotation other than Jonson's own, and added a few new texts.[42] The Folio was his choice of text for *The Alchemist*, as it was for most of the plays. David Garrick published his adaptation in 1763; owing no doubt to Garrick's stunning performance as Abel Drugger, this version was for some time the most frequently republished of the adaptations.[43] Francis Gentleman put forth a burlesque version for Drury Lane in 1770, providing a Prologue to a two-act farce called *The Tobacconist* that gave renewed attention to Abel Drugger (honouring the actor Thomas Weston, who, like Garrick, starred in this role; they both died in 1776).[44] William Gifford's edition of the *Works* in 1816 took Whalley to task for numerous perceived deficiencies, but the improvements were chiefly in the annotation and in a 'Biographical Memoir';[45] the Folio text offered and continues to offer a reliable guide for editing of *The Alchemist*, so that the emendations duly noted in modern editions derived from Whalley and Gifford are chiefly the corrections of fairly obvious typographical and copying errors. Gifford served as the model for most subsequent editions in the nineteenth century. Barry Cornwall's 1838 edition reprinted Gifford's text.

With the twentieth century came the so-called New Bibliography, emphasizing the importance of methodological investigation of all early texts, quartos and folios, along with manuscript sources, in order to determine as precisely as possible the process by which an author's writings have been transformed into various stages that could include fair copy, a playhouse script, copy for the printer, proofreading sheets, revision for later publication, and so on. Early editions during the century included C. M. Hathaway's 1903 edition, F. E. Schelling's in 1904, and G. A. Smithson's in 1907, all in modern spelling. Although Smithson introduced some new editorial stage directions, the textual advances among these editions were minor. The 1616 Folio, fortunately, offered a reliable textual guide for all these editions. Later editions, by G. E. Bentley in 1947, Douglas Brown in 1966, J. B. Bamborough in 1967, J. B. Steane in 1967, S. Musgrove in 1968, Alvin B. Kernan in 1974, and still others did not materially change the intellectual landscape of textual editing of *The Alchemist*.[46] (Helen Ostovich's more innovative editing would not arrive until 1997.)[47]

The field was thus free for Herford and Simpson to produce a thoroughly scholarly edition of Jonson in the spirit of the New Bibliography as pioneered by R. B. McKerrow and W. W. Greg, and this they did.[48] The result is an impressively scholarly edition, in old spelling, with a minimum of added stage directions or indeed anything not appearing in the original published texts, and with learned notes on sources and background. The monumental format included occasional black-letter, archaic spellings, new scenes generally marked in the 'continental' fashion at the appearance of each significant new character with a massed header of personae at the head of each scene, parentheses used to mark asides, elaborate marginalia often in Latin and Greek, numerous commendatory verses, and still more. All of this material, the editors presumed, enjoyed the author's endorsement. Percy Simpson especially, who took over the task with the abundantly valuable assistance of his wife Evelyn after Herford's death in 1931, made it his task to trumpet the textual virtues of the 1616 Folio as the primary textual source for the plays appearing in that collection. Surely, Simpson argued, the Jonson First Folio was the work of Jonson himself and should reflect in its textual method that towering presence of the author. Indeed, Jonson was undoubtedly intent on presenting his 1616 Folio as an instant classic worthy of being shelved next to the collected and annotated works of Homer, Aristotle, Virgil, Seneca, and the rest. Jonson certainly did rewrite for that folio publication. He welcomed dedicatory letters and poems from his friends and admirers, and was responsible for a large number of corrections introduced into the printed text as it made its way through the press. These would all seem to be potent reasons for privileging the 1616 Folio in a modern edition of the plays it contains (though of course the editor would need to consult the quartos as well for any hints of authorial intent misinterpreted by the Folio editors and printers). Yet, as more recent work has shown (to be discussed further in another chapter in the present volume), Simpson has overstated the case for Jonson as supervisor and proofreader of the 1616 Folio. Although many press corrections were Jonson's, many others were presumably the work of press personnel. The amount of correction tails off towards the end of the 1616 Folio, as though Jonson ran out of time and energy. Simpson was not always able to distinguish accurately between uncorrected and corrected states. Both W. W. Greg and Fredson Bowers have observed in commenting on the edition that it tends to be more an edition of the 1616 Folio itself than of what Jonson wrote.[49]

All of this has limited application to *The Alchemist*, as it happens, since its 1616 Folio text differs so little from the 1612 quarto and, though marred with misprints, seems fundamentally sound. Simpson's collation of six 1616 copies turns up essentially no interesting variants: except in the Dedication 'To the Reader', all the 37 or so variants noted are minor matters of punctuation. Thus, although Simpson's call for fidelity to the 1616 Folio in Jonson editing is substantially flawed as an argument in the case of some other works, *The Alchemist* remains unaffected because its text is so reliable and so close to the 1612 quarto. Some classicized spellings like 'praeuaricate' and 'precise' are modernized in the 1616 Folio, and, as noted earlier, a few profanities are ameliorated, but the changes are slight. The 1640–1 second Folio is essentially a reprint. Simpson's chief contribution to editing *The Alchemist* lies in the learned commentary. The work is philologically conservative and turns a deaf ear to matters of staging in many cases. Its presenting of sources and analogues normally settles for the Latin, Greek, Spanish, Italian (etc.) originals without translation, as though assuming that the edition is chiefly for the learned. The pages of the text are not reader-friendly. Still, the work is impressively knowledgeable.

F. H. Mares's edition for the Revels Plays in 1967 is more attentive to the non-specialist as well as to specialist readers. In the spirit of the Revels Plays, begun in 1958 under the general editorship of Clifford Leech and with acknowledged indebtedness to the style of editing established by the Arden Shakespeares beginning in 1899 with Edward Dowden's edition of *Hamlet*, Mares's notes and textual collations are at the foot of the page. The text is modernized, with fairly liberal insertion of editorially added stage directions. Square brackets, along with the collations, indicate where the text departs from the copy text. That copy text for Mares, as for his predecessors (and followers), is the 1616 Folio. 'It is the assumption of this edition', writes Mares, 'that the 1616 folio represents Jonson's considered intention. The text is good, and was almost certainly prepared under his direct supervision. The copy used by the printer would seem to have been the quarto of 1612, as amended by the author.'[50] Mares provides convincing particulars demonstrating that indeed certain obvious errors in the quarto have been carried over by the printers into the 1616 Folio. Mares makes more of a case for authorial revision from quarto to folio than had Simpson, including a number of stage directions normally set in the Folio as side-notes but missing, with one exception, in the quarto. Oaths are toned down, as Simpson had noted. More general is a revision of punctuation, which Mares wants to see as authorial, though this is a harder case to make since printers generally took charge of pointing the texts, and the effect in a modern edition is minimal in any case. Differences too in typography are of minor consideration in a modernized text with modernized punctuation and typography.

Thus, in substantive matters, Mares's text is largely undistinguishable from its predecessors, and for a sufficient reason. The commentary is historically learned, more ready to translate foreign languages into English than was Simpson, and more willing to gloss terms that might be unfamiliar to the academic audience to which the Revels editions are aimed. A substantial introduction, in what is by this time a standard format for Revels or Arden editions, surveys Life and Character, Alchemy, The Play, Jonson's Verse, Stage History and The Text. All this is in need today of updating, and a new Revels edition is indeed under way in the capable hands of Richard Dutton. A new complete scholarly edition, *The Cambridge Edition of the Works of Ben Jonson* (*CWBJ*), on the scale of the Herford and Simpson Oxford edition but with substantially different aims (modern spelling, chronological arrangement of the works, a searching re-examination of textual authority of the early texts, new commentary, an electronic edition to include extensive materials online, etc.), is near completion as I write in the fall of 2011.

Historical scholarship on *The Alchemist* establishes itself and rapidly gains momentum in the early years of the twentieth century. In her *Studies in Jonson's Comedy*, 1898, Elizabeth Woodbridge Morris compares the structural features of *Volpone* with those of *The Alchemist* to show how the intriguers of the earlier play, Volpone and Mosca, are reconfigured in Subtle and Face, and similarly with their victims: Celia changed into a structurally similar but very different character in Dame Pliant, Bonario similarly transmuted into Surly, and so on.[51] Morris is interested historically in the evolution of character types and roles. The title of Eleanor Patience Lumley's *The Influence of Plautus on the Comedies of Ben Jonson*, 1901, makes clear her commitment to historical method in classical source studies.[52] Alfred Remy, in 1906, looks at Jonson's creative reuse of Spanish, paying particular attention to 'Verdugoship' in *The Alchemist*; he discovers a historical Spanish organist named Verdugo and suggests that the word means 'hangman, executioner'.[53]

F. E. Schelling finds several models for Jonson's alchemical characters in *William Lilly's History of His Life and Times*, c.1681.[54] C. R. Baskervill, though concerned mainly with plays before *The Alchemist*, demonstrates how native theatrical traditions influence even a studiously classical dramatist like Jonson and continue to manifest themselves in his greatest comedies.[55] Mina Kerr surveys Jonson's dramatic development as a classicist and student of Terence and Plautus whose satirical types were to prove weightily influential on dramatists like Shirley and Brome.[56] To be sure, many of Kerr's sources-and-influences pieces of information had been gathered together in the notes of Gifford and other earlier editors. In his *Ben Jonson* (1919), G. Gregory Smith studies Jonson's development of a dramatist, proposing that *The Argument* gains some of its freedom from moral constraints from having been written after *Epicene*.[57] Byron Steel's popularizing *O Rare Ben Jonson*, 1928, attests to interest in Jonson as a dramatist.[58] Huntington Brown's 1929 note finds a Rabelaisian anecdote in the opening scene of *The Alchemist* when Face's 'Sirrah, I'll strip you –' receives Subtle's vulgar reply: 'What to do? Lick figs | Out at my –', thereby recalling Barbarossa's odd punishment of the Milanese for insulting the Empress in Book 4, chapter 45 of *Pantagruel*.[59] Another resonance may occur when Face tauntingly recalls how he met Subtle 'at Pie Corner, | Taking your meal of steam in from cooks' stalls' (1.1.25–6).[60] (To be sure, Anne Lake Prescott reminds us that such Gargantuan references are apt to be from the chapbook hero of that name, not Rabelais's own text.)[61]

In the 1930s, Eric Linklater focuses his brief analysis of *The Alchemist* on Simon Forman, John Dee, Giles Mompessom, and other figures in the shadowy history of alchemy, along with Chaucer, Gower, and literary writers attracted to the story.[62] John Palmer purveys similar information about alchemists in history, though he is mainly interested in introducing the play to readers as 'a better play than *Volpone*' because of its lucid brilliance of construction.[63] We can see here, perhaps, the influence of the so-called New Criticism, concentrating on the work of art as a thing of poetic construction. Landmark works of criticism by a prominent New Critic are to be found in L. C. Knights's *Drama and Society in the Age of Jonson* and his later published 'Ben Jonson: Public Attitudes and Social Poetry'; here *The Alchemist* is viewed as a study of greed and lust in which the Puritans symbolize avarice without guilt.[64] Harry Levin's essay on 'Jonson's Metempsychosis', 1943, offers an astute close reading of Mosca's mountebank scene in *Volpone* as the 'germ' of 'mature comedy' out of which the superb gulling in *The Alchemist* arises. Jonson, says Levin, has discovered that good and evil in this world 'are matters of opinion'; the world is divided 'not into good men and bad, but into rogues and fools'.[65] Alexander Sackton sees the dazzling display of phony jargon, both in alchemy and Puritanism, as a special kind of rhetoric in *The Alchemist*.[66] The New Critical movement has found Ben Jonson.

To be sure, historical criticism continues its study of Jonson during these same years, often with illuminating results. Charles Francis Wheeler's work on mythology in Jonson shows how Jonson combines classical references in Sir Epicure Mammon's imaginary 'Hesperian garden, Cadmus' story, | Jove's shower, the boon of Midas, Argus' eyes' (*The Alchemist*, 2.1.101–2).[67] Clifford Leech finds Caroline echoes of *The Alchemist* in Massinger, Fletcher, Brome, Davenant and Randolph.[68] Edgar Hill Duncan looks into the play's 'scientific' references by reading learnedly in medieval and Renaissance alchemical treatises that were still current in Jonson's day, concluding that Jonson did not greatly alter or exaggerate current conceptions of alchemy in what his characters profess.[69] Johnstone Parr, in the previous year, follows a similar fascination by looking at 'Non-Alchemical Pseudo-Sciences in *The Alchemist*', discovering in the process that Subtle's discourses on chiromancy, metoposcopy, astrology, and the like are usually quite accurate in their characterization of much fraudulent learning.[70] John Read looks at John Dee and Edward Kelley as likely models for Jonson's play.[71]

Freda Townshend argues (somewhat in the spirit of C. R. Baskervill's study of the early comedies) that *The Alchemist* owes more to Renaissance satire than it does to the Roman comedy of Plautus and Terence; the classical 'unities' offer too constricting a view.[72] Lu Emily Pearson's study of early modern widows looks satirically at Dame Pliant's adventures in the context of social historical research on young Elizabethan widows forced to submit to a male guardian's control.[73] C. J. Sisson argues that the gullible clerk Dapper is based on a real-life story involving one Thomas Rogers of Dorset.[74] Joseph T. McCullen Jr is also interested in Rogers as a prototype of Dapper, as is Franklin Williams.[75] (Richard Levin, in a later article, discounts Rogers's claim as unsubstantial and makes his own case for an anonymous pamphlet he calls *The Brideling*.)[76] The 'unclean birds' with their 'ruff of pride' alluded to in horror and disgust by Ananias when he sees Surly in Spanish costume (4.7.51–3) are, as M. A. Shaaber demonstrates, familiar emblems as warnings against pride. Malcolm South's article on this subject (1973) concludes that the 'vncleane birds' are Catholic priests.[77] Paul Goodman offers a persuasive Chicago-school neo-Aristotelian reading of the play, seeing the action, complete with beginning, middle and ending, as Jonson's most fully worked out comedy of deflation, in which Lovewit is representative of the play's daringly amoral sense of comic justice.[78]

Once we reach the 1950s, historical scholarship seems less in evidence than appreciative literary studies. Marchette Chute, aiming at a general audience, attracted many readers with her engaging portrayal of the dramatist and his work.[79] John J. Enck, allowing that *The Alchemist* is 'Jonson's greatest play', praises it for its construction but faults the play nonetheless for the weakness of Lovewit as an authority figure (as if some theatrical crane were lowering onto the play's fifth act 'a ponderous and desperate *deus ex machina*'), and the disproportionately specialized nature of the satire.[80] Maurice Hussey's essay on Ananias concludes too easily that Christian thought is implicitly the play's alleged norm of moral judgement.[81] Edward B. Partridge, on the other hand, shows the New Critical method at its best. Careful attention to

irony in *The Alchemist*, to inflated rhetoric and explosive epithets
that characteristically end in deflation, to martial imagery expos-
ing sexual aggression as a kind of warfare, to alchemical images
of a religious, medical, commercial and sexual nature, and to bes-
tial imagery applied to the absurd human condition (as in *Volpone*
also), all results in an illuminating reading of the play. The various
people of *The Alchemist* 'whose lives are dedicated to the acquisition of gold', writes Partridge, are doomed to 'bear some relation
to the alchemists of old'.[82]

By the 1960s, many Jonsonians seem to have learned how to
reject the stern admonitions of some zealous New Critics that we
should ignore social and political and biographical contexts to
focus intent on imagery and tone. Instead, the critical studies of
this era often favour a more harmonizing and inclusive approach
that can make critical use of background material while still viewing the work of art as a literary and aesthetic whole. An engaging
example is William Empson's essay on *The Alchemist* that appeared
in *The Hudson Review*. Empson argues against those many critics
who are so caught up in moral disapproval of the play's action that
they end up hating and despising the characters as either fools or
knaves. Too many teachers, in Empson's view, are caught up in a
mood of moral revulsion that seems to have prompted so many
readers and viewers in the nineteenth century to turn away from
the play in distaste. Such teachers, observes Empson, regard the
play as so morally distressing that it should be kept away from
impressionable students. This is nonsense, says Empson. 'One
cannot get on with *The Alchemist* without accepting its moral', he
writes. Such an acceptance requires that we understand the necessity of our half-sympathizing with the tricksters; we need to agree
with Jonson's implicit view that 'if a man can be cheated by obvious rogues like this, he deserves it'.[83] The play tells us that we are
supposed to laugh.

An Empsonian kindred spirit is to be found in C. G. Thayer.
'The world of *The Alchemist*', he writes, 'is a world turned upside
down, a world in which the motivating forces are folly and avarice.
Jonson has created a microcosm, complete in itself, not so much

a reflection of the world of ordinary experience, as one in which a single aspect of the experiential world, folly, acts as the prime mover for all that occurs.' Alchemy can be seen as 'comic art', one that, like Jonson's play, 'reduces itself to its own quintessence and becomes the ultimate sublime impossibility, the universal panacea'.[84] Moral judgement thus becomes part of the aesthetic design of the play, not a moral absolute.

To be sure, Gabriele Bernhard Jackson sees Jonson's ideal individual as 'a public man' applying to society's salvation 'man's best intellectual and spiritual qualities: clemency, manliness, critical judgment, poetic understanding'. These are the qualities by which Jonson judges his characters; *The Alchemist*, like Jonson's plays generally, is 'about moral judgment', and it is a judgement that invites us to disapprove of a character like Mammon who 'intends to spend his wealth destroying, not upholding, the qualities and relations on which society depends'.[85] Robert Knoll too insists on a moral reading of the play: 'What Jonson objects to is the excessive ambition which offends against God's ordering of things . . . *The Alchemist* is a religious, not a social, tract, and it is directed against the impious rather than the antisocial.'[86] Myrddin Jones emphasizes no less emphatically that 'the caricature of religion in the figure of Sir Epicure Mammon is strong and would have been recognized and condemned as such by the contemporary audience', if only because Mammon identifies himself with Solomon's sensuality and craving for power in 1 Kings. Jonson's moral purpose, in Jones's view, is to display at full 'the evil at the heart of an acquisitive society'.[87] The debate thus goes on, and it is one in which Jonson becomes a profoundly ambivalent figure.

William Blissett's critical approach to this same difficulty of the play's morally problematic ending is to see in *The Alchemist* a tripartite representation of World, Flesh and Devil. Subtle is the Devil, and Doll Common the Flesh; the World is more complicatedly represented by Face (Jeremy), perhaps also Sir Epicure, and, finally, by Lovewit, the man of the world who breaks no laws but triumphs over the schemers and gulls by his shrewdness. The World is like that, declares the play in Blissett's view; proverbially,

'The world will love his own.'[88] We as audience have to hand it
to Lovewit for being smart enough to win. We applaud Face or
Jeremy too, as Lovewit's closest associate. Blissett argues for much
the same sardonic and matter-of-fact conclusion as in Empson's
reading. Most tellingly, argues Blissett, Jonson himself holds the
ancient dramatists to be on his side, when he insists, in his dedicatory epistle to the Universities prefacing *Volpone*, that he has followed the example of the ancients, 'whose comedies are not always
joyful, but oft-times the bawds, the servants, the rivals, yea, and
the masters are mulcted; and fitly, it being the office of a comic
poet to imitate justice and instruct to life'.[89] The play imitates life
not according to some abstract and idealized moral template, but
according to how the world wags.

Brian Gibbons sees this remorseless candour as integral to
the spirit of what he calls *Jacobean City Comedy*. So do Jonathan
Haynes and William R. Dynes, each arguing a case for thieves
and tricksters of early modern London, vying to see 'who sharks
best'.[90] The genre of city comedy, with its relentlessly sardonic and
urbane depiction of *la comédie humaine*, is indeed ideally suited to
a satirical portraiture of shystering in a bustling and overcrowded
city like London of the early seventeenth century. Arnold Judd
similarly sees Lovewit as a seventeenth-century gallant, a type
Jonson was inclined to admire, and for whom a programme of
reforming humankind was hardly a driving passion.[91]

Alan Dessen approaches this problem of moral interpretation
by invoking the 'estates' morality, a late mutation of the genre in
the 1580s and 1590s caught up in a satirical portrayal of contemporary life in England and especially London and thus well suited to
castigate abstractions like Mercatore, Lucre and Usury. However
crude its dramatic method, argues Dessen, this genre offered a
useful model for Jonson's wry depiction of a businesslike 'venter'
in which 'the base metal of the Jacobean public can be turned into
gold or profit'.[92] L. A. Beaurline, similarly persuaded that Jonson
was 'partly indebted to the late moralities' as well as to Greek
comedy, sees *The Alchemist* as Jonson's finest example of a philo-
sophical quest for 'controlled completeness', a completeness that

can 'bring us a little closer to Jonson's design'.[93] That design is one of plenitude or copiousness, fashioned to solve the play's tendency to break up into episodes with its many characters and incidents. The encyclopedic inclusiveness is like that of seventeenth-century books on farm husbandry, health, gambling, and the like, bearing comprehensive titles like *The Complete Angler*, *The Complete Gamester*, *The Complete Parson* and *The Anatomy of Abuses*.[94]

The end of the 1960s and last three decades of the twentieth century are a time of social and political unrest: a virtual revolution in sexual mores, deconstruction in literary method, a New Historicism, and still more, altering the academic and literary landscape to a degree perhaps never seen before. Jonson criticism predictably embraces a broad scale of responses, from traditionalism to post-modern innovation. A significant figure is Jonas Barish, whose *Ben Jonson and the Language of Prose Comedy* appeared in 1960, to be followed by other significant studies. Jonson is brilliant in identifying language with character, says Barish. Subtle in *The Alchemist* is one of those 'who can within limits control their own personae, command their own metamorphoses', while the butts are those who 'try to live within an alien persona' and are doomed to fail because their ambitions exceed their capacities.[95] *The Alchemist* carries 'the subversion of justice a step farther' than in *Volpone* and *Epicene*, 'and forecloses even more sharply on the possibility of transcendent standards'. It does so by introducing for the first time 'the discomfiting element of interested judgment'.[96] Lovewit never even pretends to the kind of detachment and impartiality we see in *Epicene*'s Truewit. Little honour is to be found among thieves. Lovewit candidly admits that he has become accessory to the cheating that has gone on in his house, but hopes that the audience will not judge him too harshly, if only because he promises to redeem himself somehow with the aid of all the plunder. The final decision rests with us. We are urged to follow the line of least resistance. 'As the Jonsonian equivalence between comedy and feasting comes into sharp focus, comedy loses much of its corrective sting. . . . Only if we wish to be reckoned among the gulls will we protest too loudly.'[97] Barish thus strengthens the argument

in favour of a sardonically cheerful upending of the norms of justice – much, perhaps, as one would expect from time of upheaval
in the late 1960s and the 1970s.

Thomas M. Greene sees the circle or sphere symbolizing harmony and perfection as the great unifying image for Jonson, to
such an extent that almost everything he wrote 'attempts in one
way or another to complete the broken circle, or expose the ugliness
of its completion'. In the masques, these images are represented as
complete, with the king at the centre of the circle; conversely, in
The Alchemist, and in Jonson's other plays shortly before and after
it, the circle appears to be broken, leaving the centre to be associated with 'solitary and upright independence'.[98] The manipulating characters like Volpone and Subtle are Protean figures without
core or principle or substance. The play's closest approximation
to a moral resolution is Face's (Jeremy's) offer to give the role of
judgement to the spectators, inviting them to join in a feast of 'tolerant forgiveness of his shenanigans by their applause'. Jonson's
'appreciation of the artist-scoundrel' thereby qualifies 'his disapproval of the centrifugal self'.[99] Greene thus sides with Barish,
Empson, and others for whom the audience is co-opted into an
acceptance of the play's wild concept of poetic justice.

Michael Flachmann bolsters this argument by taking a positive
view of the play's union between alchemy and satire. The play itself
is an alchemical experiment. Alchemy is 'a powerful metaphor that
explains his [Jonson's] conception of the proper relation between
a playwright and his audience'. Jonson does not endorse alchemy
as a science, of course, but he does see in it a 'well-wrought image
which could portray his own theories on satire'.[100] The play is thus
about itself, about poetic metaphor.

Alvin Kernan advances a similar case for self-reflexivity. Both
the chicanery and the folly of *The Alchemist*'s characters are
'defined by Jonson as alchemy'. The characters are not only hop-
ing to become rich, they are intent on transmuting 'their own base
natures into something rich and strange'. Mammon is above all
the comic overreacher whose desire for alchemical transformation 'reaches truly heroic proportions'. Such characters long to

'overleap nature'.[101] Lovewit is a deus ex machina figure whose unexpected and sudden appearance helps to 'bring the plot to a comic rather than satiric conclusion', writes Kernan. With good sense and lack of scruple, Lovewit takes advantage of his opportunity. Wit, or common sense, manages at least to 'achieve what is possible for a limited creature in a limited world'.[102] James Shapiro (1991) similarly characterizes Mammon as 'a secular Faustus . . . an overreacher'.[103] We hear in self-referential analyses such as these a hallmark of post-modern criticism.

Richard Levin is no doubt right to observe that in too many moralistic and religious readings of the play, some of which we have glanced at in this survey, *The Alchemist* has ceased to be viewed as funny and has begun instead to sound 'very grim indeed'. It is 'a religious, not a social, tract', says one critic; it is 'a cynical play', says another; and so on. Levin's useful contribution is to show how such defensively conservative readings go about proving their point by explaining away the play's seeming Aristophanic irreverence; they argue that the play 'does not really mean what it seems to mean'. The very absence of reform or retribution, to one critic, 'serves to emphasize the characters' depravity', since 'they do not seem to be worth saving'. Because Face's booty is mere rubbish, argues another critic, it 'is its own best punishment'. Even for Lovewit the new possessions 'are not unmixed blessings', since they will not cover the cost of cleaning the house, and the like. Probably none of this will have changed the minds of those who have argued so, but Levin's irreverence is refreshing and, I would say, right-minded.[104]

Donald Gertmenian, in 'Comic Experience in *Volpone* and *The Alchemist*' (1977), argues similarly that the common critical desire to expect moral affirmation from comedy distorts in such a way as to see *Volpone* and *The Alchemist* as essentially alike, whereas, in Gertmenian's view, '*The Alchemist* differs from *Volpone* by being amoral and delighting.'[105] Ian Donaldson is similarly even-handed in his argument that the play's emphasis on varieties of expression forces the characters into opposing camps of equal ferocity, with plenty of low moral and intellectual stature to pass around among the contestants.[106]

This is not to say, of course, that *The Alchemist* is lacking in satirical censure, as Richard Dutton rightly observes, and yet, he freely acknowledges, the play's complexity lies in its 'baroque recognition of itself as a play'.[107] For Douglas Duncan, Jonson draws heavily on the techniques of Lucianic satire – more so than on the moralities that Alan Dessen writes about. *The Alchemist*, Duncan writes, 'is so comprehensively irreverent as to mock all critical solemnity' – it is 'rogue fiction'.[108] Aliki Lafkidou Dick suggests that Jonson's appeal to human intelligence is essentially Aristophanic, as when Face's satiric portrait of Subtle as of a 'piteously costive' beggar taking in meals of steam from cooks' stalls (1.1.28) reminds us of Aristophanes' depiction of a pale-faced and starving Socrates in *Clouds*.[109] Robertson Davies claims that Jonson's characters are unlikeable because Jonson's classically driven intent was to expose and scourge follies.[110]

The last two decades of the twentieth century have produced a quantitative growth in the number of books and essays on Jonson's *The Alchemist*. The play remains central to critical discussions of Jonson's art. At the same time, the critical explorations are not generally as revisionary or deconstructive as are critical studies of some other literary figures, notably Shakespeare. Even if, as been argued here, critical work on this play in the late twentieth century reveals necessarily some influence of rapid social change and conflict, it does so less stridently and controversially than in the instance of some other literary topics and authors. Women have contributed substantially to critical work on *The Alchemist*, starting with early pioneers like Elizabeth Woodbridge Morris in 1898, Eleanor Patience Lumley in 1901, and Mina Kerr in 1912 (see above), with a substantial number still to come, but even here, one would be hard put to characterize most of this scholarship or criticism as feminist in its theoretical concerns. Leah Marcus is successfully revisionist in her *The Politics of Mirth*,[111] but most women writing about this play tackle the same questions that have interested men.

Perhaps Jonson's *The Alchemist* invites this intellectual caution. Doll Common and Dame Pliant are hardly Moll Frith in *The Roaring Girl*, or Ophelia or Desdemona or Rosalind, or the Duchess of Malfi. One can soon exhaust the critical possibilities of Jonson's preference for satirical types in women. Similarly, a deconstructive reading of Jonson seems destined to go nowhere. Jonson is so committed generally to proving his point about how satiric comedy is supposed to work, with Jonson himself as its supreme exemplar for his own generation and upholder of the great classical tradition, that ambiguity is not what he strives for. New Historicism falls under the same constraint as a potential method of analysis: Jonson's masques can be studied as apt examples in the Geertzian mode of art forms created to enable the monarch to put itself on display and act out royal fantasies of power, but Jonson's own social and political conservatism is not comfortable with the notion that such power is illusory or that political truth is ineluctably relative.

No, Jonson's revisionism, if the term can be applied at all, lies in the great perception, of which *The Alchemist* may be his finest expression, that great dramatic art must not be constrained by conventional moral strictures; it operates according to its own laws, and must not be viewed or judged as one would judge a moral or religious tract. Even here, Jonson's critical move is humanistically conservative and traditional in the best sense of those terms, since the finest of the ancient comic writers, he insists, were aware that comedy must imitate life not in ideal terms but with a candid awareness of what life is truly like.

Some examples from the last twenty years or so of the twentieth century will, I hope, illustrate the points I've been arguing. Anne Barton sees the play as about 'transformation, as it affects not metals, but human beings'. Although Jonson had no use for real-life alchemists, he found alchemy 'a metaphoric system' well suited to his artistic purposes.[112] At the same time, his transformations in *The Alchemist* are not liberating, like those in Shakespeare. No Shakespearean miracle has occurred at the end of *The Alchemist*. It is, for Barton, 'the funniest play Jonson ever wrote',[113] because of its delightful cunning and inventive stage situations. The manipulators are without conscience, of course, but Surly is no Criticus or Horace or even Macilente striving to defend poetry, learning and the good life; he is a 'gamester' driven not by moral conviction but by professional jealousy and greed for power, like all the rest. Barton's chapter on *The Alchemist* is a wonderfully insightful essay, the method and conclusions of which are by and large compatible with those of Empson, Greene, Barish, Blissett, and others who have stood out against a moralistic reading of the play.

Wayne Rebhorn's assessment of Lovewit in 'Jonson's "Jovy Boy"' seems at first similar: Lovewit, Rebhorn argues, is triumphant at the end by virtue of 'his mental agility and shrewd ability to calculate his own advantage'. Rebhorn's analysis of scholarship on the play usefully defines 'two fundamentally opposed and seemingly irreconcilable camps', one insisting that we must condemn Lovewit on moral grounds, the other welcoming him as a vital and urbane representative of the play's compellingly eccentric view of justice as the world adjudicates such matters. Rebhorn's surprising conclusion is that at the play's end Lovewit is 'nothing less than Face's final dupe'.[114] Lovewit is fundamentally egocentric and amoral; he is animated by fantasies of power. Although he thinks of himself as the triumphant trickster, argues Rebhorn, his comic fate is to carry out Face's plans rather than his own. This argument, perhaps more ingenious than convincing, does show at least the extraordinary extent to which critics keep returning to the same conundrum of comic justice at the end of the play. If Jonson's intent was to challenge his audiences with a controversial idea, he certainly has succeeded.

One hold on the modern and post-modern literary imagination to which *The Alchemist* can legitimately lay claim is that it embodies a marked fascination with literary theory, perhaps even more so than in Jonson's other writings. In *The Alchemist*, we find Jonson 'buttressing his work with literary theory', notes Gordon Sweeney.[115] Face (Jeremy) ends the play with an epilogue, defending himself on grounds of 'decorum' (5.5.159), as though the invocation of that classical ideal would explain everything. But it doesn't, and Face is 'no simple Jonsonian apologist'. How is this 'decorum' to be reconciled with a great deal of indecorous behaviour on Face's part? And, although the play's prologue promises 'wholesome remedies' (line 15) and 'fair correctives' (line 18), Lovewit's defence of his own role flies in the face of such conventional theorizing. If he can plead that he has 'outstripped | An old man's gravity, or strict canon' (5.5.153–4), he has done so to serve what Sweeney calls 'the value of his own pleasure'. The play may be presumed to have moral significance, as called for in classical practice, but both Face and Lovewit define themselves as unique characters in a unique play, defying classical theory and prospering nonetheless. What is more, they do so by an appeal to the theatre as a vital social organ needing and deserving our support. Most epilogues resolve difficulties of moral judgement in the plays they conclude; Jonson's do the opposite, and nowhere more so than in *The Alchemist*. Face's epilogue is thus a defence of theatre, one that operates by its own rules. Acting is gulling; how can we expect Face to behave otherwise? Sweeney's astute analysis of the problem of theory in this play has the huge benefit of insisting that we re-examine the value of our own experience in the theatre. 'Are we to congratulate ourselves as benefactors of the Jacobean theater or to consider ourselves cozened, like Mammon?' Here as elsewhere, 'in Jonson's work theory and practice do not conform'; his insistence elsewhere that poetry improve and educate its spectators and readers seems oddly and yet productively at odds with Face's and Lovewit's sardonic disregard of the consequences of their own acts as characters and as actors. 'It is when we begin thinking about the play that it poses problems for us', says Sweeney. Here is a critical and theoretical argument that casts *The Alchemist* in a genuinely illuminating post-modern mode.

The importance of a sense of place in *The Alchemist* looms into view as a significant topic in recent years. The play is set in London, or, more particularly, in Blackfriars. Jonson's move towards London as his theatrical setting had already begun, argues R. L. Smallwood, with Jonson's collaborative work on *Eastward Ho!*, 1605, and was to manifest itself still further in the shift from the Italian-based quarto version of *Every Man in His Humour* (1598) to the London-based Folio version of 1616, and then again in *Bartholomew Fair* (1614).[116] *The Alchemist* abounds in local place-names. The unities of time and place are observed with special care. As William Armstrong argued earlier, the play 'achieves a concentration of space unequalled in Elizabethan drama'.[117] Certainly, the playhouse must have been the Blackfriars. The play's characters are all local denizens, and Jonson had lived in the neighbourhood at least in when he signed his Epistle to *Volpone* 'From my house in the Blackfriars, this 11 of February, 1607 [1606, new style].' 'The Blackfriars of the play and the Blackfriars in which Jonson's theatre stood are inseparable', writes Smallwood.[118] The sense of immediacy must have been overwhelmingly present to spectators. The likelihood that Robert Armin took the role of Drugger no doubt added resonance to Drugger's observation to Face's inquiry as to whether he has 'credit with the players': 'Yes, sir, did you never see me play the fool?' (4.7.68–9). Much of the play's dialogue reads like rehearsal or improvisation. The action is often about dressing up. All of this lends itself to theatrical self-awareness, aided by the interchangeability of the art of alchemy and the art of acting. Cheryl Lynn Ross's 'The Plague of *The Alchemist*' (1989) reinforces the importance of place by observing the care with which the action of the play is set in the plague year of 1610. The city is sick; it stinks with fetid fumes and acrid smoke. The effects are both practical and symbolic.[119]

Andrew Gurr's essay on Lovewit strongly supports Smallwood's thesis of local particularity in *The Alchemist*, adding the delightful suggestion that in Lovewit we are to see a representation of those theatrical persons who had in fact reclaimed possession of the Blackfriars for the King's Men in 1608 after ten years of use by a boy company; the owners were none other than Richard and Cuthbert Burbage, John Heminges, Henry Condell, and, 'last but far from least, that most famous lover of wit, William Shakespeare'.[120] W. David Kay adds further local resonances: the deceptions of *The Alchemist* that are so akin to the spirit of Jacobean City Comedy, the tobacconists and law clerks manifestly on the scene in nearby

Holborn at the Dagger Inn, the intellectual presence of Martial, Catullus, Horace, and other authors that were so much a part of Jonson's schooling in Westminster, the cooks' stalls of Pie Corner, the Puritan congregation of St Anne's in Blackfriars, and so on, all of this more important to the play than mere atmospherics.[121]

Katharine Eisaman Maus argues that *The Alchemist* belongs to a period of Jonson's artistic creativity that is increasingly diverse, prompting him to a more heightened and refined consciousness of the need for contexts and generic boundaries for a particular work. Needful rules are more necessary than ever for Jonson, underscoring the differences 'between his own artistic practices and those of playwrights who abandon moral concerns entirely'. Delight is important, but moral purposes are not to be neglected. Especially at issue, for Jonson, 'is the complicated theory and practice of what Jonson and his Roman moralist forebears call "decorum"', or 'propriety . . . in both its social and artistic manifestations'. To allow 'too wide a gap' between virtue and decorum is to invite the danger of a degeneration into 'relativist expediency'. Hence, Jonson's emphasis on verisimilitude as an aesthetic criterion, and his solicitousness about the audience's being able to enjoy pleasure. Mimesis becomes increasingly important for him in comedy. 'Decorum' is a synonym for 'naturalism', and yet audience pleasure is 'not *necessarily* dependent upon artistic verisimilitude'.[122] Eros for him tends to become peripheral or non-existent; for Doll Common, as for Ursula in *Bartholomew Fair*, 'the conventional comic reward of respectable sexual gratification is unavailable.'[123] (As William Slights also insists, ten years later, 'the days of romantic comedy with its gentle ladies, fairies, queens, and *bona fide* fairy queens were dead and gone' by the mid-1600s.[124]) The possibility of sublimation, or 'the transference of erotic energy from a base to a noble object', becomes impossible. Maus is reminded of William Hazlitt's complaints about Jonson's close attention to the body and bodily, leading the dramatist to dwell obsessively on low company, 'like a person who fastens upon a disagreeable subject, and cannot be persuaded to leave it'. Indeed, says Maus, Hazlitt's distress resembles that of the nineteenth century not only with Jonson, as we have seen, but with many of Jonson's favourite writers, most of all the satirists Horace, Persius, Juvenal and Martial, who write about things like haemorrhoids and oral sex. The 'resolute refusal to grant any but narrowly carnal aims' rules out the possibility of romance or tragedy.[125] Comedy in Jonson, as it becomes 'more and more insistently low-mimetic', more pessimistic about humanity and yet less rigorously censorious, 'begins to close the gap between the spectators and the action they witness'.[126] The London setting becomes claustrophobic. *The Alchemist*'s seemingly amoral denouement appears to violate the implicit contract of the play's start, in which Jonson invites his audience to share in his comic feast. Maus's essay is especially thoughtful in its way of locating Jonson and *The Alchemist* in the context of post-modern theory.

Other recent studies that locate Jonson fitly in our post-modern world include Julie Sanders, arguing that *The Alchemist*'s Blackfriars venue inscribes in the play the ideological values of the marginal world outside of the city walls of London that made such a significant contribution to the 'symbolic economy' of Jonson's urban world as a whole and to a 'republic of wholesale merchants';[127] Stanton Linden, with his attention to Jonson's 'keen awareness of the political and religious associations of contemporary hermetic thought' and its links to 'occult interests in radical protestantism';[128] and Richmond Barbour, taking the view that Jonson's alleged conservatism, misogyny, homophobia and revulsion against the erotic are in fact deeply ambivalent, 'by turns authoritative and subversive', and driven by his own 'fear of engulfment' by women's sexuality and a consequent 'male irrelevance'.[129] For critical studies of *The Alchemist* in the twenty-first century, see Chapter 3 in this present collection.

CHAPTER TWO

The Alchemist on the Stage: Performance, Collaboration and Deviation

Elizabeth Schafer and Emma Cox

A performance history of *The Alchemist* has to confront the fact that theatre is an intrinsically collaborative activity and that Ben Jonson sometimes found the messy, unstable process of creating performance very difficult. Famously, by the end of his career, Jonson's relationship with his co-creator of masques, Inigo Jones, was in tatters; but even in the pioneering act of publishing his plays as serious *Works* in 1616, Jonson seemed to resist the collaborative dynamic by omitting plays he had co-written with other playwrights. Any performance collaboration can deviate from what the playwright originally intended – and Jonson's intentions are sometimes spelt out very clearly – but creative theatrical 'deviations' can offer important insights into the potential dramaturgy of a play. Our performance history explores such 'deviations', or interpretations, by directors, actors, and set and costume designers, in the full knowledge that some of these would have infuriated Jonson.

Indeed, a brilliant, farce-based comedy such as *The Alchemist* cannot be fully understood unless the three-dimensional, inter-subjective, unpredictable nature of theatre is taken into account.[1] On the page, laden with footnotes, *The Alchemist* is daunting; on the stage, served up with expert comic timing, it can become a dazzling showcase for theatrical virtuosity. Richard Cave points to the astonishing theatrical brio required in act 3:

[Face] speaks in Lungs' voice through the keyhole to Sir Epicure waiting without; in his own workaday tones *sotto voce*

giving instructions to Doll and Subtle; as the Captain advis-
ing the blindfolded Dapper how to conduct himself . . . and
in squeaking falsetto as one of the elves searching the clerk for
evidence of worldly pelf.[2]

Here voice, accent, pacing and energy are critical, and actors
and directors will be able to offer more insight than editors or
readers.

Despite *The Alchemist*'s intrinsic theatricality, relatively few
Jonson scholars have engaged with the play in performance.
Robert G. Noyes's 1935 account of *Ben Jonson on the English Stage
1660–1776* was pioneering for its time and offers a methodical
survey approach.[3] Noyes maps the play's popularity during the
Restoration; he mentions how topical productions seemed after
the 1720 South Sea Bubble; he charts the play's association with
star actors such as Colley Cibber, David Garrick, Charles Macklin,
Charlotte Charke, Kitty Clive and Hannah Pritchard. He details
the cuts made by Garrick and reports on the stage life of *The
Tobacconist*, Francis Gentleman's 1770 adaptation. But Noyes is
worried by deviations from Jonson: *The Tobacconist* is a 'mon-
strous', rather than a culturally specific, and culturally revealing, response to Jonson's play.[4] Fifty years later Ejner J. Jensen's
Ben Jonson's Comedies on the Modern Stage records regret that
'only a negligible amount' of criticism on Jonson takes account
of Jonson's 'achievement as a dramatist who wrote for the stage'
and 'as a consequence [Jonson's] dramaturgical skills remain relatively unexplored'.[5] Jensen focuses on the period 1899–1972, fin-
ishing with the quatercentenary of Jonson's birth, and highlights
the recurring theatrical problem, especially during the nineteenth
century, of Jonson's frankness about bodily functions, functions
which kept *The Alchemist* off the stage. Jensen then maps a healthy
stage life for the play during the twentieth century after William
Poel revived it in 1899.

More recently, Lois Potter has argued for the importance of
theatre-centred readings of Jonson in an essay discussing the
RSC's Jonson revivals on the Swan stage.[6] Potter also notes that

Restoration theatrical memory claimed that the original players in Jonson's plays were 'taught', or directed, by Jonson 'Line by Line, each Title, Accent, Word'.[7] Indeed, Jonson's aspiration that subsequent generations of performers should also be 'taught' to perform 'correctly' inflects his published texts of *The Alchemist*; both the 1612 quarto and the 1616 folio are important first sources for a performance history because of Jonson's determination to record his staging intentions.

According to the folio's title page, the King's Men performed *The Alchemist*. Given that 'The Persons of the Play' states 'The Scene: London', information repeated in the Prologue, 'Our scene is London' (line 5), and that the play's action is located in Blackfriars, we may reasonably assume that *The Alchemist* would have been performed at the company's newly acquired Blackfriars playhouse, as well as at the Globe. Any performance of *The Alchemist* at the Blackfriars playhouse would render the play an early modern example of site-specific theatre: the play is set in, and resonates with, the environment in which it was performed. Ironically, because the playhouses were closed during much of 1610, due to the very plague that had sent Lovewit scurrying to the country, *The Alchemist* was probably first performed far away from Blackfriars in Oxford in September 1610.[8]

The folio includes a list of players but not their parts: Richard Burbage, John Lowin, Henry Condell, Alexander Cook, Robert Armin, John Heminges, William Ostler, John Underwood, Nicholas Tooley, William Eglestone. From what is known about these actors, we can speculate about which roles they performed but, despite the number of assertions currently circulating on the internet that Burbage played Subtle, traditional scholarship usually identifies Burbage's role as Face.[9] The folio does not name the boy players and it is less easy to speculate about who played Doll. Both the folio and quarto texts make few elaborate staging demands but the Prologue, ambitiously, expects the play to run at 'two short hours' (line 1). In addition, Cave has argued that Jonson's use, in both the quarto and the folio, of layout for printing intimates pacing.[10] For example, the quarto opens 1.1 with

tightly compressed lines, crammed together in a way that visually
suggests a hurly-burly atmosphere and 'a real sense of people trying to shout each other down'.[11] Jonson uses long dashes almost
as stage directions, to mark where speeches are interrupted; some
dashes are longer and more pronounced in the folio, which suggests he was not satisfied with the evocation of timing achieved by
the quarto's layout. There are also more marginal notes on action
in the folio compared with the quarto; at Doll's line in the first
scene, 'You'll bring your head within a cocks-combe, will you?',
the folio (F 609; *CWBJ* 1.1.115) comments, '*Shee catcheth out Face
his sword: and breaks Subtles glasse*', whereas the quarto does not
spell out this business. In modern texts, these annotations are dis-
played as conventional stage directions, but Cave argues that when
the folio layout is not reproduced, the effect is to deny 'access to
Jonson's evocation of the play in performance'.[12]

Some of Jonson's directions are pragmatic. For example, the
quarto (Q E3v) has '*Dol is seen*' (*CWBJ* 2.3.210), pinning down
what is implied in the text. Authorial intentions are very clear in
the folio when Jonson states '*To Surly*' and '*He whispers Mammon*'
(F 629; *CWBJ* 2.3.288, 290.1) although an actor may choose not to
'whisper' for the full five lines that are addressed to Mammon, and
might, if the performance space were appropriate, take Mammon
aside and speak in tones well above a whisper, thus ensuring all
the audience hear the lines. In 3.5, however, the folio marginal
annotations become more expansive; it may not help much to
know that Subtle is '*disguised like a Priest of Fairy*' (F 646; *CWBJ*
3.5.0), because a modern designer still has to reimagine what
this costume might look like, but '*He speakes through the keyhole,
the other knocking*' (F 647; *CWBJ* 3.5.58), like Jonson's careful
deployment of 'within' and 'without' elsewhere, creates a sense
of stage geography. In another critical scene, 4.5 (Q K2r), Jonson
uses two columns and smaller font size to indicate Doll speaking
at the same time as Face and Mammon; the folio adds '*They speake
together*' (F 659; *CWBJ* 4.5.24.1). Some folio annotations, such as
'*He kisses her*' (F 652; *CWBJ* 4.2.37), register different social conventions from today when it is not customary to kiss someone on

the mouth at first meeting; '*He falls to picking of* [Surly's pockets]' (F 661; *CWBJ* 4.6.25.1) could be deduced but is not completely necessary; '*Subtle hath whisperd with him this while*' (F 664; *CWBJ* 4.7.72.1) is theatrically clumsy, as a stage direction should signal action in present or future tense, not past. Overall, the increase in annotation in the folio compared with the quarto suggests Jonson was attempting the impossible task of *controlling* and *authorizing* the play's theatrical afterlives.

This chapter focuses on a small selection from those afterlives, a group of productions which illuminate very specific dramaturgical and artistic challenges: characterization, tone, metatheatre, Londonness, larrikinism. The productions are David Garrick's adaptation, *The Alchymist*, which was published in 1777; Jean Gascon's 1969 *Alchemist* at Stratford, Ontario; a production by Gregory Hersov in 1987 for the Manchester Royal Exchange; Sam Mendes's 1991 *Alchemist* for the Royal Shakespeare Company, Stratford-upon-Avon; Neil Armfield's 1996 production for Belvoir St Theatre, Sydney; and John Bell's 2009 *Alchemist*, which toured several Australian states.[13] While by necessity we exclude many provocative, insightful and theatrically intelligent productions, these six works, which range widely in terms of theatrical and geo-cultural context, provide a varied and instructive sample of collaborations with, and deviations from, Jonson.

When David Garrick made Abel Drugger the star of the play, he introduced one of the most radical creative divergences from Jonson's *Alchemist*, in terms of characterization, in the play's performance history. But Garrick's foregrounding of Drugger continued a process that had begun much earlier: *The Imperick*, the droll printed in Francis Kirkman's 1662 publication *The Wits*, is largely given over to exhibiting Drugger (1.3, 2.6) and, to a lesser extent, Ananias (2.5).[14] While Garrick first acted Drugger on 21 March 1743, over subsequent decades he frequently changed and adapted the role; the published text of *The Alchymist* indicates some overall trends of Garrick's adaptation. Cutting is often deep, and bawdy jokes are marked as unplayable. Garrick gives Drugger extra, amazed interjections in response to Face's or Subtle's

alchemical spiels, as well as lines which repeat what another character has just said, making him sound dopey. *The Alchymist* does
not record, however, the moment which Garrick describes in his
'Essay on Acting' as part of a mock comic discussion of his own
playing of Macbeth and Drugger:[15]

> When *Abel Drugger* has broke the *Urinal*, he is *mentally
> absorb'd* with the different Ideas of the *invaluable* Price of
> the *Urinal*, and the Punishment that may be inflicted in
> Consequence of a Curiosity, no way appertaining or belong-
> ing to the Business he came about. Now, if this, as it cer-
> tainly *is*, the Situation of his Mind, How are the different
> Members of the Body to be agitated? Why Thus, – His *Eyes*
> must be revers'd from the Object he is most intimidated
> with, and by dropping his *Lip* at the some [sic] Time *to* the
> Object, it throws a trembling *Languor* upon every *Muscle*,
> and by declining the right Part of the Head *towards* the
> *Urinal*, it casts the most *comic Terror* and *Shame* over all the
> *upper* Part of the Body, that can be imagin'd; and to make the
> *lower* Part equally ridiculous, his *Toes* must be *inverted* from
> the *Heel*, and by *holding* his *Breath*, he will unavoidably give
> himself a *Tremor* in the *Knees*, and if his *Fingers*, at the same
> Time, seem *convuls'd*, it finishes the compleatest low Picture
> of *Grotesque Terror* that can be imagin'd by a *Dutch* Painter.

Garrick's description is worth quoting at length because it is such
an incisive deviation from Jonson, which seized on Drugger and
expertly repackaged him to appeal to contemporary taste. While
the comic deployment of urinals, or specimen bottles, is something
that has recurred through much of *The Alchemist*'s performance
history, the broken urinal supposedly originated with 'old Cibber':
Thomas Wilkes claims that in one performance, Theophilus
Cibber, as Drugger, inadvertently broke a glass vial; his reac-
tion, in character, to this accident so pleased the audience that
they demanded he repeat the comic business in subsequent performances.[16] The terror performed by Garrick's Drugger helped

create comic sympathy but it also helped to build a subsequent joke when Drugger shapes up to take part in the assault on Surly in 4.7; as Surly departs in confusion, Garrick's Drugger asks proudly, 'Did not I behave well?' and 'He won't be here | In a hurry, I believe', convinced his pugnacity has driven Surly away. While it is ironic that two of Garrick's most memorable comic moments as Drugger were *inspired* by Jonson rather than *written* by him, this creative collaboration between Jonson and Garrick generated physically comic theatre which helped keep *The Alchemist* on stage for a large part of the eighteenth century.

A recurring theme in critical responses to Garrick's Drugger is wonderment at Garrick's ability to transform himself; one night he plays King Lear, the next he plays Drugger.[17] Although the roles of both Face and Subtle would have given Garrick even more chance to demonstrate his ability to switch rapidly from one persona to another, he found in Drugger a comedy grounded in pathos as well as silliness, something which other notable Druggers have identified in the role. In 1932, Ivor Brown described Cedric Hardwicke's performance:

> Drugger became in his hands a superb simpleton, whose bland expectant smile continually atoned for the absence of a big speaking part. The make-up, with a clown's tuft of hair and upturned snout, was a masterpiece of plastic creation, and this great actor's boundless skill was evident in the complete success with which he made an almost speechless role dominate a stage which was otherwise a flood of roaring eloquence.[18]

In 1947, Alec Guinness's Drugger inspired even higher praise. Kenneth Tynan claimed Guinness's performance confirmed him as 'the best living English character-actor':

> Mr. Guinness manages to get to the heart of all good, hopeful young men who can enjoy without envy the society of wits. I was overjoyed to watch his wistful, happy eyes moving, in

dumb wonder, from Face to Subtle: a solid little fellow, you felt, and how eager to help! At last he puts in a tolerable contribution to the conversation. O Altitudo! His face creases ruddily into modest delight, and he stamps his thin feet in glee. . . . Drugger is commissioned by Face to bring him a Spanish costume as disguise. He trots away, and returns shyly, clad in its showy cloak and hat. Waiting for Face to answer the door, he begins to execute timid dance-steps under the porch. He treads a rapt, self-absorbed measure with himself, consumed with joy. Then Face appears: and, not regretfully or pathetically, but smartly and prosaically, he sheds his costume and hands it over. It is most touchingly done.[19]

While 'most touchingly done' does not sound Jonsonian, there was a significant theatrical pay-off in Guinness's interpretation.

Characterization is almost inevitably a major area where modern theatre will deviate from Jonson, simply because so many modern actors are trained in Stanislavski-inspired approaches, which seek nuance where Jonson deployed cartoon. And most boy players would have had trouble competing with Jane Casson's cleavage, which featured in production photographs and reviews of Jean Gascon's 1969 *Alchemist* at Stratford, Ontario. Casson's Doll was praised for her ability to switch 'from nun to whore to fairy to thief with expert timing';[20] she was 'first-rate, a lovely bawd made up of rouge, beauty marks, protuberant bosom and an utter capacity for the consummate swindle';[21] and she 'can, and she does, imitate Marilyn Monroe'[22] – something it is safe to say Jonson never envisaged.

Gascon's *Alchemist*, which toured widely in the United States and Canada, polarized reviewers and provides a particularly useful case study for examining the challenge of tone, of how robustly the comedy of *The Alchemist* should be played. The production's farce/comic balance generated much discussion: one review praised the 'sight gags, the bold bawdy gestures and the wildly inventive Rube Goldberg-like contraptions';[23] meanwhile, another complained of 'the limited but standard Stratford sight gags of breast-pulling and crotch grabbing'.[24] The pacing was hilarious, 'reminiscent of French bedroom farce';[25] or it came close to 'a traffic disaster'.[26] The production's visual comedy was increased by the use of an alchemical machine that would 'spew forth steam whenever the clients need impressing'.[27] It was 'a sort of gothic boiler on wheels, armor plated, adorned by a set of matching crocodiles that look like tin armadillos. Atop it is a jungle of beakers, retorts, flasks and tubing and it is invaluable in helping the alchemist fleece the fleeceable.'[28] Gascon placed alchemy centre stage, both thematically and physically, although the machine risked upstaging the performers – and Jonson's words.

Despite the production's commitment to *The Alchemist*'s London location – the soundscape was dominated by cockney vowels[29] – some reviewers found a Molièresque flavour. This had the potential for political loading in 1969 Canada, when francophone and anglophone relations were deteriorating as the FLQ campaign escalated in violence. And although in terms of 1969 Québécois politics, Gascon, a French Canadian, was far from hard-line, he had a history of sustained commitment to the francophones' classic playwright;[30] indeed, in the previous year at Stratford, in a theatre largely dedicated to English high culture, he had directed a very successful *Tartuffe*, which was being revived in 1969. Despite intersections between *Tartuffe* and *The Alchemist* – two neoclassical comedies, full of biting satire, written fifty years apart – for one reviewer, 'a Molière-oriented intelligence is not the most felicitous to turn loose on the extravagance of Jonson';[31] another commented that Powys Thomas's Subtle 'kept reminding me of Tartuffe, a hard surface with something close to wizardry beneath it'.[32] Meanwhile, Martin Gottfried, who began his career as a classical music critic, took Gascon to task for directing 'as if it [*The Alchemist*] were a comic-ballet of Molière's' and 'sandwiching a slow second act between the first and third acts, as if the play were a concerto', something redolent of Molière 'whose plays are very much stage concertos'.[33]

One reason this production was susceptible to being seen as Molièresque was because William Hutt, who had played Tartuffe, and was about to reprise the role, was Mammon. But Hutt's performance, like most aspects of the production, divided the critics. In the 'naked between my succubae' speech (2.2.41–95), one reviewer found subtlety of characterization:

> He speaks with faint relish of the pleasures of table and bed, but one knows at once that for all his long life he has been a victim of acid indigestion and sexual timidity. We see him now as an old man, turning to the practitioners of the grey art in the sad hope of tasting at last the pleasures that have always been denied him.[34]

And yet Hutt's Mammon was also described as 'eyes goggling, lips salivating' and eventually quivering 'away in lusty exhaustion',[35] 'a figure of ecstatic pornography. He struts and roars like an oversexed lion, preens himself, roars, rants and almost literally brings down the house.'[36] Broad comedy was also to be found in Thomas's playing of Subtle: 'looking like a strange cinematic amalgam of Svengali and Ghengis Khan', Thomas 'plays the fake alchemist with enormous gusto, rolling the meaningless periods of scientific gobbledy gook off his tongue with the zeal of a Welsh preacher'.[37] He was 'a thrift shop Merlin', 'fondling his astrological charts, peering into his glass globe, knocking a knuckle on a handy skull'.[38] These descriptions all suggest a physicality in performance that was comically robust.

Overall, Gascon's *Alchemist* was far more positively reviewed at Stratford than on tour; the production developed and changed during its extended run, but on the open main stage at Stratford, it worked better than in the tour venues, most of which were proscenium arch theatres.[39] A rather different approach to the challenge of touring was adopted in Gregory Hersov's 1987 *Alchemist*, for the Manchester Royal Exchange;[40] this production took its stage space with it. This *Alchemist* was always performed in the round, in a space very evocative of the unlocalized Jacobean playhouse stage, on a portable stage replicating the Royal Exchange's dimensions.[41]

Like most productions, Hersov's had to work with the play's insistent identification of its location as London. A production staged in Manchester, which toured the north of England, has to have a different relationship with the play's Londonness compared with, for example, an *Alchemist* at the National Theatre in London, which (as the programme for Nicholas Hytner's 2006 production claimed) is close to the original Blackfriars playhouse. Even the name 'Blackfriars' reads differently in Manchester, where it evokes a tower-block-dominated area in Salford. Locale at the end of the production also functioned differently. After the cast dismantled the entire set in seconds for the move to outside Lovewit's house, a very large crowd of neighbours entered. Local amateur dramatic societies provided these neighbours when the production was on tour; these amateurs were led and managed by the two professional company members playing Neighbours 1 and 2, who spoke all the Neighbours' lines. The local actors murmured, hummed at, and reacted to events onstage, creating an enthusiastic and distinctively localized 'rabble' (5.3.74). Few professional companies today can hope to assemble 'Forty o'the neighbours' (4.7.112), but this production deployed far more than is usual.

While the Royal Exchange theatre-in-the-round configuration placed specific constraints on staging – no flats – the production's set, 'Lit by Michael Calf in the mellow tones of a Rembrandt night scene' was 'dominated by furnace, bellows and retort, and overhung by a flickeringly-candled chandelier from which dangle cabbalistic signs'.[42] The characters constantly circled around the object of desire, the powerhouse of alchemy, and Face, Subtle and Doll regularly pumped the central stove with bellows, producing clouds of smoke. Offstage, behind the audience, an area 'was used as an echo chamber for tormented voices and exploding, smoking cauldrons',[43] an effect which helped catch the audience in the embrace of the action; they too were part of the circle of alchemy and had been conned into giving money to watch Face, Subtle and Doll perform.

The opening scene of this production was understated, with Jonathan Hackett's Face, Michael Feast's Subtle and Alyson Spiro's Doll keeping their distance from one another, lobbing abuse across the space. This blocking diluted the intensity of the action, but it played to every angle of the theatre and took in every section of the audience. In the magic circle of the stage space, Hackett's Face became a superb shape-shifter or 'the ideal rep character actor',[44] someone who could play any required role in any production. There was broad physical comedy as he performed a Quasimodo version of Lungs, fighting ludicrously with his behumped costume; he then became an icily puritanical Jeremy at the end of the play. Meanwhile, Feast's Subtle overacted with gusto for all the gulls, 'a wonderful diabolical figure swirling a great cloak, holding a druid's staff aloft, glaring transfixed into a bubbling glass flask'[45] and 'swooping on victims like Kenny Everett playing Dracula',[46] although his 'final rage after being cheated contains something of Malvolio's compressed bitterness'.[47] Feast rendered the alchemical jargon a glorious, ridiculous hocus-pocus. The alchemical catechism was hilarious, palpable nonsense delivered with a gleeful sense of improvisation, or even theatre sports in play. One minute Subtle was enthusiastically stripping off to join the Anabaptists in mortifying their flesh; then he was pulling on his reversible coat and completely transforming his appearance; the next he was ad-libbing (or appearing to) as the gate into the playing space got stuck.

Like Gascon, who used 'lugubrious melodramatic incidental organ music',[48] Hersov deployed music – Carl Orff's 'Fortuna' from *Carmina Burana* – to help 'fuel the atmosphere of mediaeval necromancy and astrological craft'.[49] Costume was Jacobean, but Hersov stressed how relevant the play was to 1987: 'After years of "Thatcherism", England seems to me to be dedicated to lust, greed, avarice and the fulfilment of fantasies. . . . The parallels of A.I.D.S., get-rich-quick, advertising, Big Bang seems to make "The Alchemist" particularly relevant to 1987.'[50] Hersov adds, 'At the end, Face's final speech to the audience comes from the past right into the present'; certainly, Caryl Churchill's play

Serious Money, which opened in London in March of that year, satirized many of the same targets identified by Hersov. The left wing *Tribune* felt the cast played 'with the accuracy and fervour of stockbrokers making their first million' and that the play's action offered

> the perfect metaphor for the post-Big Bang yuppie wealth trail. That VDUs and computers are used now instead of alembics and crucibles doesn't alter the essential identity. Props apart, the name of the game is to take someone else's money and call the process wealth creation.[51]

A memorable sound effect, the chink of money being dropped into a moneybox every time a gull handed over any cash, generated a powerful sense of the booty that was accumulating.

Hersov slimmed the text strategically, cut deeply into the Kastril plot-line, and updated vocabulary ('bitch' for 'brach', 1.1.111). The actors managed to have fun with words that could have no meaning for modern audiences; for example, 'chiaus' in 1.2.26, 30 and 35 became 'chouse', an affected choice of vocabulary, probably a malapropism, trotted out by Dapper to the great amusement of Face who then played around with the word.[52] Overall, Hersov's production exhibited finesse in its use of space, locale and metatheatre, and broad, knockabout comedy in its energized, exuberant performances.

An indication of how difficult it can be to please reviewers over the question of comic balance in relation to *The Alchemist* appears in the critical responses to Sam Mendes's 1991 RSC *Alchemist*.[53] Generally, there was high praise for this *Alchemist*: it was a 'vigorous and brilliantly acted production';[54] 'Zestful, shrewd and often extremely funny';[55] 'gloriously entertaining'.[56] One reviewer, however, complained that the 'extra rapacious edge – the darker side of Jonson' was 'absent' and 'the black comedy' had 'gone missing'.[57] For another, there was 'little sense here of Jonson's lashing of vice or the bitterness of his vision. Indeed you find yourself suspending all judgment on the unholy trinity of Face, Subtle, and Doll

Common because they are such stylish, inventive villains.'[58] A reviewer of the 1992 revival commented, 'This is an exceptionally good-natured production' with the satire 'gently administered'.[59] And yet, David Bradley's Subtle offered 'clever, involuntary hints of the character's destitute background',[60] and his 'defeat' was 'enraged'.[61] Certainly, the *Times Educational Supplement*, with more time to reflect than reviewers in the daily papers, found that the production's 'ever-inventive humour lightly conceals a swinge-ing indictment of that most meretricious of decades, the 1980s'.[62] Mendes himself stressed that Face, Subtle and Doll 'need money, they are also starving. Acting becomes their livelihood'; he argued the play was 'not about criminality; it's about gullibility; about the need to believe' and that 'the crushing of [the gulls'] dreams is a terrible thing'.[63] He also found the scenes between Mammon and Doll 'sad and very desolate'.[64]

The performers were working with a space, the largely unadorned Swan Theatre, which was one step up from bare boards: 'five doors and a table and a light bulb'.[65] So the chal-lenge to Jonathan Hyde as Face, David Bradley as Subtle and Joanne Pearce as Doll was how to use actorly craft to create what the gulls – and the audience – wanted to see. One major point of reference for Mendes was the theatricality of street traders:

> You go down the Walworth Road now . . . and you go down the market, and it's the same guys. They've got endless tricks. They're endlessly inventive. We spent some time talking to market traders. Because it's that sort of street nous that they use. You're looking all the time to try to find a way of demon-strating the artistry, with nothing, out of nothing.[66]

For several reviewers, this *Alchemist* evoked David Mamet's 'salesmen-in-extremis' plays such as *Glengarry Glen Ross*.[67] When con-merchants are roguishly entertaining, it becomes easier to overlook their illegality. But because Mendes 'inserted a whole host of visual gags that seem to owe more to vaudeville than clas-sical theatre',[68] he could also be read as underlining the levels of theatricality in play, something which could offer a comically Brechtian distancing and commentary, as well as securing laughs.

A particularly clear example of Mendes's creative collaboration with Jonson appeared in the production's representation of Doll (Figure 2.1). Although she initially appears to be an excellent role for an actress, Doll has fewer chances to display virtuoso acting skills than her partners in crime, and her great comic moment as the Queen of Fairy comes at a point when the sometimes exhausted audience can see that the play is galloping into the last furlong. Pearce's Doll was an unusually strong presence – 'both funny and sexy' and 'moving with great assurance from feisty slut to high-class whore'.[69] As the Queen of Fairy Pearce recognizably imitated Queen Elizabeth II, speaking in a cut-glass accent which contrasted strongly with Doll's usual broad cockney. Because she was balancing on Face's shoulders – Face was largely covered by Doll's gigantic flouncy skirts – this Queen of Fairy was able to caress Dapper 'with all four hands'.[70] Elsewhere Pearce's Doll was

Figure 2.1 *Joanne Pearce as Doll Common in The Alchemist, RSC, 1991. Directed by Sam Mendes. Photograph: Michael Le Poer Trench. Reproduced with permission.*

a 'sassy smokey-voiced Bonnie to Bradley's Clyde',[71] and aroused
Mammon 'to ecstasy by rhythmically stroking his dangling money
bag' in 4.1.[72] Nevertheless, Mendes felt Pearce was frustrated in
the role: Doll 'doesn't have any gags' and 'she's not funny: she
doesn't have the comic motor of the play'.[73] What this production gave to Pearce was more room to manoeuvre than Jonson did.
Pearce's Doll was frequently to be seen roaming the long stage
gallery, hidden by the shadows, during scenes when she was supposed to be offstage, such as 1.2 and 2.1. Spying and eavesdrop-
ping as she prowled around the gallery, this Doll was a particularly
strong and sometimes threatening presence; this staging decision
also made good plot sense as Doll was seen to be keeping up with
the latest plot developments and was clearly ready to shift into
whatever role might be required next.

Alongside Pearce, Bradley's Subtle, brought 'a wonderful fer-
rety fervour and a prodigious gift for esoteric mumbo-jumbo to
his various impersonations of the alchemist'.[74] Hyde as Face went
'through a series of lightning disguises, accents and manners';[75]
when he 'has to revert to his "real" self as Jeremy the butler at the
end, this last role seems, in its creepy mock-meekness, no more
authentic than, say, his uproarious impersonation of "Lungs"'.
Finally, Hyde's Face 'tries to bribe the audience to acquit him,
hinting at our complicity in what has gone on. Here he throws
what looks like a heavy handful of sovereigns into the stalls. Only
instead of landing with the crash of coins, they float and flutter
in the air, sparkling, weightless confetti.'[76] This theatrical gag – a
variation on a pantomime favourite whereby a bucket of 'water' is
thrown at the audience and the 'water' turns out to be bits of shiny
paper – offered one final chance for the audience to see themselves
as gulled among the gulls.

Mendes's *Alchemist* was costumed in a mixture of Jacobean and
modern modes; Dapper wore a doublet and hose made out of pin-
stripe material; Surly wore plus fours. In addition, Lovewit's house
contained a flushing loo and electric lights. While the first director to put *The Alchemist* into modern dress, Tyrone Guthrie, was
castigated in 1962 for his contemporarized Old Vic production,

since then many directors have followed Guthrie's lead.[77] In 2000, Barry Edelstein, who was directing *The Alchemist* in New York, argued for viewing *The Alchemist* 'through a double lens of 1610 and 2000, with one foot in early modern London and the other in post-modern New York'.[78] This notion of a 'double lens' sits very comfortably with Mendes's production.

Similarly, Neil Armfield's *Alchemist*, produced by Company B, Belvoir St Theatre in Sydney in 1996,[79] had to negotiate a 'double lens', grounded in the fact that audiences would in all likelihood approach the play with an awareness of it (and themselves) being simultaneously in-London and not-in-London. This compounded the dualities produced by historical distance, crystallized in designer Stephen Curtis's mixing of the mock-Jacobean and the contemporary: a section of neo-Tudor panelling looming over modern interior squalor. But Sydney is a very long way from London, and it is perhaps the case that Armfield's production was not as culturally and imaginatively freighted by the London-centrism that affects theatre in Britain, particularly performances of English canonical texts. For British productions that originate outside London, going to the capital remains an important measure of success. The task that faced Hersov in Manchester might, as far as extricating his *Alchemist* from the overwhelming dominance of London is concerned, have been more acute than that faced by Armfield, a major player in an Australian professional theatre scene that by the mid-1990s had set aside the burdens of cultural cringe. In terms of centre–periphery relations, Sydney – Australia's London, the big, restless, multifarious, greedy city – was inextricably present in Armfield's *Alchemist*.

This geo-cultural resonance exists despite Armfield's characteristic resistance to any self-consciously 'localized' idea of place, whether Sydney, London, or otherwise. Armfield emphasizes the role of the theatre space in doing the bulk of the imaginative work, commenting in an interview for the national broadsheet, 'The skill is achieving your own and particular world for that play and not trying to say this is happening in London of 1610 or we've updated it to [Sydney's] Kings Cross.'[80] Several critics were more interested in international resonances than local ones, including Mamet's *Glengarry Glen Ross* (a comparison also invoked, as we have noted, by critics of Mendes's production); Tarantino's *Reservoir Dogs*;[81] the British theatrical inheritance of Garrick and Guinness as Abel Drugger;[82] the emergent impacts (and uncontrollable trajectories) of the internet and genetic science;[83] and contemporary New Age 'self-help gurus [and] get rich quick schemes'.[84] Others were interested in the local, with one reviewer maintaining that despite Armfield's general approach, the production had a sense of contemporary Sydney: 'Neil Armfield has said he always sets productions of the classics "on the stage", but his version of this savage satire of life in the back streets of Jacobean London seems awfully familiar when we walk out of the theatre into the back streets of Howardean Sydney.'[85]

Although *The Alchemist* is not often staged in Australia, it is tempting to suggest that the play finds a natural home in a nation that stereotypically values certain qualities that are hallmarks of this comedy: an irreverence that runs roughshod over certain social formalities, delight in mocking excessive seriousness or pretension, boisterous physicality and inventiveness with language. These are traits of the Australian larrikin, a figure so iconic that it has become a cultural cliché. The term 'larrikin' has undergone a shift from its derogatory meaning in settler culture as a tough hooligan to its current affectionate connotation; Melissa Bellanta emphasizes the importance of Australian vaudeville theatre from the 1890s to the early twentieth century in popularizing the larrikin identity, citing the bawdy double-act 'Stiffy and Mo' (Nat Phillips and Roy Rene).[86] If, as Penny Gay argues, the larrikin 'insist[s] on the integrity and right to speak of . . . subaltern individuals',[87] *The Alchemist*'s protagonists seem to fit the bill – it would not be a stretch to imagine Subtle, Face and even Doll as the kind of people who, some 150 years after Jonson wrote the play, might have found themselves on a convict ship bound for Australia.

Armfield's dynamic Subtle and Face, Geoffrey Rush and Hugo Weaving, can to a large extent be mapped onto vaudeville antecedents. The actors offered an inventive, subversive theatrical larrikinism, unencumbered by cultural–nationalistic sentimentalism. Many of the Lecoq-trained Rush's comic and tragicomic stage performances owe at least as much, in terms of embodiment and characterization, to European stage clowning traditions and the Australian vaudeville theatre to which Bellanta refers than to post-Stanislavski techniques.[88] Weaving's commanding, at times imperious physicality as Face complemented Rush's fluidity as the wily Subtle. The duo generated a great deal of comedy out of verbal ripostes and slapstick interactions.

Characterization and vaudeville-larrikin comedy in this actor-focused production (played in Belvoir's 340-seat theatre, configured as a corner thrust stage enclosed by two of the building's external walls) are best understood in terms of deviations, and even *deviousness*, in costume, language (including accent) and non-verbal work. Kym Barrett's costumes gave particular insight into characterization and were a grungy celebration of shape-shifting (as well as time- and place-shifting) and actorly artifice. Rush's mercurial Subtle first appeared as a dirty, ratty figure in threadbare long johns, his face faintly whitened (as were the other actors'), eyes outlined in black and his teeth dark with rot between the gaps. He reappeared in the first scene with Abel Drugger (Arky Michael, hunched and peering dimly through thick spectacles) in a long black gown, skullcap and Jacobean-style white neck ruff. Rush also shifted gear physically in this scene, reining in Subtle's roving limb and hand movements and adopting a solemn, hushed demeanour (Figure 2.2). His subsequent costume changes eliminated any sense of the character occupying an identifiable time or place: Subtle appeared as a barefoot guru in sarong and turban, his body daubed in white, and later robed himself in swirl-patterned satin dressing gown and waved a peacock feather about in an outrageous performance of New Age conjuring. A charismatic Face, Weaving wore a British naval officer's jacket and tight black trousers; as Jeremy, he was dressed suavely in a black suit and sunglasses, his hair tied up and briefcase in hand. Only as Lungs did he shed this businesslike veneer, appearing in overalls and apron, with a gas mask pushed up on top

Figure 2.2 *Geoffrey Rush and Hugo Weaving as Subtle and Face in The Alchemist, Belvoir, 1996. Directed by Neil Armfield. Photograph: Heidrun Löhr. Reproduced with permission.*

of his head. As Doll, Gillian Jones's costumes drew on theatrical signifiers of a prostitute that were closer to contemporary urban than Jacobean – a short red skirt over white stockings and platform heels; a pink minidress; and as Queen of Fairy, a white skirt with silvery trim topped with a black bodice – most of these items worn past their best.

The production omitted the Prologue, moving straight from the acrostic Argument into the explosive opening.[89] Subtle's crude first line, and the audience's response to it, can be something of a barometer of how the vulgarity and farce are likely to play. Rush's vocal work helped things along. While not using the comically broad local inflections that marked out some of the production's dim-witted characters, he lingered a beat on open-mouthed long 'aa' vowels (an identifiably Australasian sound), bookending the joke with a rhyming repetition: 'Thy worst. I fart at thee' (1.1.1), became, '*Aah*, thy worst. I fart at thee', followed by another minor addition to Jonson's text that produced the same sound: 'Lick figs | Out at my *arse*' (the last word overlapping with Face's forceful 'Rogue').

Armfield retained most of the exchange between Subtle and Face in 1.2, allowing for high-energy interplay between Rush and Weaving. The words most savoured or emphasized by the lead actors were in many cases modifications to Jonson's text: 'my arse'; 'You pathetic whelp, you coward'; 'cramped and consti-pated, with your ugly great nose'; 'boot boy' (Subtle's insult to the knee-high-boot-clad Face); 'dog vomit'; 'stink-marks'. Other words, in particular Jonson's repeated 'mongrel', translated very easily into a familiar Australian vernacular – this word was, in fact, made more prominent by the alteration of Face's line, 'You might talk softlier, rascal' (1.1.59) to 'Keep your voice down, mon-grel', and 'Hang thee, collier' (90) to 'Yes, I hang thee, mongrel.' The modification of Doll's 'Rascals' (166) to 'Puritans' accorded with one of Armfield's 'what I love about' Jonson statements, which were printed in the programme: 'I love the way the play hates puritanism and all those who impede the pleasure of play and of people laughing at themselves.' Some of the production's more obvious textual 'violations' included Face's 'loose lips sink ships'; Pliant's idiotic 'is it French?'; Surly-as-Spaniard's 'que sera, sera' and 'hasta la vista, baby'; and Face's panicked 'Fuck!' upon Lovewit's return. The enthusiastic laughter that these lines attracted hinted at a collective delight in humour that, in contrast to many of Jonson's jokes and references, demanded of the audi-ence no cultural translation whatsoever.

The production crucially deviated from Jonson in 1.1 when Jones's Doll threw a full chamber pot over Subtle – an act that drew a wave of repulsed laughter from the audience – followed by the barked out addition, 'clean it up'. As Armfield explains, this coup was a last-minute innovation:

It was only on the morning of opening night that we decided Doll . . . would tip the chamber pot all over Subtle. . . . We'd had Subtle throwing it over Face . . . within the first four or

five lines of the opening scene and it never really worked,
because it was actually defusing the fight too early. We spent
a couple of hours that morning and changed it.[90]

As well as avoiding a too-soon quelling of the fight, Doll's action
here prevented her from being swept aside in the maelstrom of
Subtle's and Face's bravado. But while she was no timid collabora-
tor, Jones's Doll did appear in an anxious state, her lines prior to
the first knock at the door, a modification of Jonson, spoken with
desperate urgency: 'we're in it up to our necks, we could drop for
this'. The stakes, at least as far as she was concerned, were life or
death, encapsulated in a textual change from 'I'll not be made a
prey unto the marshal' (1.1.120) to 'I'll not be made a prey unto
the hangman'. Jones moved in a twitchy, agitated manner, with an
addict's air of being caged. Sitting close to Mammon (Max Cullen,
a preposterous dandy in suit and cravat) in 4.1, she awkwardly
rearranged her long cape, the mechanics of seduction not coming
naturally. As Queen of Fairy, her con-artistry was accompanied by
some nervous toe-tapping and nail-biting. With this unease, Jones
offered compelling textures of characterization that tempered the
production's raucousness, even if reviewers tended to be preoccupied by the extraordinary duo of Rush and Weaving, about
whom they were universally effusive: Rush gave a '*tour de force*',[91]
'magnificent'[92] performance 'to be treasured'[93] and Weaving was
'suave and calculating',[94] and 'dashing'[95] 'in one of his superior
stage performances'.[96]

Strategic use of regional and international accents delineated
differences in class and intelligence, producing immediately recognizable (for local audiences, with their specific geo-cultural
competencies) – and outrageously funny – associations. While the
production's audacious mixing of voices suggests, in part, a cultural abandonment of lingering anxieties about the 'proper voice'
in which to perform Renaissance plays, it also highlights the particular function of accent in comic work. Drawing on his pho-
netic analyses of selected Australian productions of Shakespeare,
Rob Pensalfini observes that Standard British English accents

frequently remain the default in non-comedic roles.[97] Pensalfini understandably laments this apparently imperial theatrical hangover, but in this context it is worth expanding upon the implication that, in Renaissance comedies at least, accent variation may become a potent tool. Accent (and more broadly, sociolect) bypasses the meanings contained in words and sentences, connecting with audiences at a very deep level. As such, accent is one of the most acute weapons in a comedian's arsenal, something Australia's most successful stage and screen comedians (including Barry Humphries, Jane Turner, Gina Riley and Chris Lilley) understand very well.

Arky Michael's Drugger had a very broad Australian accent, with characteristic long, flat vowels, marking him out as a stolid simpleton, while Daniel Wyllie's Kastril and Rebecca Massey's Pliant spoke, much to the audience's delight, in thick New Zealand accents to indicate a similar deficit of sophistication and nous. Cullen's Mammon adopted an approximation of Received Pronunciation, inflected with a lisp. Tribulation and Ananias, played by Frank Whitten and Keith Robinson as buttoned-up men, spoke with approximate Standard British English accents, while Ralph Cotterill's Lovewit had an English West Country lilt. This combination of voices reflects a specific set of geo-cultural perspectives, which not only attributes certain ideas of class and intelligence to a broad Australian accent, but also registers the voices of other nationalities, New Zealand and British, as having clear significations which are ripe for mockery. Not all of the production's accent varieties were as blatant: in each other's company, Rush's Subtle, Weaving's Face and Jones's Doll used General Australian accents, but their inflections shifted slightly in scenes of con-artistry, when their characters were 'acting'. As the alchemist, Subtle's tone shifted towards Standard British English, as did Doll's accent in her play-acting scenes. As the alchemist's assistant, Face used a broader Australian accent, signifying low status.

While accent or sociolect can expedite certain effects of characterization, from Armfield's directorial perspective *The Alchemist* required a lot of work in terms of what had to exceed the text. Shortly after the production's opening, he commented:

> *The Alchemist* was exhausting for me. It was a particularly hard one to do, much harder I have to say than *Hamlet*, because of the constant demand for comic invention. Each scene of *Hamlet* has an organic, imaginative glow to it that actors just have to hook on to and the scene then plays itself. With *The Alchemist* you all have to work so much harder than that.[98]

The comparison seems to suggest that while *Hamlet* – so often held up as a theatrical Everest – offers a ready framework for performance, Jonson's text is demanding to the extent that it must be met with a robust and comprehensive physical language on stage. These demands were answered with extratextual fun in Armfield's production. A spirit of inventive, intersubjective play was achieved most decisively in farce-based visual gags and the appearance of improvisation, helped by the fact that the intimate Belvoir corner space lends itself to a potent complicity between actors and audience.[99]

Much of this complicity derived from the audience being 'in' on the duping of the gulls, but on other occasions, it meant watching as an individual audience member became an object of fun. In the first scene with Abel Drugger, Subtle ostentatiously mimed a séance and then sprayed the room with air freshener after Drugger's departure, grimacing at the audience as if in sympathetic disgust at Drugger's halitosis that had offended them as much as him. In 2.6, Subtle encoded Drugger's name in chalk on the wall by drawing a bell, a crude outline of a person with a 'D' on the chest, and a defecating dog accompanied by a canine growl; Drugger's good-natured stupefaction, standing on one spot, arms clamped to his sides, contrasted directly with Subtle's and Face's dynamic use of the stage, and his delayed comprehension of the chalk scribbles drew applause from the audience in the production recording analysed. A cup of tea shared with the uptight Ananias and Tribulation became a pretext for audience participation when Rush (cheekily intoning, 'c' mon, it'll be fun') pulled a person on stage to join the tea party, then upon releasing him a few moments later, threw a biscuit at him with the prepared, and explicitly Australian, ad-lib, 'You can have an Iced VoVo. Did you know that Jonson invented the word Iced VoVo?'[100] Of course, the element of unpredictability that comes with participatory techniques demands actorly quick-wittedness, as hinted in a review of a preview performance that refers to 'a couple of hilarious attempts at getting a stubborn audience member to participate'.[101]

As the play progressed, interactions between Subtle and Face increasingly took on the chaotic quality of a vaudeville-larrikin double-act: a brilliant farce interlude saw Subtle knocked out cold when a trapdoor in the downward-tilting ceiling broke open, releasing a jumble of pots and pans. Face resuscitated him using an iron brandished like a defibrillator, holding it to Subtle's chest repeatedly and calling out, 'clear'. As the pair swept the pots and pans into a trapdoor in the stage floor, dancing about as they worked, Rush's prepared ad-lib, 'we do anything in this bit', was followed with theatrical bows from the pair. In addition to these visual gags, an ongoing aural joke consisted of a series of different tunes for the doorbell, including Hal David and Burt Bacharach's 'Raindrops Keep Fallin' on My Head', and Scott Joplin's ragtime classic 'The Entertainer', which was memorably revived as the theme music of the 1973 film about a pair of con-artists, *The Sting*. A clever prelude to the 5.1 transition to outside was the exploitation of Belvoir's unique stage geography: a door exiting on to the street. Face threw Doll out of this door, with Subtle hot on her heels, as passing cars and streetlights came into view, producing a wonderful metatheatrical breach of the play's imaginative borders, as well as its interiority. At the play's denouement, Weaving's Face appeared alone, eating an apple and sitting nonchalantly in a chair; his final line, which put him in the position of a Master of Ceremonies, was a casual, 'well, you are the audience', at which point he threw his apple core at one of the doors, bringing out the rest of the cast for a jubilant curtain call.

If, in Armfield's production, Sydney obscured London as far
as imaginative, cultural and theatrical inheritances are concerned,
the intervening 13 years and an accelerated globalization helped to
frame John Bell's 2009 *Alchemist* in terms of a kind of multilocal
imagination. In part, its geo-cultural unfixedness is a consequence
of performance conditions: a co-production by the Sydney-based
Bell Shakespeare Company and the Brisbane-based Queensland
Theatre Company, it premiered in Brisbane, before touring to
Sydney, Canberra and Perth.[102] But the work also seemed to tap
into certain transnational discourses, much of which it did not
actively seek. In a promotional video, Bell connects the themes of
greed and gullibility in *The Alchemist* to contemporary economic
woes, but prefaces the observation by noting, 'we shouldn't always
be looking for, "is it a play about us"',[103] and the company's online
promotional material did not engage the link. Nevertheless, just
as Hersov's production was read through the lens of Thatcherite
cut-and-thrust capitalism, a contemporary meme informed critical interpretation of Bell's work, with almost all reviewers commenting on the global financial crisis, or on modes of scamming
in a globalized world. A Canberra reviewer inferred the resonance
of the economic crisis as a creative intention, describing the production as 'a work that director John Bell aims squarely at the
present economic debacle'.[104] A Sydney reviewer commented,
'Wall Street shows us not much has changed in 400 years',[105] while
another praised the production for helping 'to pull theatre-lovers
from the dark depths of the global financial crisis'.[106] Some critics
drew more general contemporary connections: a reviewer of the
Brisbane season wrote that *The Alchemist* might 'be a play whose
time has come. Anyone who has ever been e-mailed by a Nigerian
millionaire dying to share his loot will know that suckers are born
every day.'[107] One critic offered an extended contemporary analogy, reproducing a scammer's e-mail that had recently 'plopped
into the inbox'.[108]

Notwithstanding this interest in modern allusions, a play
so intensely concerned with the chameleonic as *The Alchemist*
resists too-easy insertion into an economic or political thematic

basket. Bell was concerned to avoid 'anything too naturalistic', and told designer Bruce McKinven, 'Let's have a totally open space: there is no set . . . a bit like a theatre rehearsal room.'[109] The venues to which the production toured are all configured as end-on proscenium spaces, with capacities ranging from 398 at the single level Sydney Opera House Playhouse, to 618 at Canberra's three-level Playhouse, to 850 at the two-level Queensland Performing Arts Centre Playhouse in Brisbane and 1,200 at Perth's Edwardian Baroque His Majesty's Theatre. McKinven's design used several metatheatrical devices: two costume racks flanked the stage on each side, providing exits and entranceways – as well as a frame – for the actors. Behind one of these racks, a stage scaffold was visible, and the assistant stage manager, Jennifer Buckland, sat in view of the audience. An old stained couch decorated in ripped and faded floral was the centrepiece of much of the action, and opposing it was a make-up mirror and chair. Proximate spaces were littered with recognizable detritus of modern consumption: a box of cornflakes, a tea towel, a cardboard soft-drink cup and straw, a dish-rack, dishes, cups, pink washing up gloves, a teapot and pan, a milk carton, a tin of baked beans with a utensil left in it, a spray can, old suitcases. Perhaps the most effective metatheatrical design element was the enormous mirror across the back wall of the stage, which intensified the theatrical duality, revealing actors and props from behind and making the audience privy to certain mechanics and to 'hidden' things – an unadorned back of a table or chair, or the unfastened back of Subtle's ill-fitting disguise – that were not ostensibly part of the 'picture' of alchemy. When Patrick Dickson's Subtle formed Drugger's name 'in some mystic character' (2.6.15) on the mirror, the effect was to reflect his acting self to himself, just as his face became visible (the face of the trickster, mid-trick) to the audience in reflection. An additional level of theatrical self-referentiality consisted of the glimpses that some audience members – depending on where they were seated – could catch of themselves in the mirror, laughing, reacting, submitting to the illusion.

Costume in this production was also fundamentally metatheatrical, the cast wearing items selected from the Bell Shakespeare Company and Queensland Theatre Company wardrobe stocks. The actors had some input in selecting what they would wear, in a 'controlled negotiation'[110] with McKinven and Gayle MacGregor, the then Head of Wardrobe at the Queensland Theatre Company, which acknowledged the function of costume in a performer's characterization process – and democratized that process. McKinven describes how the work of creating costumes for the production differed from the professional norm:

> [F]or this production, where we are using the artifice of theatre to expose the deceit of the play, we decided to throw open the collaborative process somewhat . . . The costumes become more like found-object sculptures, each one taking you on an individual journey. I think you need to be far more trusting of your process to know that this will work . . . I also really enjoy that some pieces of clothing hidden in stock for so long, are getting another run onstage.[111]

The resulting costumes ranged wildly in terms of period, style, colour, fabric, and even gender- and age-appropriateness, and reinforced the point that characterization was here derived from a series of exteriors being trotted out and presented to the gullible of the play, and of the theatre.

Dickson's Subtle wore a range of dressing gowns over grubby pyjamas, a woollen hat, a gold star pendant and beaded necklaces (giving him an ageing hippie appearance that he accentuated by occasionally pressing his hands together in a *namaste* gesture); as the alchemist, he wore a girl's gingham dress over his regular clothing. As Doll, Georgina Symes clattered with jewellery and switched from denim miniskirt, cowboy boots over fishnet stockings, a leopard-print shirt and a long black wig (evoking, as several reviewers noted, the late British soul singer Amy Winehouse), into a slinky red evening gown for her assignation with Mammon (during which she undressed to white and pink lingerie) to a gaudy dress as Queen of Fairy, made up of mismatched fabrics and red feathers. Andrew Tighe's Face was comparable in appearance to Weaving's, his eighteenth-century British naval officer's uniform alternating with a blue boiler suit, workman's apron and protective eye mask as Lungs. But this Face did not exhibit the reckless confidence that Weaving brought to the role, Tighe's Face being imbued, as one reviewer put it, with 'precision and steadiness', a concentration that left him 'exhausted, at the play's end'.[112]

David Whitney's Mammon was a kind of grotesque whiteface clown, clad in a very obvious fat suit over the top of a red and gold embroidered frock coat, a colourful waistcoat, white trousers and knee-high boots, glittering rings on each finger, and a pair of devilish horns protruding from his head. Lucas Stibbard's Drugger wore an apron and knitted vest, a flat cap over his greasy red hair. As Kastril, Scott Witt's outfit consisted of a mink coat, a floral shirt, gold necklaces, trousers with feather tassels, a cowboy belt, oversized sneakers with extralong shoelaces and a too-large baseball cap. His sister Pliant, played by Liz Skitch, wore a similarly discordant concoction: a slinky silver dress over pink stockings, long white gloves with rings on top, a colourful feather fascinator over tight blond curls, all set off by the stuffed toy elephant that she carried around with her. Peter Kowitz's Tribulation wore a long black frock coat, a wide brimmed straw hat and had a thick grey beard, giving him an Amish appearance. When disguised as the Spanish Don, Sandro Colarelli's Surly strutted about in a flamboyant satin matador's costume, a contrast to Surly's top hat, maroon tails and riding boots. Such a motley collection of signifiers gave the production a cosmopolitan sense of being located in many places at once, or nowhere but the theatre itself (also a hallmark of Armfield's theatrical approach).

The prepared ad-libs and farce interludes that were so effective in Armfield's production were not as prominent a feature of Bell's *Alchemist*; nonetheless, Bell's direction drew appreciative laughter from extratextual elements – characters' outrageous appearances and mannerisms and visual gags. Doll's assignation with Mammon in 4.1 was a slapstick burlesque centrepiece, culminating in

Mammon stumbling, half-dressed, his preposterous fat suit protruding, after Doll, and then struggling, his love-heart motif boxer
shorts fallen to his ankles, to resuscitate Subtle-as-doctor by hammering on his chest. Pliant's ridiculously high-pitched, idiotic
laugh was a hit with the audience, and her exit, in fits of giggles
as she was carried out by Surly dressed as the Spaniard, elicited
an uproarious response. The cashed-up Lovewit (Russell Kiefel,
who played Surly in Armfield's production), all-gauche, golf-club
swinging, gum-chewing bravado, was an immediately recognizable
contemporary 'type'.

As a means of characterization, accent again played an important comic function. Witt's posturing Kastril, continually rehearsing his fighting moves, bouncing on the spot like a terrier, used a
broad Australian accent, delivered (absurdly for the Angry Boy)
at a high pitch; along with Witt's small stature, these elements of
characterization gave Kastril's feistiness an inherent comic irony.
Like Arky Michael in Armfield's production, Stibbard's Drugger
spoke in a very broad Australian accent, his tone rising at the end
of each sentence, a local speech pattern that, when caricatured,
conveys a sense of perpetual uncertainty. The actor's dopey
demeanour, his arms hanging by his sides, head thrust forward,
was also remarkably evocative of Arky Michael's in the same role.
Whitney's effete Mammon spoke, as had Cullen's, with plummy
RP vowels. Kowitz's Amish appearance as Tribulation was accompanied by his approximation of a southern US accent (and sometimes the singsong tones of a Southern preacher). These idiolects
carried direct class and cultural implications.

The production omitted a large chunk of the elaborate exchange
of insults between Subtle and Face in 1.1 and consequently Doll
spoke a greater proportion of text. Symes played to this opportunity to come more to the fore: easily manhandling Subtle in
1.1.149, by the end of the scene she positioned herself between
Subtle and Face on the couch and spoke calmly, an arm around
each in a domineering position. Their flattery at 174–9 ('Royal
Doll', 'thou shalt sit in triumph', etc.) reinforced her stature – in
Armfield's production these lines were cut. While Jones's Doll

spoke feverishly of being made 'prey unto a hangman', Symes's was concerned merely with being made 'prey unto the sheriff'. A tall, striking performer, she was, like a kind of female version of Weaving's Face, empowered by her glamour. If a contemporary theatrical manifestation is to be found of the 'larrikin girl' that Bellanta has sought to recuperate in an essay on this most masculine of Australian identities,[113] Symes's Doll may just have been it.

Jonson's fighting address 'To the Reader', which prefaces the 1612 quarto, employs a telling phrase that goes to the heart of our performance history of *The Alchemist*. Jonson attacks the 'Multitude' for, among other things, commending 'Writers, as they doe Fencers, or Wrastlers; who if they come in robustuously, and put in for it with a great deale of violence, are receiv'd for the braver fellowes.' Many productions of *The Alchemist* over the centuries have been criticized precisely for coming in too 'robustuously' even though just how 'robustuously' *The Alchemist* should be played will always be up for debate; it is certainly impossible to access Jonson's own standards of theatrical energy, pacing and tone, all which are impossible to pin down in writing, and which within any one production will vary from performance to performance, depending on audience response. But while the productions we have discussed illuminate a range of dramaturgical possibilities, it is the issue of tone and comic balance – precisely of whether a production comes in too 'robustuously' – which emerges as critical. Was Garrick too robustious in hijacking *The Alchemist* and making Drugger the star? What about the physical and visual comedy of Gascon's *Alchemist*? Rush's claim that Jonson invented the Iced VoVo? Was this too robustious or was it inspired riffing, which helped get the Australian audience onside? When was Symes's larrikin Doll collaborating with Jonson and when was she deviating from him? On the other hand, was the lack of darkness in Mendes's production not robustious enough?

The liveness of theatre means that the areas focused on here – characterization, Londonness, (meta)theatricality and comic tone – will be revisited and reworked in every *Alchemist*. The play's original site-specificity – at least when it was performed at the Blackfriars playhouse – has to undergo fundamental reorientations in productions such as the ones we have discussed. For modern practitioners and audiences, the imaginative work of (re-)presenting, comprehending and deriving enjoyment from *The Alchemist* will always be inflected with an awareness of certain transhistorical and sometimes transnational dualities: London and not London; London now and London then; boy player and actress. And the theatricality that exists between Jonson's lines – pacing, costume, soundscape, accent – will always create space for robustiousness.

Much work remains to be done in terms of performance-centred Jonson studies, and *The Alchemist*, in particular, would benefit from more in-depth, as well as critically rigorous, performance histories. Ideally, the insights offered by performance histories of early modern plays should always be fully integrated into any exploration of their potential dramaturgies. The productions examined here suggest that Jonson's play succeeds best nowadays when directors, actors and designers collaborate with him, and rework *The Alchemist*, rather than respecting every dash in the Folio text. But which elements of such reworkings are 'collaborations with', and which are 'deviations from'? And how, indeed, do the two elements work together? However, these questions may be reconciled, while Jonson continues to attract international theatre practitioners, wholly prepared simultaneously to work within and test the boundaries of his meticulous authorial designs, *The Alchemist* will continue to conjure up explosive, unpredictable alchemy in the theatre.

CHAPTER THREE

The State of the Art

MATTHEW STEGGLE

'Like all mega-writers', observes Charles Nicholl, 'Jonson supports a small industry of research'.[1] Certainly *The Alchemist*, which for its intellectual density, complexity and importance deserves to be called a mega-play, has by itself been the subject of a great deal of scholarly work since the year 2000. Across that body of work there are many recurring themes and concerns, although the chapters and articles in question are not always fully in dialogue with one another. In this survey of the state of the art, I bundle recent work into a series of loose categories which suggest, in the process, various opportunities for new explorations of the play.

The categories are as follows: editions, *The Alchemist* in Jonson's career, space and place, time, historical contexts: The Blackfriars in 1610, historical contexts: gender and masculinity, histories of science, histories of economics, performance, other approaches, my conclusion.

Editions

The one major new edition of the play in the new millennium is that of Peter Holland and William Sherman for *The Cambridge Works of Ben Jonson*, the long-awaited project which promises finally to supersede Herford and Simpson and to change the whole field of Jonson studies. In the case of *The Alchemist*, Holland and Sherman's edition includes a modern-spelling text freshly edited from first principles, and a fresh collation of copies of both the 1612 quarto and the 1616 folio. The resulting text bases itself upon F, but occasionally adopts readings from the 1612 quarto edition of the play when F seems in error. They conclude that for this play, at least,

> Jonson participated in the production of F1 and was respon-
> sible for most if not all of the significant changes in the text.
> Whether or not they all represent Jonson's 'considered
> intention' (as Mares put it), there is no compelling reason in
> this case – unlike some of the other plays in this edition – for
> reverting to Q.[2]

The text also comes with a full, up-to-date, and scholarly commentary. It is prefaced by a short and elegant introduction, organized by the subheadings 'date and time' (both extra- and intra-diegetic); 'place and space' (discussing both cultural geography and staging issues); 'materials for perfection' (a section which includes discussion of sources, and possible topical allusions); and 'theatre and print'. It will, undoubtedly, be the standard text of the play for decades to come.

In terms of editions, the only other noteworthy development, since 2000, has been the astonishing resurgence of two much older forms of the play: the Felix Schelling edition of 1904, and what one might call 'the 1616 text' – a letter-by-letter transcription of the play exactly as it appeared in the 1616 folio. Both of these have spread primarily in electronic media. To ground this discussion, I will preview the opening of Jonson's play as it stands in *The Cambridge Works of Ben Jonson*:

> [*Enter*] FACE [*with his sword drawn*], SUBTLE [*holding a glass containing a liquid, and*] DOLL COMMON.
> FACE Believe't, I will.
> SUBTLE Thy worst. I fart at thee.
> DOLL Ha' you your wits? Why, gentlemen! For love –

The text is modern spelling, the speech-prefixes are regularized, and square brackets mark in the editorial additions to the original stage directions. As noted above, an introduction and running notes, including a textual apparatus, accompany the play. These factors seem, on the face of it, not too exceptional, exemplifying current scholarly practice which has already been applied to *The Alchemist* in most of the best currently available pre-2000 texts of the play, such as the editions of Martin Butler, Gordon Campbell or Helen Ostovich. And yet this style of edition is out of step with the texts of the play that many readers have, in practice, been using in the years since 2000.

Since the later 1990s, standard scholarly databases including *Literature Online* (1994–), *Early English Books Online*, and the University of Virginia's e-text site have published *The Alchemist* electronically, in the form of an old-spelling transcription of the play exactly as it is printed in the First Folio. The transcription's opening lines, here reproduced exactly, indicate the general tenor:

Face, Svbtle, Dol Common.
Beleeu't, I will.
Svb. Thy worst. I fart at thee.
Dol. Ha' you your wits? Why gentlemen! for loue –[3]

The primary problem with this '1616 text', of course, is not so much its deficiency as a text per se – as discussed above, the best current scholarly edition makes only a few substantive changes to its readings – but rather its user-unfriendliness. As the opening lines exemplify, it is in old spelling, and formatted as a seventeenth-century playscript. Thus, it offers no explanatory stage directions, abbreviated speech-prefixes, and conventions such as the omission of speech-prefix for the first speech of a scene. What is more, translation of such a play-text into purely digital form tends to remove the layout cues which a reader might use to distinguish, for instance, stage directions from speech-prefixes. Even Herford and Simpson's edition – something of a byword for uncompromising austerity and difficulty – seems positively user-friendly compared to this version of the text. Thus, a very easily obtainable 'standard' electronic edition of *The Alchemist* exists, but it is far from suitable for reading.

Its principal electronic rival, on the other hand, goes to the other extreme, being highly readable at the expense of being less clear-cut about its relationship with the original. The Schelling edition, as it appears in its digitized form, opens as follows:

> A ROOM IN LOVEWIT'S HOUSE.
> ENTER FACE, IN A CAPTAIN'S UNIFORM, WITH HIS SWORD DRAWN, AND SUBTLE WITH A VIAL, QUARRELLING, AND FOLLOWED BY DOL COMMON.
> FACE. Believe 't, I will.
> SUB. Thy worst. I fart at thee.
> DOL. Have you your wits? why, gentlemen! for love —[4]

Again, few substantive differences in the dialogue occur between this text and the Holland/Sherman, a reflection of *The Alchemist*'s relatively 'clean' textual history rather than of this edition's own due diligence. Its handling of stage directions is rather free, as this opening shows: it does not use square brackets to mark editorial interventions, and it localizes the scene to '*A room in Lovewit's house*', in the overofficious manner of a nineteenth-century playscript. There are – in most of this text's online iterations – no textual or explanatory notes, although an alphabetized glossary is sometimes attached. Its introduction, which calls Jonson, at one point, 'the first literary dictator', is more or less what one would expect of an edition a hundred years old.

The power of Schelling's text, on the other hand, lies in the fact that it is out of copyright. Project Gutenberg has digitized it and the accompanying material, in effect releasing it into the wild, so that Schelling's edition has become the default choice for many computer applications based on making use of a freely available e-text. For instance, it is the version of *The Alchemist* that tends to turn up on e-book readers. In addition, the edition is re-emerging in paper form. At the time of writing, in marketplaces such as

Amazon and Abebooks, many firms are offering what appear to be new recent editions of *The Alchemist*, bearing publication dates between 2000 and 2012. These turn out, on closer inspection, to be print-on-demand titles, which seem simply to print out the Schelling e-text. (If any searching or previewing is permitted, then that phrase, 'the first literary dictator', is one very useful litmus test to identify such editions.) Some of the marketplace offerings further obfuscate their nature by bundling in other material, such as Jonson's current Wikipedia entry, facilitating Schelling's return to print. As noted elsewhere, one effect of copyright laws is that much of the information freely available on the internet is rolled back to the latest out-of-copyright textbook available.[5] In this respect, *The Alchemist*, too, is presented most often in a text which predates the work of the New Bibliography. The labours of Herford and Simpson and of later textual editors have, in the jargon of the internet, been reverted.

In fact, this situation continues to change, and e-texts (albeit not free-to-air ones) of more recent editions are also starting to become available. A digitized version of Herford and Simpson itself is now available bundled in the subscription package *Oxford Scholarship Online*; Michael Jamieson's 1966 Penguin edition, complete with brief footnotes, is now available as part of the bundle of texts offered by *Literature Online*. The current Oxford World's Classics edition is for sale as a download for e-book readers, and the new Cambridge Jonson is shortly to be available electronically as well as in paper form. It is worth stopping, though, to mention some more unusual forms of the play conveniently available in free-to-air form, which may sometimes be of use: an HTML transcription based on the 1692 Folio,[6] a Google Books facsimile of Peter Whalley's edition of the play,[7] a Google Books facsimile of its successor, Gifford's 1816 edition,[8] and an OCR'ed text of Garrick's eighteenth-century adaptation.[9] While it is easy to cavil about the profusion of older texts of the play now available, at the same time the easy availability of such versions offers a whole raft of new research opportunities.

So much for editions: now for scholarship and criticism, organized into a series of loosely linked thematic areas.

The Alchemist in Jonson's career

I start with work that sees *The Alchemist* in the frame of Jonson's
career as a whole. For instance, in a brief and richly suggestive
section of an essay in *The Cambridge Companion to Ben Jonson*,
David Bevington puts *The Alchemist* alongside Jonson's other
major comedies, particularly *Volpone*, of which *The Alchemist* is
'to a remarkable degree, a replay'.[10] Both plays are beautifully
structured, satirically sophisticated explorations of the multiple
relationships between folly and crime. Bevington also offers an
interesting – indeed, provocative – formulation of the tone of the
end of the play:

> [Lovewit] thus encapsulates the spirit of comedy in *The
> Alchemist* and its stunningly amoral (though not immoral)
> ending. He presides genially over the defeat of all unwar-
> ranted aspirations and rewards wit for its own sake[.][11]

This question of morality, or its absence, is one which many other
recent analyses of the play take up.

Ian Donaldson's recent and magnificently detailed biography of
Jonson has a different perspective, coming to its main discussion
of *The Alchemist* within a chapter titled 'Employment 1607–10'.
In it, *The Alchemist* rubs shoulders not with the other great comedies but with a much less familiar subset of Jonson's works. These
include the largely lost *Merchant Tailors' Entertainment* of 1607,
provided to accompany a spectacularly sumptuous guild feast
whose total budget was in excess of £1,000; the almost entirely
lost *Entertainment at Salisbury House* (1608), celebrating Cecil's
appointment as Lord Treasurer of England; the recently redis-
covered *Entertainment at Britain's Burse* (1609), commissioned
to celebrate Cecil's opening of a major new shopping centre; and
The Masque of Queens (1609), which far exceeded its assigned

budget of £1,000. For Donaldson, *The Alchemist* shares flavours with these works, and what particularly jumps out is the intoxicating power of money, expressed in images of feasting and lavish entertainment. Donaldson observes the similarities between Sir Epicure's imagined feast and those for which Jonson had provided entertainments in the preceding years. And he comments: 'Social change (in Jonson's perception) is driven entirely by gold: even Mammon's cook – once Subtle has perfected the elixir – can now go out to buy himself a knighthood.'[12] For Donaldson, this social mobility through entertainment speaks to Jonson's own experiences in these fast-moving, high-budget years, in which 'Like Jeremy the Butler or Captain Face, Jonson himself needed swiftly to adapt to changing circumstance.'[13]

Derek B. Alwes's 'Service as Mastery in *The Alchemist*' also considers the biographical, taking up a dialogue with Thomas Greene's idea of the 'centered self'.[14] Alwes follows up on Face's challenge in the first lines of the play: 'Why? Who | Am I, my mongrel? Who am I?' Face's protean identities seem to challenge Greene's assertion that Jonson thought of a single, 'real', selfhood underlying the various contingent identities adopted by Face in the course of the play. Indeed, if Face has a real identity, it is one defined reciprocally in his mutually beneficial servant/ master relationship with Lovewit. This condition makes him, in some ways, like Jonson himself, who famously defined himself as the court's 'servant, but not slave'. Alwes explores the paradoxes of whose servant Jonson might be constructed as: the court's, or the theatre audience's. While holding back from fully identifying Face with Jonson, Alwes does suggest that the play toys with such possibilities.

Space and place

In recent years, more and more attention has been paid to how to talk about the play's interest in space and place. A number of critics have written on this topic, and what is interesting, too, is that the terminology of space and place also comes up in essays covered in many other sections of this survey. It is not too much to say that discussion in terms of space and place has become one of the dominant modes of critical discourse about the play.

Russell West's book *Spatial Representations and the Jacobean Stage* was an early entrant in what has become a burgeoning field, place-based studies of Renaissance drama. Starting from the premise that Jacobean theatre was an 'ostentatiously spatial art-form', and using the terminology of Lefebvre among others, West explores the links in that theatre between physical and intellectual spaces. In the case of *The Alchemist*, West argues that there is an 'isomorphism'[15] between the space of the tricksters' house and the space of the theatre: and that the 'stage space . . . is heavily semanticized as a generator of power or wealth'.[16]

Andrew Hiscock considers the play in his monograph, *The Uses of This World*. For Hiscock, as for West, space is not an inert and neutral container but something which can be contested, manipulated and renegotiated. In Hiscock's analysis, *The Alchemist* is interesting in that it develops a form of 'provisional space',[17] an imaginary geography which transcends the physical limits of the plague-surrounded house, and offers a path to encounters with the Other. For Hiscock, the play uses space to question the usual understandings of identity itself, both at a personal level and at the level of communities.

Shona McIntosh's essay on 'Space, Place, and Transformation in *Eastward Ho!* and *The Alchemist*' offers an extended comparison between the two plays named in the title. Both share a concern with ideas of social mobility, the sort of transformation in which McIntosh is most interested. While *Eastward Ho!* is expansive in its use of locations, ranging around the city of London, *The Alchemist* confines its scene to a single house. While *Eastward Ho!* seems to offer a genuine hope of social mobility within the society of London, the latter play, in her analysis, is far more sceptical. Thus, McIntosh argues that *The Alchemist* 'is to some extent a recantation or qualification of [Jonson's] own "venture tripartite" (1.1.135) with Chapman and Marston, one with considerably more conservative implications' (66).[18]

James D. Mardock's discussion of the play in the monograph *Our Scene Is London* also compares the play to *Eastward Ho!*, in terms of its differing use of space.[19] Drawing explicitly on Michel de Certeau's terminology of *lieu* and *espace*, Mardock distinguishes 'urban place' from 'theatrical place', arguing that the latter – in the form of the alchemical laboratory, itself a metaphor for the Blackfriars theatre – actually has a TARDIS-like potential to represent a much wider range of spatial meanings. Mardock offers a fascinating reading of the plague, that phenomenon which imposes a strange geography of its own, and of the liminal status of the Blackfriars itself, only recently incorporated within the city of London. For Mardock, the play is a celebration of 'the space of the author', Jonson's career-long fascination with representing and manipulating ideas of place and space.

Time

A number of the most recent interesting studies of place have linked it to the question of time. For James Loxley, for instance, the most pregnant detail about this play is its setting in the 'unreal city', the city of plague-time:

> [The venture] is growing out of control in London's ruins, in the space abandoned by the city's natural rulers. . . . When Subtle is subsequently disguised in Act III as a 'priest of Faery', and Dol as the Faery Queen herself, the device seems highly appropriate. Their world too is a shadowy, night-time realm, coexisting with – but not in the full sight of – the quotidian daylight world of early modern London. It is just that the prolongation of the plague allows that realm an extended spell in which to articulate its form and its promise.[20]

Loxley comments too on the dreamworld of Mammon, with his longing for 'succubae'. In its opening up of an alternative fantasy world, other than normal daytime, *The Alchemist* sounds, for a moment, like an urban version of *A Midsummer Night's Dream*.

Sean McEvoy's approach is productively different, stressing precisely the extent to which time, in the play, does line up with what Loxley calls 'the quotidian daylight world'.[21] McEvoy's essay on *The Alchemist* offers a general introduction and some interesting remarks about recent productions of the play, but it is particularly good on the treatment of time, quoting Walter Benjamin's remark that 'a clock that is working will always be a disturbance on the stage. Even in a naturalistic play, astronomical time would clash with theatrical time.'[22] For Jonson, though, argues McEvoy, stage time runs entirely in synchrony with time as perceived by the audience:

> This is not a separate imaginary world on another temporal plane into which the audience can look: the time on stage claims to be the same minute of the same day in which the audience are alive. . . . There is thus a significant sense in which the audience of *The Alchemist* are participants in a kind of game, rather than discrete spectators of a work of art.[23]

McEvoy's essay, in turn, is at an interesting angle to Ian Donaldson's essay on the play, 'Clockwork Comedy: Time and *The Alchemist*'. In it, Donaldson argues that 'time, and the attitudes which people show towards time, are a central preoccupation of the play'.[24] Donaldson documents the various gradations of time within the play, contrasting Jonson to Shakespeare and Beckett in the uses of the idea of time and divine ordering. Loxley, McEvoy and Donaldson form a noteworthy trio of readings on the idea of time in *The Alchemist*.

Historical contexts: The Blackfriars in 1610

In recent years, several scholars have, in different ways, looked to relate *The Alchemist* specifically to the theatrical context of its first performance at Blackfriars in 1610.

Anthony J. Ouellette provides a detailed and considered account of the play in terms of the return of the King's Men to the Blackfriars in 1608, an important move in that it marked a resumption of professional playing inside the City of London whereas other playhouses remained out in the liberties. This relocation, Ouellette suggests, was also a sign of the growing self-confidence of the King's Men, an increasingly dominant and prestigious force in the culture of early modern London. Ouellette reads the play in terms of contrasts between the city and the less-favoured regions outside the walls, frequently referred to in the text, and draws attention to the play's metatheatrical elements. Finally, and intriguingly, Ouellette argues that the epilogue seeks to renegotiate the relationship between playgoers and players. At the increasingly self-confident Blackfriars, they are honoured 'guests'; elsewhere, the implication runs, they are merely consumers.[25]

Melissa D. Aaron, by contrast, considers a hitherto little-discussed aspect of the 1608 takeover. When, in 1608, the King's Men had taken over the Blackfriars Theatre, there had been some controversy. The goldsmith Robert Keysar, a shareholder in the building's previous occupants, the Children of the Queen's Revels, claimed that he had a stake in the property, and that the King's Men had moved in without his permission:

> [T]he said Richard Burbage, Cuthbert Burbage, John Hemminges, Henrye Condell and others, have entred in and upon the said playe howse, and all the said goodes, apparell, and premisses and have soe Continewed in the possession for a longe tyme and made profitt theirof[.][26]

He therefore demanded a share of the profits made by the King's Men at the venue. It is unclear how the suit played out, and it was probably settled out of court. But Jonson and his audiences, suggests Aaron, must have been aware of it, and it makes for an interesting 'economic reading'[27] of the first performance which gives a particular edge to the critical consensus that Lovewit's house functions as a metatheatrical metaphor for the theatre itself. Like

Lovewit's house, the Blackfriars theatre in the Keysar lawsuit is a property whose ownership is contested and whose profits are up for grabs. Unfortunately, due to their near-simultaneous publication, Aaron's article is not in dialogue with Ouellette's, given that the authors read similar material to quite different conclusions.

A third article in this category draws attention to *The Alchemist*'s similarities to another Blackfriars play. In 'Carrying Tempest in His Hand and Voice: The Figure of the Magician in Jonson and Shakespeare', David Lucking draws attention to similarities between *The Alchemist* and Shakespeare's *The Tempest*, performed at almost exactly the same time, and possibly in the same theatre.[28] Lucking notes, for instance, striking similarities between Prospero's speech to Ariel (beginning 'Dost thou forget | From what a torment I freed thee?', 1.2.250–93), and Face's speech to Subtle (beginning, 'Do but collect, sir, where I met you first', 1.1.23–46). Also Subtle's self-description, which forms the epigraph to the article, likens an alchemist to a maker of tempests. Lucking's clever reading opens the possibility of seeing *The Alchemist* as a work which offers an imaginative engagement with Shakespeare's masterpiece.

Comparison between *The Alchemist* and *The Tempest* also informs an essay by Arlene Oseman, meditating on the 'relationship between these two artistic minds'.[29] For Oseman, Shakespeare's interest in completion, wholeness and consummation is in vivid contrast to Jonson's mental world, symbolized by the broken compass and the unattainability of *The Alchemist*'s Philosopher's Stone.

The 1610 context features, then, in accounts of the playhouse, and in accounts of the relationship to *The Tempest*: it figures in a different light again, in recent articles on this play's relationship to plague. Melissa Smith, for instance, discusses the relationship between playhouse and plague house in a number of plays, putting *The Alchemist* in the company of *The Revenger's Tragedy* and *The Broken Heart*.[30] For Smith, all three plays are witnesses to the early modern belief in the interconnection of emotion and disease, and all three can be thought of as psychologically defensive responses to the 'mass trauma' inflicted upon London by the infection. Patrick Phillips calls *The Alchemist* 'the most overt depiction of plague-time London in all of English drama', and draws attention to the fact that the plague was still a real and terrifying medical threat at the moment when the play was being staged.[31] The paradoxical situation – of audience members crowding in at the Blackfriars to watch a play about contagion – can be addressed, Phillips suggests, by reference to contemporary medical theory, which thought that mirth could serve as a 'wholesome remedy' against plague itself. Phillips provides a wealth of evidence from contemporary medical textbooks, and from this platform offers a convincing reading of an *Alchemist* in which fearless action actually drives away the plague. Plague also features centrally in Mathew Martin's article on the play, discussed below under 'Performance'; Boluk and Lenz's, discussed under 'Histories of Economics'; and, more glancingly, in several other studies, as we shall see.

Historical contexts: Gender and masculinity

Writing in 1998, Julie Sanders, Kate Chedgzoy and Susan Wiseman commented on the relative dearth of approaches to Jonson and sexuality, Jonson and gender.[32] One of the most interesting developments in *Alchemist* criticism since 2000 has been the emergence of more gender-sensitive readings of this play.

In 'The Repudiation of the Marvelous: Jonson's *The Alchemist* and the Limits of Satire', Ian McAdam takes up the challenge of the play's interest in gender and the erotic. This play is not, for McAdam, primarily about Face and Lovewit; instead his focus is on the trio of Subtle, Doll and Sir Epicure Mammon, three characters who do not meet with success at the end of the play but still between them articulate, McAdam suggests, something of a vision of a better world. McAdam starts with Sir Epicure Mammon, often written off as a deluded monomaniac, but draws attention to his hope of curing the plague: 'in a play where ruthless competition and aggressive self-interest seem the general

rule, Mammon is the only character to entertain, at least temporarily, thoughts of human charity'. This can be linked, McAdam
suggests, to Subtle, still pursuing the possibility of a genuinely
transformative alchemy, and to Doll Common, who despite per-
sistent denigration, offers a vision of female strength and gender
equality which challenges the unthinking misogyny of Face and
many other male characters through the play. This ideal, argues
McAdam, chimes with the erotic symbolism of alchemy itself,
with which Jonson's relationship is famously ambivalent, and
which celebrates a yin-and-yang-like equality between the gen-
ders. 'Behind the rampant competitiveness of the men in *The
Alchemist*', he argues, 'lies the intimation of a deep dependency on
female power'.[33] At the centre of the play, in McAdam's nuanced
account, is Sir Epicure's vision of an erotic relationship with Doll
based on gender equality:

> Mammon's behaviour, though exposed as delusional and
> outrageous through the play's satire, nevertheless implicitly
> ironizes the limited possibilities that most of the other men
> in the play – and men in general in Jonson – imagine for
> women and for social relationships.[34]

Particularly brilliant in this essay is the reading of the house at the
end of the play, with its cracked vessels, and 'MADAM, with a
dildo, writ o'the walls'. McAdam comments:

> With this image of male imaginative and sexual failure, the
> play repudiates the marvelous perhaps because the real mar-
> vel is missing; as Subtle subtly reveals to us in the first scene,
> Face has been conversing with cobwebs since his 'mistress'
> death hath broke up the house' (58); that is, Lovewit's wife
> has died and presumably left no heir. Without this wife and
> potential mother no real transformation is possible[.][35]

McAdam's chapter offers a fascinating new approach on the play's
treatment of femininity. In new work, published for the first time

in this volume (127–39 below), McAdam returns to the play's treatment of gender, suggesting that masculinity, too, is put under the microscope in this play: and that this play is far from acquiescent in its treatment of Lovewit, a representative of the 'conservative, landed patriarchal social order'.

Similarly psychoanalytical in tone, but taking cues more strongly from the approaches of Edmund Wilson and William Kerrigan, Lynn S. Meskill writes on 'Jonson and the alchemical economy of desire: creation, defacement and castration in *The Alchemist*'. Meskill reads Subtle and Face in terms of a father/son relationship gone psychologically sour, with Oedipal overtones. The plot structures of Shakespeare, a figure of fatherhood and rivalry, lurk troublingly in the background, and Jonson's imagination is characteristically metatextual, worrying about the fate of the text itself at the hands of its consumers: 'a literary imagination which leaps to its own posterity in the very moment of its conception'.[36] The result is full of interesting observations about the sexual energies within the play – for instance, the acute remark that Hieronimo's cloak, borrowed from *The Spanish Tragedy*, functions as a 'symbol of authorial virility';[37] but I am a little dismayed by the extent to which, in this account, *The Alchemist* seems to exist primarily to refer to itself. In the claim that the play 'in its relentless self-referentiality . . . enacts a regression into the womb'[38] the article may alienate some readers.

In contrast, Caroline McManus's article on the representation of Doll Common in the play is grounded in a safely external referent.[39] Each year on Maundy Thursday, Queen Elizabeth would take part in a ritual in which she washed the feet of poor women, and gave away some clothing to them. McManus provides a richly historicized description of this ritual, and notes the parallels between it and Doll's blessing of Dapper in her disguise as the Fairy Queen. This provides McManus with a way into consideration of how *The Alchemist* recycles the sacred into the secular; how it approaches the relationship between money and faith; and how Doll's various disguises offer reflections of that exemplar of a certain sort of womanhood, the dead Elizabeth I.

Regina Buccola's recent monograph on fairy lore contains a substantial essay on Doll which would make an interesting dialogue with McManus's: 'The Fairy Quean: Fairyland Meets the Fifth Monarchy in Ben Jonson's *The Alchemist*'. Buccola's monograph as a whole puts *The Alchemist* alongside a number of Shakespearean plays that represent fairy lore, including *A Midsummer Night's Dream* and *The Merry Wives of Windsor*, arguing that fairies, unruly women and Roman Catholicism form a thematic trio in the Renaissance imagination. Buccola offers a detailed and convincing account of how Jonson's play interacts with contemporary fairy belief, both popular and elite. Using this material, Buccola is able to situate the play's treatment of the Fairy Queen figure in terms of urban issues – social change and gender politics in the citizen classes; and in terms of the play's relentless satire of contemporary Puritan radicalism. Puritans, Buccola shows, had a particular antipathy to fairy belief. But, '[b]y having Dol the prostitute impersonate in rapid succession both the fairy queen and a gentlewoman run mad with studying biblical genealogy', argues Buccola, Jonson links Puritans to the very thing they particularly detest. For Buccola, the Fairy Queen scenes are at the very heart of *The Alchemist*.[40]

While McAdam, McManus and Buccola consider the play's treatment of femininity, a number of pieces of work have looked at the play's treatment of masculinity. Mark Albert Johnston, for instance, focuses specifically on that pre-eminent symbol of the masculine, the beard. His work has appeared as an article, 'Prosthetic Absence in Ben Jonson's *Epicoene*, *The Alchemist*, and *Bartholomew Fair*', and also in a monograph, *Beard Fetish in Early Modern England*. Johnston notes Abel Drugger's anxiety to possess a full beard, a marker of maturity which would be appropriate to his status as a newly established freeman of the city. Drugger's beard is, however, far from satisfactory, and he has bought a 'receipt to make hair come', a detail which reveals both his anxieties and his vulnerabilities. As Johnston notes, 'This confession – that he has already paid a barber for a concoction to grow facial hair – indicates that he will make a fine gull.'[41] Face, by contrast, has a different relationship with his beard. Throughout, the play makes apparent that the beard he bears is a false one, which he must shed to return to his identity as the smooth-faced and boyish butler Jeremy. Johnston, then, is interested in Jonson's 'play with gender prostheses': not just women's clothing, the most obvious gender prosthesis, but equally, and in strange parallel to it, the male beard, which signifies both in its presence and in its absence. *The Alchemist*, suggests Johnston, is one of Jonson's plays which explores not merely the constructed nature of women, but also, more transgressively, of men: it is interested in the possibility that 'masculinity and its prerequisite privileges are also prosthetically constructed and inherently artificial'.[42]

Another recent piece of scholarship also worries about beards: Lois Potter's 'How Quick Was a Quick Change? *The Alchemist* and Blackfriars Staging'. Lois Potter is interested in the scene at the start of act 5 that seems almost deliberately 'filler', to cover Face's transformation back into Jeremy. Face must, in theory, have his beard shaved off offstage, although, as Potter notes, in practice its removal would not have been a problem, since the beard would have been a false one held on with adhesive:

> Removing it would only take moments. Face's butler costume might well have been worn under his captain's gear. It would have been an easy costume change. The odd thing is that Jonson attempts to make it look so difficult.[43]

Potter puts it in the context of the many pieces of virtuoso quick-changing required by the play – the disguises of Subtle; the alterations in voice and costume required of Doll. She also considers the quick-changes required in other contemporary plays, arguing that in them 'most quick-changes are not really very difficult, but are presented as if they were, both because the impression of breathless speed and danger is inherently funny and also because the situation draws attention to the actor's skill'.[44] This analysis of the quick-change, in turn, poses questions about the actor who played Jeremy, who must be clean-shaven for the run of the play: unless he was wearing a 'chin-clout', a bald wig for the chin. In fact, she argues, the moment of Face's shaving opens up a series of questions about the nature of theatrical illusion, and indeed the status of the actor in early modern society. Potter's work and Johnston's are not (yet) in dialogue with each other, and interesting possibilities might open up in comparing their perspectives.

Masculinity also informs the account of the play offered in Jennifer A. Low's monograph, *Manhood and the Duel*, which devotes eight pages to considering duelling in *The Alchemist*.[45] In its ritualized body language and spoken language, duelling functions as a system for creating meaning, Low argues, and in particular for affirming masculinity: the play shows this discursive system creating meaning, even in the chaotic world presented in the play.

One final take on what it means to be a man – a particular sort of man – in this play is provided by Anthony Ellis's article, 'Senescence in Jonson's *Alchemist*'.[46] Ellis is concerned with the discourses of old age in Jonson's England. In particular, suggests Ellis, by a common elision of microcosm with macrocosm, old age is associated in the Renaissance imagination with the current state of the world, on its last legs and lurching towards the apocalypse. Ellis observes that old men constitute two of the lynchpins of this play. Lovewit's advanced age is obvious enough, but also, and more surprisingly, Ellis draws attention to the numerous references to the age of Doctor Subtle. *The Alchemist*'s interest in rejuvenations, in various senses, is linked by Ellis to a much wider cultural concern: the question of what it means to be an old man, and what it means to be living in a world which is itself senescent. Ellis's monograph, *Old Age, Masculinity, and Early Modern Drama*, revisits this material, comparing the play with Dekker's *Old Fortunatus* in terms of its representation of masculinity and ageing.[47]

Histories of science

Since 2000, a number of articles and studies have considered the play relative to histories of science. The best overview of the play's relationship to science generally, and one which sounds a number of notes explored at greater detail in the other studies below, is by Katherine Eggert. Linking the play to Jonson's masque *Mercury Vindicated from the Alchemists at Court*, Eggert argues that *The Alchemist* cannot straightforwardly be signed up to a narrative of new science overtaking old medieval practice. Rather, she argues, it belongs to 'a period of both transition and overlap' between different scientific practices.[48] Eggert offers a cogent account of early modern natural philosophy, heavily invested as it was in the interconnectedness of all things, and in ideas of a perfect Edenic language. Eggert reads this into the play's interest in names and naming. The essay talks about the social, even theatrical aspects of contemporary experimentation, and it also observes that, whereas modern science strives to be dispassionate, early modern science was heavily invested in ideas of jokes, play and fun. This concept, Eggert suggests, has fascinating and still relatively little-explored implications for *The Alchemist* itself.

Anthony Miller's article 'Ben Jonson and "the Proper Passion of Mettalls"' has appeared both in the journal *Parergon* and in a festschrift for Christopher Wortham.[49] In it, Miller argues that 'Ben Jonson's works display an unusual knowledge of minerals and the technology of metalworking.'[50] Imagery of blacksmithing, forging, tempering and smelting runs through Jonson's whole canon, perhaps most famously in the image of the poet as a blacksmith, hammering hot metal 'Upon the *Muses* anvile'. Jonson frequently returns to imagery of metalworking, notably in *Sejanus* with its images of 'forging' (that pointedly ambiguous word). Thus, *The Alchemist*, dominated by its offstage furnace and its talk of purifying metals, can be contextualized in a pattern of imagery, throughout Jonson, exploring the metaphors of metalworking. In Miller's analysis, the play is as much about metallurgy as about alchemy, and Miller concludes with a long analysis of Jonson's ambivalent relationship to Ovid's myth of the Golden Age.

John Shanahan, meanwhile, aims to change the terms of reference of the discussion of the play's engagement with science. In 'Jonson's *Alchemist* and Early Modern Laboratory Space', Shanahan argues that the play is important in the history of science, not so much for its engagement with specific alchemical ideas, but for its imagination of the *idea* of scientific research, specifically scientific research taking place in a space dedicated to the purpose: 'its dramaturgy produces new images of space and time and models new kinds of relationships useful for the conceptual development of laboratory experience.'[51] Whereas modern readers of *The Alchemist*, consciously or unconsciously, tend to inherit a 'two cultures' model of an antithetical relationship between science and humanities, Shanahan proposes that much early modern science was defined in terms of its demonstrations for patrons. (There are, obviously, overlaps here with Eggert's work.) Documenting these claims, Shanahan goes on to ask: 'How and when was an experimental trial not merely a performance in the sense of theatrical playing, but also something potentially more stable and significant intellectually?'[52] Among the many contemporary reference points woven into Shanahan's argument is Jonson's contemporary Francis Bacon, who proposed a 'Solomon's House', a well-funded public space established on a professional footing specifically set up for scientific experimentation. The complex and long-recognized metatheatricality of *The Alchemist* is given an extra twist by the play's fascination with the idea of a space given over to science: a space, such as a theatre.

Henry S. Turner weaves the play into an analysis of *The English Renaissance Stage: Geometry, Poetics, and the Practical Spatial Arts*. The monograph as a whole is framed by the argument that the new epistemologies of the Renaissance – including mathematics, land surveying and other forms of technology – are linked throughout the period to new ways of conceptualizing drama and the dramatist. In this analysis, *The Alchemist* is a play about methods of knowing:

> The complexity of *The Alchemist* lies in the way that Jonson undertakes an examination of several different practical epistemologies of his period – alchemy, astrology, early industrial 'projects', applied mathematics – and compares them directly to the arts of the theatre. In this sense, the play

is nothing less than an examination *through* performance of the many operative and quasi-empirical modes of knowledge that flourished prior to the 'new science' of the seventeenth century.[53]

Noting that 'plot' can denote both a series of events and a physical ground-plan, Turner links the concept, in this play, both to Jonson's reading of Heinsius and to his own experience as a bricklayer.

Finally, on another scientific front again, a brief and cheerfully sarcastic note by Richard A. Levin considers Subtle's pseudo-magical instructions to Drugger on how to arrange his shop to best effect. This, Levin notes, sounds very much like the ancient Chinese art of *feng shui*, which was reputedly in existence at the time Jonson was writing, and which has of course emerged in recent years as a lucrative field in its own right. Levin does not demonstrate a particular mechanism of transmission by which Jonson might have come across *feng shui*, beyond speculating that the Silk Road may have been involved. There may well be more to say which could historicize this idea, although for Levin the delight of the parallel lies primarily in linking Subtle to the twenty-first-century *feng shui* consultants who might be considered his spiritual descendants.[54]

Histories of economics

For many observers, though, the alchemy depicted by the play more cogently resonates with economic rather than scientific terms. An article by Jonathan Haynes from 1989 has acted as something of a godfather to this strand of recent criticism, being very frequently cited in it, and therefore requires mention here. In 'Representing the Underworld: *The Alchemist*', Haynes argues that whereas much contemporary rogue literature tends to romanticize its rogues, Jonson is interested in the hard economics of crime: in effect, treating crime as a form of capitalism. This has unlocked a number of readings of the play in terms of economic criticism.[55]

In Peggy Knapp's analysis, for instance, alchemy is interesting not so much for its history-of-science significance but rather for what it does: 'the social and cultural work of a discourse encapsulating expansive hopes for the natural and human worlds'.[56] Here a Marxist analysis of the progress of economics supplies the terms of reference. Knapp argues that Chaucer's *Canon's Yeoman's Tale*, followed later by *The Alchemist*, both use alchemy as an overarching metaphor, considering the human condition during the transition from a feudal to a proto-capitalist society. For Knapp, 'Jonson's alchemical lab is both a metaphor for capitalism and an instance of capitalist structures of feeling. Every kind of thing is for sale.'[57] Knapp traces the progress, through the play, of words including *venture* and *commodity* as part of her argument that the play is a witness to, and sardonic comment upon, the emerging 'alchemy of capitalism'.[58]

Eric Wilson applies some of the same intellectual tools, heavily inflected by the discourse of psychoanalytical criticism. For Wilson, too, the play is a symptom of a stage in the evolution of a capitalist economy, and it offers a psychoanalytically dense pottage of ideas of commodities, value, trade, signs and meaning. Wilson devotes considerable time to Drugger's shop sign, which he suggests might make a contemporary audience think in particular of the title page of Dekker's *The Bellman of London*.[59]

In some ways, similarities between Knapp's and Wilson's approaches herald that taken nine years later by Stephanie Boluk and Wylie Lenz, in an article with the eye-catching title 'Infection, Media, and Capitalism: From Early Modern Plagues to Postmodern Zombies'. The reference points for Boluk and Lenz are Defoe's *A Journal of the Plague Year*, and the modern zombie films *28 Days Later* and *Shaun of the Dead*. All four take place in London, and all are concerned with the aftermaths of contagious outbreaks. In the later films, 'the relatively new rhetorical figure of the viral zombie', they argue, 'stands in place of and performs a function similar to the more venerable plague[:] . . . [the texts are] vehicles for expression of the ever-accelerating viral nature of global capitalism'.[60] With this as a starting point, Boluk and Lenz return to *The Alchemist*'s imagery which links infection with the structures of capitalism. Relatively lightly read in other *Alchemist* criticism, Boluk and Lenz's article is nonetheless stimulating in unlocking some vivid new analogues by which to reimagine Jonson's play.

Ceri Sullivan, in a refreshingly different analysis of the economics of the play, takes issue with one of the cornerstones of neo-Marxist readings, including Haynes's. Such analyses often describe the play as being inflected by 'the mysterious workings of nascent capital':[61] Sullivan emphasizes, instead, the extent to which it has continuities with the self-descriptions of seventeenth-century merchants. For Sullivan,

> the play responds to the merchants' sense that trade is an
> art of adequation between the demand (esteem) for differ-
> ent goods[.] . . . [It stages a] deliberate precipitation of an
> inflationary spiral through the translation mechanism from
> cash to hope.[62]

Sullivan focuses on the nitty-gritty of the operation; precisely what the various coins are worth; the bookkeeping used; the careful management of supply and demand; the nature of the credit they trade in. For Sullivan, what is striking is not so much the element of fraud in the scheme, as the extent to which it resembles good business practice as represented in contemporary mercantile handbooks.

Complementary to Sullivan's argument – and, again, it would be fascinating to stage a dialogue between these two pieces of writing – is an essay by Elizabeth Rivlin on the play's treatment of the idea of work, a topic which is itself emerging as an interesting new field across Renaissance studies. Rivlin too takes issue with the suggestion that *The Alchemist* depicts a new world of capitalist free-for-all, noting instead the fettering discourses of 'service' and 'work' that run throughout the play. (Alwes, as we have seen, also discusses 'service' in the play, but to rather different effect.) Rivlin shows that not just the dupes, but also the rogues themselves, are victims of illusory promises of wealthy leisure:

> The quandary that Face, Subtle, and Dol face – the more strenuously they try to avoid the commitments of labor and service, the more inextricably they are bound to them – reveals the limits of socio-economic change for those at the lower levels of the social hierarchy.[63]

Indeed, at least most of the dupes have some sort of independent income stream to fall back upon; the rogues do not. Rivlin's thoughtful chapter concludes by drawing analogies between the working conditions of the rogues, and the working conditions of the theatre company at the Blackfriars, thus tying this economic section back to the ideas of the Blackfriars context raised earlier in this chapter.

Performance

Since, by common consent, *The Alchemist* is a play that considers its own performance conditions, it is a particularly useful test case for ideas of performance in general, and several recent articles on the play are linked by their concern with the idea of performance in the abstract. Mathew Martin's article on the play takes its epigraph from Artaud:

> If the essential theatre is like the plague, it is not because it is contagious, but because like the plague it is the revelation, the bringing forth, the exteriorization of a depth of latent cruelty, by means of which all the perverse possibilities of the mind, whether of an individual or a people, are localized.[64]

This epigraph is the jumping-off point for a reading of the play in terms of 'unlicensed theatre', a plague-time double of the regular theatre in which 'desire governs the processes of knowledge' and imagination runs riot. And yet this imaginative space, argues

Martin, is shown within the play as a limited one: 'In contrast to Marlowe's *Doctor Faustus*, whose fictional reality is magical, from the beginning *The Alchemist* attempts to separate the realm of magic from the realm of the real.'[65]

Mary Thomas Crane, in a not entirely dissimilar vein but to rather different effect, uses *The Alchemist* as a glass through which to examine the whole early modern idea of performance. New Historicist critics of early modern drama, she observes, have often betrayed a lingering antitheatricality, positing a clear dichotomy between the authentic and the merely 'performed'. In fact, notes Crane, this dichotomy has become increasingly untenable in recent years: 'One of the central discoveries of postmodern criticism has been the role of performance in constituting many of the things that modernity took to be unequivocally real.'[66] *The Alchemist*, for Crane, is a test case for early modern understandings of performance, which by no means share the New Historicist perspective. Instead, in *The Alchemist*, performance – true performance, rather than mere representation of the sort favoured by dimwits like Drugger – is seen as something which is, potentially, genuinely transformative, like alchemy itself. *The Alchemist* is a witness to the proposition that in early modern drama there was, as Crane writes, 'at least a possibility that the act of performing itself constituted an "exercise" that effected material change in the world'.[67] Thus, whereas Martin sees Jonson's theatre as mocking the whole idea of transformation, Crane's Jonson is more favourable to the idea that theatre could change the world.

Sean McEvoy reaches not dissimilar conclusions to Crane, in an essay published in the *Ben Jonson Journal* commenting on the power of Jonson's plays in modern performances. McEvoy quotes Kent Cartwright's analysis of earlier humanist theatre in terms of a 'mysterious doubleness' of reality and unreality, actor and role, and argues that this term could apply equally well to *The Alchemist* and Jonson's other mature plays: 'The great comedies do not represent the world, but, in reveling in this "mysterious doubleness", they participate in it; they intervene in it.'[68] Their performance constitutes a moral challenge for the audience.

A fourth angle on the idea of performance in the play is provided by Rick Bowers, in a section of his book, *Radical Comedy in
Early Modern England*. For Bowers, *The Alchemist* is a specimen
of 'Ben Jonson's supersized comedy', a genre celebrating excess
and vitality in a world of almost post-modern intellectual chaos.
Bowers argues that *The Alchemist*, in particular, is a commentary
on the central process of the Renaissance, the 'change of state from
accepted faith to speculative possibility'.[69] This acts as a gloss on
the play's repeated fascination with secrets and explanations.

> [Subtle] pronounces as follows with all the searching grav-
> ity of crackpots and tricksters everywhere: ''twere absurd |
> To think that nature, in the earth, bred gold | Perfect, i'the
> instant. Something went before.' [2.3.137–9] Anyone who
> enquires – defensively, scornfully, or even vaguely inter-
> ested – as to what that 'something' is will become a part of
> the overwhelming process. Don't ask. They'll tell. The char-
> acter Surly, for all his defensiveness, falls into the trap[.][70]

For Bowers, the intellectual world of the play is a carnivalesque
one in which 'the party never ends'.[71] If, for Martin, Crane and
McEvoy, the play is about ideas of performance, then for Bowers,
the play is more or less pure performance, with a 'wonky clockwork brilliance'[72] which offers a radical challenge to all forms of
authority.

Other approaches

Finally, a group of studies of the play are united by the fact that
they do not fit easily into any of the preceding categories.

Raphael Shargel offers a fascinating analysis of a little-discussed
but historically important adaptation of *The Alchemist*: David
Garrick's adaptation, which opened in 1743 and remained a staple of the theatre's repertory for decades thereafter. As Shargel
demonstrates, Garrick took the surprising decision to make Abel
Drugger the central character, and the result is a lopsided and

unfamiliar play. Parallel passages, before and after adaptation, show the strange effects of Garrick's rewriting, which eliminates most of the linguistic pyrotechnics of characters such as Subtle, Face and Sir Epicure Mammon: '[Garrick] removed anything that might steal Drugger's fire.'[73] Garrick's adaptation, in turn, spawned Francis Gentleman's version, retitling the entire play *The Tobacconist* and producing something even more conventional and unthreatening. Shargel relates these changes to what Henry Fielding called, dismissively, 'genteel comedy'. Garrick and Gentleman, concludes Shargel, impoverish the play, 'preserving Jonsonian drama in their century only because they dilute the potent aspects of his work for which he wished to be remembered'.[74]

Donald Beecher's article, 'Suspense Is Believing: The Reality of Ben Jonson's *The Alchemist*', is grounded in the languages of cognition and of evolution.[75] *The Alchemist* functions as a test case for Beecher, who is interested in the paradox whereby narrative uncertainty can have effects upon the limbic system of the reader of the fiction. Beecher suggests, to put it bluntly, that the play can be read as speaking to our evolutionary instincts, because it offers a case study in the 'psycho-evolutionary "arms race"' between community benefit and individual benefit. Subtle, Face and the rest are examples of individuals trying to beat the system, and hence they raise an emotional response in readers:

> Thus, while we are presumably not emotionally concerned with the rising and falling fortunes of the protagonists *per se*, except as representative players within an economy of cooperation and cheating, we are vitally concerned with the mechanics and evaluations of that computational economy, perhaps because what we learn about those exchanges through provisional practice may be essential to our future well-being.

I find the approach of this article oddly utilitarian in its approach to aesthetics. It recalls Sidney's *Defence of Poesy*, with its suggestion that comedy fundamentally consists of a series of practically applicable life lessons about social interactions:

> This doth the comedy handle so in our private and domestical matters as with hearing it we get as it were an experience what is to be looked for of a niggardly Demea, of a crafty Davus, of a flattering Gnatho, of a vain-glorious Thraso; and not only to know what effects are to be expected, but to know who be such, by the signifying badge given them by the comedian.[76]

This vision seems to substantially reduce the richness and subtlety of comedy. The principal difference between Sidney's formulation and that offered in this article seems to be that, in the twenty-first-century version, the audience are no longer the morally educable gentlepersons imagined by Sidney. Rather, the audience are baboons, taking notes on the best ways to cheat other troop members, and periodically picking fleas off one another.

Among briefer mentions of the play over the past 12 years, Julie Sanders considers the play's treatment of the myth of Danaë, a recurring reference point in early modern drama.[77] Duncan Salkeld identifies 'deaf John' (1.1.85). He was, it turns out, an inmate of the charitable hospital at Bridewell, and this is one of a number of references by Jonson to that institution.[78] In an appreciative essay, Amra Raza celebrates the play's range of language.[79] Nicholas McDowell has some interesting comments on *The Alchemist*'s Puritans in the course of an article, 'Early Modern Stereotypes and the Rise of English: Jonson, Dryden, Arnold, Eliot'.[80] The Jonsonian stage caricature, argues McDowell, cast a long shadow over subsequent constructions of Puritans as philistines, remaining influential even into the twentieth century.

Conclusion

The 40 or so scholarly books and articles considered above give an almost stratigraphic cross-section through the current state of the art of Jonson criticism in general: moving away from an older vision of Jonson as a towering, pedantic, solitary moralist, and towards a sense of a pragmatic, engaged and playful body of work spread across nearly 40 years. The critical practices used vary considerably, but many of them are recognizably within a reinvigorated and broadly defined historicism, with particular interests (for instance) in space and place, gender and historicized performance studies. One thing is certain: there is more to say about this rich and intriguing mega-play, starting with the essays in the succeeding chapters of this book. *The Alchemist* will continue to invite new guests into its house of mysteries.

CHAPTER FOUR

New Directions: Space, Plague and Satire in Ben Jonson's *The Alchemist*

MATHEW MARTIN

'May dogs defile thy walls, | And wasps and hornets breed beneath thy roof' (5.5.113–14). Ananias's bathetically apocalyptic curse, which concludes his own stream of invective against the newly returned owner of 'this cave of cozenage' (115), Lovewit's house in Blackfriars, projects London momentarily into a post-civilized space, a wilderness in which London's buildings have been given over to the wild and its topographies. Dogs mark their territory on London's walls, and insects erect their own civilizations in the eaves of its ruins. Ananias is slightly mad, of course, and the play satirizes and dismisses him and the rogues' other clients in order to clear the way for Lovewit's marriage to Dame Pliant and the restoration of civilized, patriarchal London space through a different species of breeding. If at the play's opening the death of Lovewit's first wife 'broke up house' (1.1.58) and gave Lovewit's butler 'credit to converse with cobwebs' (57), the play's conclusion sweeps those cobwebs over the back wall and promises the refurbishment of urban space and the re-establishment of domestic economy after its temporary interruption by plague, death and feral interlopers. On the strength of this promise depends the strength of the play's satire. Hence, the play's oft-remarked insistence on the neoclassical unities of space, time and action. The play's gulls are taken from all strata of London's society – 'No clime breeds better matter for your whore, | Bawd, squire, imposter, many persons more' (7–8), the Prologue tells us – and their fantasies, which the three rogues coin into profit, are carefully calibrated to their respective social positions. Yet, all the fantasies involve the rearrangement or imaginative revision of London's space, a topographical sublimation that the play mordantly desublimates through its almost tautological insistence on the inflexible nature of the spatio-temporal structures of reality: a house in Blackfriars is a house in Blackfriars (and all the places it is not are to vanish like smoke at the play's end). The stability of the copula is suspect, however, threatened not only by such things as madam's pliancy (a common cynical gesture at the end of city comedies, one perfected by Thomas Middleton), but also by the fact that by 1610 vermin, plague and death were endemic to London. The real fantasy in which the play indulges is its attempt to purge London's civic spaces of its feral, disruptive and grotesque elements. Although by the play's conclusion rogues and gulls alike have been dispersed, London's urban spaces have been rezoned in ways that establish ostensibly temporary plague-time structures as permanent fixtures of London's landscape.

Within its walls and in its suburbs and liberties, early modern London was a highly regulated urban space. Early modern Londoners daily navigated their way through the spaces of a city whose water supplies, marketplaces, buildings, gates, pedestrian and transportation routes, clocks and other material aspects of quotidian life were ordered by regulations articulated and enforced by various levels of municipal government, from city council to parish constable. According to recent historians such as Stephen Rappaport and I. W. Archer, earlier historians' characterizations of early modern London as squalid and perpetually in crises caused by epidemics, famine and riots overstate the bleakness of existence and the extent of disorder in this expanding urban centre. 'No claim is made here', Rappaport writes, 'that Londoners lived in an absolutely stable society, devoid of tension or untouched by conflict, and the existence of social problems in Tudor London is undeniable, but chronic instability cannot be counted among them.'[1] In spite of destabilizing forces, Rappaport contends, London, unlike some continental cities, remained a relatively stable urban space. Essential to this stability was the decentralized and participatory nature of early modern London's municipal government. Guild membership and municipal citizenship provided a framework within which Londoners across a wide social spectrum could participate in the maintenance of order in the urban spaces they inhabited, and Rappaport suggests that at the end of the sixteenth century one in every ten London males served the city in one elected office or another.[2] The result, Archer argues, was considerable cohesiveness among London's inhabitants:

> The multi-layered structure of City government through companies, wards, and parishes set up a complex of interlocking loyalties which helped identify many Londoners with the regime. The loyalties were differently felt at different social levels. . . . But all found themselves appealing to communal and neighbourhood values at some time.[3]

Such interlocking loyalties imbued London's spaces with the hegemonic social values of early modern commonwealth ideology, at whose centre was the patriarchal household. Archer writes:

> The household stood in the front line in the maintenance of order throughout early modern English society. Sixteenth-century Englishmen regarded all social and political structures as having their origins in the family, and widely interpreted the fifth commandment to cover obedience to all superiors. As Professor Collinson observes, the writers of conduct manuals assumed 'a perfect congruence of domestic government with the government of the commonwealth'. Heads of households were vested with kingly authority within the domestic sphere, while the emphasis on the responsibilities of family patriarchs for the catechising of their children and servants underlined the household's role as a seminary of the church.[4]

If the reproductive, patriarchal household stood at the centre of London's socialized urban space, then threats to the hegemonic culture it epitomized were pushed to the margins or otherwise spatially regulated. As actors well knew, masterlessness, homelessness and unemployment were crimes: the 'idle' poor could be publicly whipped and returned to their parishes of origin.[5] Vagrancy – the spatial mobility of the poor, the homeless and the unemployed – was countered by regulations intended to fix the offending vagrants in place. Foreign workers and immigrants from other parts of England faced similar spatio-social marginalization, massed largely outside London's walls and outside the guild structure that would give them rights as municipal citizens.[6] The transgressive spaces of theatres and brothels were also located beyond the city's walls in the suburbs. If the former threatened the hegemonic culture through the actors' flagrant violation of such class regulations as sumptuary legislation (a common target of attack by antitheatricalists) and other forms of social miscegenation, the latter challenged the patriarchal organization of sexuality through its commodification of sex for pleasure rather than reproduction.[7] Other spatial structures, such as prisons and hospitals, existed to contain other sources of disorder. Poor houses, playhouses, bawdy-houses, madhouses, hospitals and houses of correction: the regulated spaces of London's urban topography housed sources of disorder in order to contain them, making them visible and socializing them as marginal to the hegemonic culture materialized in the patriarchal household.

Early modern London was not static, however. Its dynamism was driven by a rapidly expanding population that had transformative impact. Paul Griffiths summarizes that 'London's size and shape were changed speedily, and people felt that they were losing the city that they once knew. The population inside and outside the walls nearly quadrupled between 1500–1600, reaching roughly 200,000, and it almost doubled over the next five decades to around 375,000.'[8] Immigration, rather than the reproductive forces of the patriarchal household, fuelled the population explosion: in contrast to London's growth, death rates over the period

exceeded birth rates.[9] The immigrants were 'strangers' from other
parts of England and 'aliens' from abroad, rendering London
an increasingly 'strange' place.[10] The pressure exerted by the
population growth on London's spaces generated responses that
included, on the one hand, the subdivision of houses into tenements despite legal prohibition and, on the other hand, the construction of extravagant townhouses in what had previously been
common green space.[11] Changing ideology also had a transformative effect. The English Reformation made London's liberties,
zones previously under ecclesiastical control and outside municipal jurisdiction, available for secular use but with an uncertain
jurisdictional relationship to municipal authority.[12] According to
Steven Mullaney, the liberties 'stood in a certain sense outside the
law, and so could serve as privileged or exempt arenas where the
anxieties and insecurities of life in a rigidly organized hierarchical society could be given relatively free reign'.[13] James Burbage's
refurbishment of a monastic hall in the liberties of Blackfriars as
an indoor theatre for the Lord Chamberlain's Men in 1596 exemp-
lifies the radical spatial reconfigurations enabled by the liberties'
'exempt' or 'privileged' status.[14] Such spatial reconfigurations
could create conflict, however. Burbage's company was prevented
from using the hall theatre until 1608 because the liberties' residents protested to the Privy Council that the theatre would attract
'all manner of vagrant and lewde persons that, under cullor of
resorting to playes, will come thither and worke all manner of
mischeefe'.[15] The residents also worried about 'the great pestring
and filling up of the same precinct, yf it should please God to send
any visitation of sicknesse, as heretofore hath been, for that the same
precinct is allready growne very populous.'[16] Certain spatial innovations, however, were designed to proclaim London's growth in a
triumphant light. Such institutions as Gresham's Royal Exchange,
built in 1568, and the later New Exchange were visible symbols of
London's emergence as a hub of European commerce and a centre of conspicuous consumption. Visited and named by Elizabeth
in 1570, Gresham's Exchange declared the new power and position of capital in England's social order. Similarly, in 1609 James

presided over the opening of the New Exchange in the Strand, an occasion celebrated in Jonson's *Entertainment at Britain's Burse*.[17] Yet, as Jonson's contemporaneous *Epicene* illustrates, these two architectural monuments to London's commercial prosperity also represented vehicles and symbols of the nascent capitalism that was contributing to the breakdown of the regulation of London's urban space.

The urban literature that developed alongside London's dynamic expansion registers that dynamism in various ways. In his *Survey of London* (1598), John Stow attempts to contain London's growth within a vision of London as an ideal commonwealth memorialized in the city's architecture and spaces, its bridges, walls, gates, houses, streets and fountains. In his prefatory address to Mayor Robert Lee, Stow states that 'What London hath beene of auncient time men may here see, as what it is now every man doth beholde.'[18] What London 'hath beene', according to Stow, was an ideal commonwealth. Discussing cities in general, Stow argues:

> At once the propagation of Religion, the execution of good policie, the exercise of Charity, and the defence of the countrey, is best performed by townes and Cities; and this civill life approcheth nearest to the shape of that mistical body whereof Christ is the head, and men be the members.[19]

London in 'auncient time', specifically the time of King Stephen in the following passage, was precisely this kind of political body: 'in those dayes, the inhabitants & repayers to this Citie of what estate soever, spirituall or temporal, having houses here, lived together in good amity with the citizens, every man observing the customes & orders of the Citty.'[20] Although such losses as the decline in private charity and the dereliction of folk festivities generate considerable nostalgia in Stow's survey,[21] his verdict on 'what it [London] is now' is that 'the present estate of London [is] yet still growing to better',[22] and he concludes the survey with a prayer that 'Almightie God . . . grant that her Majestie evermore rightly esteeme & rule this Citie; and he give grace, that the Citizens may answere duty, aswell towards God and her Majestie, as towards this whole realme and countrey.'[23]

Although deeply historical, Stow's *Survey* is one of a multitude of early modern English texts that Lawrence Manley groups under the rubric of 'fictions of settlement', socio-symbolic attempts to domesticate and render knowable the bewilderingly new urban environment of early modern London.[24] As Jean Howard has recently argued, the period's theatre advanced these fictions of settlement in the 'London comedies' it presented on its stages, themselves relatively new urban spaces. In its dramatizations of London, according to Howard, the theatre 'participates over time in rendering the city ideologically knowable, in regulating conduct within it, and in negotiating the most vexed issues with which Londoners were confronted'.[25] Many of these dramas reiterate Stow's commonwealth vision even while acknowledging the emergent forces pressuring that commonwealth. The Royal Exchange, for example, is a central space in Thomas Heywood's *If You Know Not Me, You Know Nobody, Part II*, which in Howard's analysis 'dramatizes a version of history that makes protagonists, not of monarchs, but of exemplary figures from London's citizen classes' yet at the same time 'points to rents in the social fabric of that citizen group as well'.[26] Conversely, although Jonson celebrates the New Exchange in *The Entertainment at Britain's Burse*, in *Epicene* it becomes, along with the theatre, a space of class and gender disruption. In its concluding marriage between the aristocratic Roland Lacy and the merchant class Rose Oatley and in the reconciliation it contrives between their antagonistic fathers, Thomas Dekker's *The Shoemaker's Holiday* presents London as the scene of the consolidation of harmony among social classes. Similarly, Dekker and Webster's *Westward Ho!* offers an urban version of festive comedy in which London as a regulated patriarchal space is sexually threatened, but the potential transgression mostly occurs outside the city in the town of Brentford, and the concluding return to the city, like the concluding return to Athens in *A Midsummer Night's Dream*, is a return to patriarchal order.

The play's three citizens' wives, who have joined three gallants for a night's stay beyond the city walls at an inn in Brentford, refuse the gallants' sexual advances and delight in the thought that their 'Jest shal be a stock to maintain our pewfellowes in laughing at christnings, cryings out, and upsittings this 12. month' (G4r).[27] The three wives' laughter reaffirms the rituals of the reproductive household while trivializing transgressive sexuality as a joke. The play's witty plotter, Master Parenthesis, counsels their jealous husbands to support this reaffirmation:

> what a glory it will be for you 3. to kisse your wives like forgetfull husbands, to exhort and forgive the young men like pittifull fathers: then to call for oares, then to cry hay for London, then to make a Supper, then to drowne all in Sacke and Suger, then to goe to bed, and then to rise and open shop, where you may aske any man what he lacks with your cap off, and none shall perceive whether the brims wring you.
>
> (H4r)

The three husbands have suffered sexual humiliation even though their wives have proven to be chaste, but their return to London will restore them to their households and to their symbolic positions as household heads, positions they will be able to occupy with their caps off, without fear of shame.

London comedy did not always endorse the application of the conventions of romantic comedy to London's urban environment, however. The satirical city comedies of such playwrights as Jonson and Thomas Middleton highlight instead the disjunctions between the socio-symbolic order embedded in these conventions and London's economic and sexual realities. They are fictions of unsettlement. Thus Middleton's *A Chaste Maid in Cheapside* moves from the domestic disorder of several broken households and separated romantic lovers to the restoration of those households through the production of an heir and the marriage of the lovers. But the patriarchal order thus restored is wholly undermined by the manner of its restoration: the Kix and Touchwood households are reassembled only because Touchwood Senior has administered to Lady Kix the miraculous 'water' (2.1.186) that the impotent Kix is incapable of supplying, and the two lovers, Touchwood Junior and Moll Yellowhammer, are reunited only because Lady Kix's pregnancy has economic implications that render the main obstacle to the match, Touchwood Junior's rival Sir Walter Whorehound, bankrupt.[28] In this satirical drama, however, the real winners are the Allwits, whose domestic arrangements parody the reproductive patriarchal household. The household is funded by Whorehound, who has made Mistress Allwit his mistress and has had by her a number of children, all of whom have been christened as Allwit's. Allwit rejoices in the situation: 'I live at ease, | He hath both the cost and torment' (1.2.54–5). Not at all daunted by Whorehound's bankruptcy and imprisonment, at the end of the play the Allwits plan to move their anti-patriarchal household further into the heart of the city: 'Let's let out lodgings, then' (5.1.160), Mistress Allwit declares, 'And take a house in the Strand' (161).

The plague heightened the pressure on the socio-symbolic order of London's spaces, especially its central location, the household. The government's plague policies intensified the regulation of urban space; the intensified regulation encountered popular resistance and the plague's reconfiguration of London's spaces. Plague policies tightened the regulation of public spaces, closing theatres and other spaces of large communal gathering. These policies also mandated the regulation of domestic space: households with plague-stricken members were to be isolated for at least six weeks.[29] Such measures, Dekker writes in *The Wonderfull Yeare*, converted London into 'a vast silent Charnell-house'.[30] Although early modern London was unwilling or unable to implement the comprehensive plague policies established in most other European cities, the plague incited a discourse of permanently heightened regulation of urban space and permanent cleansing of the city through the elimination of the spaces, such as theatres, that were held to be moral and medical incubators of the plague. As Foucault argues in relation to plague regulations in seventeenth-century France, the plague opened up utopian possibilities in the imaginations of those in authority, and the plagued city provided the spaces in which those possibilities could be enacted: 'The plague-stricken town, traversed throughout with hierarchy, surveillance, observation, writing; the town immobilized by the functioning of an extensive power that bears in a distinct way over all individual bodies – this is the utopia of the perfectly governed city.'[31] Foucault is of course aware that what he is describing is a 'political dream', a totalitarian fantasy of 'omnipresent and omniscient power' that no early modern state could realize.[32] During the plague, moreover, most of London's major public officials fled: mayors, aldermen, doctors, the clergy and the rich quickly abandoned the city. Those officials who remained to implement the plague regulations faced the problems of insufficient funds to relieve those confined, inadequate and often corrupt minor officials with which to enforce the orders, and the general unpopularity of and resistance to the orders.[33] Nonetheless, as the Blackfriars residents' petition to the Privy Council demonstrates, even in times when it was quiescent in London, the plague incited regulatory discourse: the residents trope their desire to prevent Burbage from using his new theatre as a prophylactic measure taken against 'the great pestring and filling up of the same precinct, yf it should please God to send any visitation of the sicknesse'.[34]

Inevitably, however, the impetus to regulation was countered by equally forceful movements of disorder. The grim conditions of London during the peak periods of plague mortality provided a macabre setting and motivation for carnivalesque behaviour. According to contemporaries, drunkenness, dancing in graveyards and infected houses, promiscuous sexual behaviour, and looting the abandoned houses of the rich were common.[35] The denial of spiritual and secular order in the ludic, anarchic and carnal pursuit of life in the fleeting moment is understandable: death was imminent, public plague policy and Galenic medicine were ineffective, the plague appeared to distinguish not between just and unjust but between rich and poor, and many had little left to lose. Spiritual responses could be equally disruptive. Robert

Lerner argues that one of the primary responses to the first out-
break of the plague in Europe in 1347–50 was to fit it into current
eschatological paradigms as a sign of the imminence of the millennium: 'Europeans tried to comprehend the fury of the plague
with the aid of what might be called a prophetic "deep structure"',
and prophecies 'foresaw contemporary storms being succeeded by
wondrous times of peace and Christian triumph'.[36] Many early
modern English responses to the plague can be placed within this
apocalyptic tradition, often figuring plague-stricken London as a
type of Jerusalem, the city of God's chosen people being pun-
ished for their sins. John Donne's sermon on the 1625 plague, for
example, presents London during the plague as the 'Holy City' in
which God's judgement was revealed: its unrepentant inhabitants
had cried out

> let us eat and drink, and take our pleasure, and make our
> profits, for tomorrow we shall die, and so were cut off by the
> hand of God, some even in their robberies, in half-empty
> houses, and in their lusts and wantonness in licentious
> houses.[37]

The plague transformed London into an apocalyptic space.

In *The Alchemist*, the plague displays its transformative power,
paradoxically, in the dramatic unity of the play's setting, a house
in the liberties of Blackfriars. As the play's point of departure
and return, Lovewit's house represents the patriarchal space
that Archer places on the front lines of social order. At the play's
beginning, we are informed that Face's 'mistress' death hath
broke up house' (1.1.58). If Lovewit's wife died of the plague,
the plague has assaulted the patriarchal order at its reproductive centre. Even if not, the plague has still evacuated the play's
space of its patriarchal authority figure: 'The sickness hot, a
master quit, for fear, | His house in town, and left one servant
there' (Argument.1–2). Only when the plague mortality rates
have abated to 'one a week' (4.7.116) 'within the walls' (117) does
Lovewit return to re-establish patriarchal order by reclaiming his

house and resubmitting it to the regulatory regime of municipal government: 'The house is mine here, and the doors are open' (5.5.26), Lovewit tells the officers whom the enraged gulls have brought to arrest Subtle, Face and Doll; 'If there be any such persons as you seek for, | Use your authority, search on o'God's name' (5.5.27–8). By this time Subtle and Doll are long gone, however, and Face has desublimated himself back into his subservient position as Jeremy the butler within Lovewit's patriarchal household. Lovewit consolidates the return to patriarchal order when he marries the young Dame Pliant and thus reforms the reproductive household broken up by the plague at the play's beginning. Within the boundaries delimited by Lovewit's departure and return, however, the plague transforms the house in Blackfriars into a deregulated space whose transgressive potential appears even in its liminal, seemingly empty moments. Before the house becomes home to the alchemical con-game of the play's satirical action, its only occupants are Jeremy, 'the rats' (1.1.50), and 'cobwebs' (57), poor company perhaps but with subversive potential: Jeremy is a temporarily masterless man with a home, and he soon attracts the similarly masterless roommates Subtle and Doll. Likewise, when Lovewit enters his house at the end of the play, he professes that the only damage he can see to his property is to 'find | The empty walls, worse than I left 'em, smoked' (5.5.38–9). But the walls are not quite empty: there is the small matter of some graffiti, 'madam with a dildo writ o'the walls' (42), an advertisement for commercial, non-reproductive sex that not only echoes Surly's earlier charge that the house 'is a bawdy-house' (2.3.298), but also casts an ominous shadow over what Lovewit next confesses to having found in his empty house, 'one gentlewoman . . . | That is within, [who] said she was a widow' (5.5.44). The scene, however, has not changed. Unlike the urban festive comedy *Westward Ho!*, in which transgressive action occurs in locales outside London's ordered space, *The Alchemist* reveals through the plague the plasticity of urban space: the same house in Blackfriars is patriarchal household, a harbour for masterless men and a bawdy-house.

The plasticity of London's spaces during the plague is precisely what the play's three masterless rogues count on and manipulate when they set up their alchemical con-game in Lovewit's house. As Cheryl Lynn Ross has argued, the socio-symbolic resonance of their squatting only reinforces the plague's transformation of urban space:

> When Subtle, the waste product that effaces boundaries, and his smokes, stinks and fumes that spread and swirl incontinently, enter the social body by invading Lovewit's house in Blackfriars . . . he eclipses the strong borders that lend a society its symbolic identity, integrity and strength. The effect is the social equivalent of putrefaction and plague.[38]

Yet, in defiance of plague orders, the newly infected house is the destination of a torrent of traffic: 'Ladies and gentlemen', 'Citizens' wives', 'knights', 'coaches', 'oyster-women', 'gallants', 'Sailors' wives' and 'Tobacco-men', according to Lovewit's Blackfriars neighbours at the end of the play (5.1.3–5). The crowd is, significantly, socially heterogeneous, a collection of characters from all walks and stations of life. Arguing that *The Alchemist* is an updated version of the estates morality play, Alan Dessen sees the play's characters as types, each a representative of a different social estate and illustrating that estate's corruptness: Jonson 'has transformed the traditional conflict between a Vice or set of Vices and a group of representative "estates" into a "literal" conflict between a group of business-like rogues and a panoramic cross section of figures from English society'.[39] As Dessen's characterization of the three rogues as 'business-like' suggests, however, Jonson's satire is not moral so much as it is social and economic. If, according to Dekker, plague-time London sprouted numerous 'jolly Mountibanks', who routinely 'clapt up their bills upon every post (like a Fencers Challenge) threatening to canvas the Plague and to fight with him at all his own severall weapons',[40] then Lovewit's house provides its 'jolly Mountibanks' with the headquarters from which they are able to multiply the range of scams by which they can convert the plague into a quick profit by exploiting their customers' social desires. The rogues transform Lovewit's house into a commercial space, as the play's argument makes clear. Face sublets his absent master's house to Subtle and Doll: 'wanting some | House to set up' (6–7), Subtle and Doll 'contract' (7) with Face, 'Each for a share' (8). Like the Royal Exchange and the New Exchange, the transformed house, the traffic it attracts, and the profits that accumulate in its cellar testify to London's fertile commercial environment. What the rogues are selling, moreover, is ostensibly a cure for the plague, the philosopher's stone, but is really the plague's further spread out into London's socio-symbolic order. Jonathan Haynes remarks that 'the victims' relations with the cony-catchers are all based on unsettled ambitions within the social order and/or dreams that would explode it'.[41] The philosopher's stone and the other magical items and services that the rogues offer their clients allow those clients to live out fictions in which all impediments to social mobility and the acquisition of symbolic capital vanish. Dapper will 'blow up gamester after gamester | As they do crackers in a puppet-play' (1.2.78–9); Drugger will encounter no opposition to his meteoric rise through the ranks of his company; the stone will instantaneously establish the Brethren as 'lords' (3.2.52) of 'a faction | And party in the realm' (25–6); and in Mammon's fantasies the entire world – including the poet 'that writ so subtly of the fart' (2.2.63) – will without hesitation allow itself to be bought.

Radically reconfiguring London's spaces and disrupting the social hierarchies by which those spaces are ordered, the plague enables the alchemical con-game that functions as the vehicle for the play's satire. Significantly, however, the three rogues' transgressive actions take place within the context of the constant threat of regulation and repression. Even Mammon's seemingly unrestrained fantasies of infinite wealth do not ultimately escape regulation. While wooing Doll, Mammon promises her that, should she become his companion, 'the jewels | Of twenty states [will] adorn thee' (4.2.141–2). This conversion of political symbol

into sexualized fashion accessory does not go unchecked, however.
Doll asks:

> in a monarchy, how will this be?
> The prince will soon take notice, and both seize
> You and your stone, it being a wealth unfit
> For any private subject.
>
> (4.1.147–50)

Doll's regulatory threat involves spatial relocation, either to 'a
loathed prison' (153) or to 'a free state, where we will eat our mul-
lets | Soused in high-country wines' (156–7). Similarly, Subtle
plays on the Anabaptists' zealous approval of coining by invoking
the threat of punishment. Although the Brethren have declared
'That casting of money is most lawful' (4.7.78), Subtle defers
their hopes once again with his reply that 'here I cannot do it: if
the house | Should chance to be suspected, all would out, | And
we be locked up in the Tower forever' (79–81). On a smaller scale,
Face whets Dapper's appetite to meet Dr Subtle by claiming that
the law has made Subtle reluctant to take clients: 'the law | Is
such a thing', he tells Dapper, 'and then, he says, Read's matter |
Falling so lately –' (1.2.16–18). Moreover, the threat of regulation
and repression weighs not only on the fantasies engendered by
the alchemical con-game but also on the rogues themselves. In the
quarrel with which the play begins, Subtle, Face and Doll invoke
informal community regulation as well as the severest forms
of legal punishment, which constitute a complex of regulatory
threats that appear as ever-present dangers to the rogues' trans-
figuration of urban space. Plagued space is also paranoid space.
The neighbours' ears are never far away: 'Will you have | The
neighbours hear you? Will you betray all?' (1.1.7–8), Doll asks
the arguing Subtle and Face, each of whom subsequently both
demands that the other lower his voice and raises his own voice
to gain tactical advantage. According to Doll, the ears belong to
'A sort of sober, scurvy, precise neighbours' (164), who 'Would
run themselves from breath to see me ride, | Or you t'have but a

hole to thrust your heads in' (167–8). Although they have established themselves in the house in Blackfriars, the rogues face the
constant threat of eviction. The neighbourly nature of local polic-
ing can always lead to carting, the stocks, or the gallows. Doll
reminds Subtle and Face of these regulatory dangers in order to
put an end to their 'civil war' (82), and to make the 'abominable
pair of stinkards, | Leave off [their] barking and grow one again'
(117–18). In the heat of the argument, however, Face turns those
words against his fellow rogue:

> I'll bring thee, rogue, within
> The statute of sorcery, *tricesimo tertio*
> Of Harry the eighth – ay, and (perhaps) thy neck
> Within a noose for laundering gold and barbing it.
>
>   (111–14)

At the end of the play, Face proves that these were not entirely
empty threats, preventing Doll and Subtle from taking the chest
of valuables with them as they flee by telling them that 'Here will
be officers presently. Bethink you | Of some course suddenly
to scape the dock, | For thither you'll come else' (5.4.135–7).
London during the plague is not an entirely carnivalesque space:
the unruly behaviour unleashed by the plague does not fully
escape the law's regulatory mechanisms. Nonetheless, whether to
defraud their clients or to combat each other, the rogues do not
submit to these regulatory mechanisms so much as they appropriate them for their own subversive ends. The members of the
'venture tripartite' (1.1.135) are plague-time poachers on the
commonwealth's sovereignty, dispersing its power through their
own rebellious subjectivities.

To transform London's spaces the rogues employ their
plague-time agency not only in conflict and collaboration with
each other but also in collaboration with their clients. If for the
three rogues the house in Blackfriars is primarily a commercial
space, for their clients it is what Ian Donaldson has aptly termed 'a
sounding-board for the imagination',[42] a magical house that seems

capable of inverting the spatial relations between inside and outside. As he relates his alchemical dreams to his companion Surly
at the threshold of the house, Mammon proclaims:

>   Now, you set your foot on shore
> In *novo orbe*. Here's the rich Peru,
> And there within, sir, are the golden mines,
> Great Solomon's Ophir! He was sailing to't
> Three years, but we have reached it in ten months.
>
>   (2.1.1–5)

In Mammon's imagination, the door of this London house opens
upon the vast expanses of a new world. This world is golden; its
gold, like the plague, is virulently contagious and transformative, spilling out of the spatially inverted house in Blackfriars
to gild all of London. James Mardock suggests that Mammon's
'purchase of the alchemist's magic is imagined in terms of
acquiring the power to define the spaces and places of the city'.[43]
Mammon's imagination is drawn to particular locales, however.
Subtle's remarks upon observing Mammon approach the house
are telling. He sees Mammon 'entering ordinaries | Dispensing
for the pox, and plaguy-houses, | Reaching his dose, walking
Moorfields for lepers' (1.4.18–20), and 'Searching the spital to
make old bawds young | And the highways for beggars to make
rich' (23–4). Mammon's philanthropy leads him to London's
marginal spaces and people: ordinaries patronized by syphilit-
ics, plague houses, zones of wasteland set aside by municipal
authority for such figures as lepers and the homeless, hospitals,
bawdy-houses, and highways, the routes of vagrancy. Mammon
himself promises 'to fright the plague | Out o'the kingdom in
three months' (2.1.69–70). Yet, Mammon's Midas touch will
only replace the plague with an even more powerfully deregula-
tive force as it liberates the bodies of London's marginal subjects
from their containment in marginal spaces and provides them
with the resources to continue their wayward, transgressive
practices.

The fantasies of the rogues' other clients are not as grandi-
ose but involve a similar reconfiguration of urban space. Drugger,
for example, is 'building | Of a new shop' (1.3.7–8) and con-
sults Subtle to know 'Which way I should make my door, by
necromancy. | And where my shelves' (11–12). Subtle's advice
addresses multiple aspects of the shop's future spatial existence,
from its orientation to its appearance. 'Make me your door, then,
south; your broad side west', Subtle recommends, 'And on the east
side of your shop, aloft, | Write *Mathlai, Tarmiel,* and *Baraborat*'
(63–5). 'Beneath your threshold bury me a loadstone | To draw
in gallants', he adds, 'And on your stall, a puppet with a vice, |
And a court-fucus to call city-dames' (69–73). Set up according
to Subtle's strictures, Drugger's shop will become a replica of the
house in Blackfriars: its alchemical magic will draw clients, such
as gallants and city wives, who will pay for drugs and potions that,
like the elixir of life, hold out the promise of restorative effects, for
consumption by the ounce or the jarful. Moreover, the shop, its
owner and its function will presumably continue after the plague
has abated, permanently establishing the reconfiguration of urban
space that the three rogues can, at least in this play, effect only
temporarily. The shop's alchemical design will have an immedi-
ate effect on Drugger's social location: 'This summer', Subtle
predicts, 'He will be of the clothing of his company, | And next
spring called to the scarlet' (35–7). Drugger's shop will establish
the rogues' plague-time disorder at the heart of London's ordered
socio-symbolic space.

Within the reconfigured space of the house in Blackfriars, the
play displays another kind of transformation, the disciplining and
regulation of the clients' bodies in an anti-patriarchal economy
of consumption. Kastril provides the paradigm. '[A] gentleman,
newly warm in's land', Kastril is worth 'some three thousand a year'
of landed income and 'does govern | His sister here' (2.6.57–60),
Dame Pliant. He represents, then, the reproductive patriarchal
order that Jonson celebrates in such poems as 'To Penshurst'. Yet
Kastril, like Sir Amorous La Foole and the other gulls in *Epicene*,
has come to London from his country estates during plague-time

in order to consume his economic and sexual patrimony, to marry off his sister and 'To learn to quarrel and to live by his wits' (61). Granted, Kastril expects his participation in consumption to be only temporary and devoid of long-term effects: after his stay in London, he intends to 'go down again and die i'the country' (62), and he has vowed that he will not marry off his sister 'Under a knight' (51). The rogues have other ideas, educating Kastril not only in the niceties of quarrelling but also in the tactics and logic of the consumer economy in which they hope to entrap Kastril permanently. They envision no return to the country for Kastril. '[W]hen your land is gone' (3.4.83), Face tells Kastril, Kastril will benefit from the various dubious commercial schemes that Subtle can now (for a fee, of course) teach him. Significantly, all these schemes require that Kastril remain 'in town' (89). Controlling these and other tactics, such as gambling, is the ultimate consumer logic, that of living on credit. Thus, Face tells Kastril that he must 'spend' (50) himself through gambling to transform himself into a witty gallant: gambling, like the philosopher's stone, 'will repair you when you are spent. | How do they live by their wits there that have vented | Six times your fortunes?' (51–3). Dame Pliant's fate even more tellingly illustrates the transformative potential of the rogues' plague-time practices. 'A wife, a wife, for one on's' (2.6.85), Face exclaims to Subtle after the two rogues have persuaded Drugger to bring Kastril and his sister to the house for a consultation, and by the end of the play Dame Pliant has become Doll's substitute in the liaison the rogues have arranged with the Spanish Don.[44] The considerations that dictate Dame Pliant's body's redeployment in the anti-patriarchal economy of non-reproductive sex are wholly commercial: 'All our venture | Now lies upon't' (4.3.64–5), Face tells Subtle after both realize that they have double-booked Doll with Mammon. To 'make the widow a punk' (102), however, threatens to destroy her value within the patriarchal, landed economy within which she is one of her brother's assets. 'Marry a whore?', exclaims Subtle, who possesses no real estate whatsoever; 'Fate, let me wed a witch first' (90). 'This match will advance the house of the Kastrils' (4.4.88), declares the duped Kastril. Ironically, though, it promises a disappointing loss of revenue even to the house in Blackfriars: 'Would Doll were in her place to pick his pockets now' (4.5.108), Subtle laments, and his comment reminds us that not even the rogues can fully master plague-time's risky consumptive economics.

The rogues' other clients are similarly disciplined and regulated. 'Spend what thou canst' (1.3.83), Face urges Drugger, and the rogues' customers do just that, throwing away their money in the hope of recovering it in the future in the form of realized wishes. Subtle and Face stoke Dapper's transgressive desire with fantasies of social mobility that involve not just Dapper's frictionless accumulation of capital through gambling but also a life of consumption floated by the credit he thus obtains. 'He will win you | By unresistable luck, within this fortnight, | Enough to buy a barony' and will consequently, 'for the whole year through, at every place, | Where there is a play', have 'The best attendance, the best drink, sometimes | Two glasses of canary, and pay nothing' (3.4.58–65). Yet, of course, Dapper must pay for the magical fly that will produce this scenario. 'There must a world of ceremonies pass' (1.2.144) before Dapper can take possession of his good luck charm, and each stage of the rituals that Subtle prescribes for him requires payment. The final ceremony demands that he 'throw away all worldly pelf about him' (3.5.17), and Dapper complies as he is blindfolded, pinched, and ultimately gagged with mouldy gingerbread and shoved in a privy. His reward is to kiss Doll's 'departing part', a crude visual inversion of the 'proper' patriarchal reproductive sexual relationship that Dapper accompanies with the promise to sign away to Doll his 'forty mark a year' (5.4.57–8). Mammon's unruly desires are similarly regulated and disciplined. He participates in London's plague-time economy as capitalist as well as consumer. In response to Surly's jibe that the possessor of the philosopher's stone must be 'pious, holy, and religious' (2.2.98), Mammon states that 'That makes it, sir, he is so. But I buy it' (100). Such a purchase, however, is impulse shopping on a compulsive and grand scale, involving the constant outlay of funds. Even when 'the works | Are flown *in fumo*' (4.5.57–8), shattering the sexual fantasies Mammon has been entertaining with Doll, Mammon's 'itch of mind' (93) still has its terminus in 'A hundred pound to the box at Bedlam' (86). The rogues' alchemical con-game, then, disciplines the clients' bodies and their desires to function within the anti-patriarchal, consumer economy incubated in the plague-time space of the house in Blackfriars.

The point of the play's satire, of course, is that the clients' fantasies will never escape the realm of more or less utopian social fiction. They reveal the clients' social and psychological deformities rather than exercising any real force on London's topography, plague-time or otherwise. Through its dramatic unity, in fact, the play seems to insist on the obdurately untransformable nature of urban space, especially the house in Blackfriars, which constitutes both the play's scene and its first performance venue. As R. L. Smallwood demonstrates, the play's dramatic unity constructs an 'absolute topicality and simultaneity' between the rogues' temporary home and the King's Men's new hall theatre:

> An audience in a theater in the autumn of 1610 pays money to pass what the Prologue promises will be two hours (and an interval), to watch three masters of pretense, in the autumn of 1610, take two hours (and an interval) to deprive a number of representative gulls of their money.[45]

The identity extends even to the response each theatre receives from its neighbours. As Smallwood notes, Blackfriars residents several times complained against the commotion caused by the King's Men's performances, as do Lovewit's neighbours at the play's end. The collapse of fictional and real space, however, raises the disturbing question of logical if not ontological priority: which space is the replica? As Smallwood's vocabulary suggests, the King's Men's hall theatre, like Drugger's shop, reproduces the rogues' plague-time disorder within and as a regular part of London's ordered socio-symbolic space.

The abatement of the plague ends the alchemical con-game, and Lovewit's return seemingly rezones the house in Blackfriars back to its pre-plague status as a patriarchal household: Lovewit asserts his authority as owner of the house, as master of his servant, and as potentially reproductive husband of a young wife. Yet, in Lovewit's cellar remain the rogues' earnings, and Lovewit takes possession of these as well. When in 5.4 Doll, Subtle and Face count up their profit, the list of items in their trunks contrasts starkly with the items in the rhetorically similar lists that Mammon produces when he elaborates upon the wealth that the philosopher's stone will bring him. Mammon's lists contain exotic, spectacularly valuable items to be consumed, from 'jewels' (4.1.141) to 'butter made of dolphins' milk' (160). The items in the three rogues' inventory are commonplace and of small value individually: 'Mammon's ten pound' (5.4.108), 'The jewel of the waiting maid's' (110), 'The fishwife's rings' (113), 'the whistle that the sailor's wife | Brought you' (115–16), 'the French petticoats | And girdles, and hangers' (118–19), some of Drugger's tobacco (121), along with 'Mammon's brass, and pewter' (4.7.127). They constitute the untransmuted stuff of everyday life, and their accumulation, like the stink of the privy from which Dapper exits at the play's end, persists through the house's multiple rezonings: from the plague-time fantasy space of the alchemical laboratory, through the restored patriarchal space of Lovewit's household, to the theatrical space of the King's Men's hall theatre. The play concludes with Face/Jeremy/the actor who played Jeremy declaring that 'this pelf, | Which I have got, if you do quit me, rests | To feast you often, and invite new guests' (5.5.163–5). Pelf: it is such base stuff that makes and is made out of dreams, and like the plague this stuff has become endemic to London, accumulating in the cellars of houses in Blackfriars. The concluding lines extend into the audience the three rogues' efforts to discipline and regulate their clients. They invite the audience to continue consuming and accumulating pelf in exchange for the privilege of being fed fantasies. The metatheatrical gesture suggests an ironic reading of the satirical intentions Jonson expresses in the play's Prologue: by inviting audience members to 'see and yet not own' (Prologue 24) the 'natural follies' (23) of the play's gulls, Jonson invites them to adopt precisely the self-ignorant attitude that, like the plague, enables the alchemical con-game. Jonson's 'fair correctives' (18), like Mammon's elixir, banish the plague only to replace it, rendering audience members the vectors of its permanent residence in London's urban spaces.

CHAPTER FIVE

New Directions: Staging Gender

IAN MCADAM AND JULIE SANDERS

Masculinity in *The Alchemist*

IAN MCADAM

Masculinity in Jonson is surprisingly complicated. In a 1994 article, Douglas Lanier claims that the Jonson canon 'has, with some [notable] exceptions, remained relatively unamenable to gender-oriented criticism', but suggests that such 'barrenness' from the perspective of a feminist reading can be rectified by 'shifting critical attention away from Jonson's admittedly jaun-diced view of the feminine and towards his conception of the masculine'.[1] While the exclusion of one term from the gender binary constitutes, theoretically, a tricky proposition, and while more recent feminist readings have further challenged the alleged 'barrenness', there is no doubt that Jonson's own moral and artis-tic obsession with 'Things manly'[2] renders a focus on masculin-ity potentially illuminating. The illumination can be particularly striking in the case of *The Alchemist*, which, I argue, appears at a critical moment in the evolution of Jonson's conceptions of masculinity. *The Alchemist* unsettles a depiction of a conservative, hierarchical masculinity with a radically individualized – and ulti-mately more creative, less oppressive – masculinity. Jonson's satire may be directed at the extreme individualism, even megaloma-nia, of occultists, Puritan 'enthusiasts' and millenarian thinkers, but the play opens up an interesting ideological space within this project, supported by Don E. Wayne's crucial observation that,

after *Volpone*, 'Jonson begins to show signs of a disturbed awareness that his own identity as poet and playwright . . . depended
on the same emerging structure of social relationships he satirized in his plays.'[3] Thus, the edge of Jonson's satirical attack on
anti-authoritarian forces in *The Alchemist* is substantially blunted,
reflecting a political (and psychological) development increasingly
evident in his ensuing plays.

In an excellent review of trends in Jonson criticism, James
Loxley examines the theoretical importance of Wayne's landmark
chapter:

> Wayne's revision of [L. C. Knights] is an attempt to politi-
> cize the reading of Jonson's drama. . . . It is not simply that
> he does not think the plays can be adequately understood as
> repudiating passions or follies which are the permanent stuff
> of human nature . . .; he considers that an account of their
> functioning should not be constrained within the model of
> a satirist consciously and purposively working through the
> definition and treatment of a problem. What Jonson thought
> he was doing, in other words, . . . is not the appropriate hori-
> zon of interpretation.[4]

Loxley supports a more sophisticated Marxist reading that strives
to uncover the material contingency of what earlier critics unprob-
lematically designated as 'human nature' in order that, politically,
'it might one day be changed'.[5] While my own readings of 'human
nature' are less suspicious of transhistorical behavioural patterns,
I do agree that the greatness of Jonson as an artist often lies in his
creation of works that transcend his own conscious moral (and
satirical) purposes. That the *unconscious* meaning of works like *The
Alchemist* surpasses – not just in potential social progressiveness,
but in psychological perceptiveness – the *conscious* moral or satirical meaning may be related to the complexity of the playwright's
conceptions of masculinity.

Upon closer consideration, some of the striking contradic-
tions and paradoxes in Jonson's artistic and moral temperament

may seem less surprising, if not less complicated. The conservative Jonson is closely allied with his neoclassical stance – the value of civil order and hierarchy – yet his classicism also emphasizes individual virtue; that is, the more pagan or secular values of self-discipline and (moral and political) independence. Transplanted into the theologically grounded hierarchical structure of early modern England, Jonson's classical values can take on dangerously republican overtones. Moreover, a classical Jonson is certainly recognizable in his echoes of 'the neostoic conception of the embattled yet resolute self expressed in Plutarch, Seneca, and Tacitus'; but if, in Lanier's terms, Jonsonian 'masculinity entails the maintenance of a rigorous self-identity and autonomy',[6] the 'embattled' aspects lead to such aggressive, at times violent, competition between men in Jonson's work – painfully evident as well in his own personal relationships – that the independence or autonomy of a 'centered self' becomes highly suspect.[7] His emphasis on the importance of homosocial bonds and male friendships can be traced to his low social status – Sara van der Berg argues that 'As a man without the advantages of family, rank, or privilege, Jonson considered friendship not only an ideal but a necessity' – but when such relationships failed, and ideals were compromised, he could make 'art of rage and betrayal, of envy and contempt, as well as of affection and respect'.[8] A writer of masques, in Jonson's case some of the era's most notable, by the very definition of the genre must honour aristocratic authority, but subordination to patrons, though an important source of income, could come humiliatingly close to 'iDollatry', and 'To My Muse' significantly defines 'manly' writings as 'not smelling parasite'. Jonson's neoclassical poetics emphasize 'the proper relationship between nature and art', which leads to 'an idealized version of the temporal regime of a landed, patriarchal social order',[9] evident in poems such as 'To Penshurst', but his plays reveal an artistic obsession with the kind of competitiveness, already noted, which flourishes in 'artificial' urban contexts, particularly London. For all of Jonson's elitist pride in humanist and classical education, through which he aspired to be the kind of moral centre he identifies in *Volpone*'s

'Epistle' – 'men . . . will easily conclude to themselves the impossibility of any man's being the good poet without first being a good man'[10] – the most vital and memorable characters in his drama apparently flourish without the assistance of the two sister universities honoured in the dedication to that play, or any other educational institutions for that matter. Rather, through a school of hard knocks and the acquisition of street-savvy, they discover the necessary tools of their survival, which seem, for the most part, to have little to do with what moralists call goodness.

In the face of such multifaceted implications, arising from peculiar combinations of Jonson's innate elitism and conservatism in conflict with his individualism, more radical humanism, and personal ambition, I want to suggest that *The Alchemist* can be read as a kind of allegory of warring concepts of masculinity in the psyche of the playwright. The celebrated opening in fact directly expresses this conflict: the tension between the conservative and radical conceptions of masculinity embodied respectively by Face and Subtle. The two men do not simply struggle for domination within the 'venture tripartite' (1.1.135). They represent different social origins, connections, talents and aspirations, temporarily held in suspension through their collusions with Doll Common. The first scene in fact clearly establishes Face's and Subtle's different political and psychological leanings through their different attitudes towards their female compatriot. Doll finally manages to pacify her male partners' 'civil war' (82) – ironically after descending to the level of masculine aggression by seizing Face's sword and breaking Subtle's alchemical vessel. When she has re-established the two men as 'My noble sovereign and worthy general' (172), Subtle responds gratefully, 'Royal Doll! | Spoken like Claridiana, and thyself!' (174–5). The irony here is pleasant, and complimentary. The prostitute can hardly be 'royal' – just as the alchemist cannot be 'Sovereign' – because, as Doll herself asserts, the 'venture tripartite' (135) is a 'republic' (110), 'the work . . . begun out of equality . . . All things in common . . . Without priority' (133–6). Jonson may (consciously) be satirizing Subtle's elevation of Doll, and, by implication, his self-subordination to a woman.

Such a foolish gesture is immediately and ruthlessly deflated in Face's response:

> For which, at supper, thou shalt sit in triumph
> And not be styled Doll Common but Doll Proper,
> Doll Singular. The longest cut at night
> Shall draw thee for his Doll Particular.
>
> (176–9)

The Cambridge editors, Peter Holland and William Sherman, claim that common, proper, singular and particular are grammatical terms, adding 'But "Common" and "Proper" may also stand for two kinds of legal ownership and of sexual conduct';[11] as I have argued elsewhere, 'Face implies that the winner at drawing straws, or perhaps the most generously endowed [physically], will receive her particular sexual favors.'[12] Face's comment drastically reduces Doll to simply a sexual object, to what she in fact is (socially): a punk or whore. In doing so, however, he shows much less sensitivity and imagination than either Doll or Subtle, between whom there is a distinct and thematically crucial sympathy.

The epithet that Subtle applies to Doll, 'Claridiana' (175), alludes to the heroine of a popular romance translated from the Spanish as *The Mirror of Princely Deeds and Knighthood* (1578). While the name implies 'bright divinity', or perhaps 'famous virginity' (fuelling Face's comical cynicism), such romantic idealization recurs later in the play when Sir Epicure Mammon, believing Doll to be the sister of a nobleman, addresses her as, ''Fore God, a Bradamante, a brave piece' (2.3.225), identifying her with the female warrior in Ariosto's *Orlando Furioso* that influenced Spenser in his depiction of Britomart. When Mammon later approaches what he expects will be blissful sexual union with Doll, he exclaims to her, 'There is a strange nobility i' your eye, | This lip, that chin! Methinks you do resemble | One o'the Austriac princes'. The idealization is again sneeringly undercut by Face: 'Very like: | Her father was an Irish costermonger' (4.1.54–7). Admittedly, the conscious level of the play's satire is on

Face's side, yet Face's drolleries are rather depressingly grounded in his surprisingly rigid acceptance of social limitations, in terms of both class and gender. (How much revolutionary spark does it take, for instance, to realize that Austrian princesses are not always beautiful, or that lower-class individuals can be exceptionally so?)[13] In the subtext which more concerns me here, there is an intriguing and unexpected connection between Subtle and Mammon – that is, between con-man and dupe, lower-class rogue and foolish knight – in their ability to imagine greater (social) possibilities for both themselves and for Doll.

Before tracing further the secret sympathies between Subtle and Mammon as well as the more overt psychological and political connection between Subtle and Doll, I want to first clarify what I have called the 'conscious' level of the play's satire, which as I have suggested is focused on, or through, the character of Face – the other con-man bound by, and ultimately obedient to, the traditional hierarchies of early modern society. Alchemy in the play is, obviously, a complete scam,[14] a game facilitated by Face, who, if he does not own the means of production, possesses the keys to the arena where the production takes place. All those attracted to alchemy's possibilities are therefore fools. The dupes at first glance possess disparate desires, ranging from the sexual monomania of Sir Epicure Mammon to the completely self-serving politico-religious aspirations of the puritan Anabaptists. John Mebane helpfully explains the disparity: 'The Puritans and the occultists obviously had their differences, but in *The Alchemist* Jonson emphasizes their very real similarities. Most importantly, he links them together because both are "enthusiasts" who regard their own subjective inspiration as superior to any institutional authorities.' For Mebane, the conservative point of Jonson's satire is indisputably clear: Jonson's gulls are deluded into 'thinking they can establish a new political, social, and religious order', and therefore the playwright illustrates 'his belief that the rhetoric of individualism and reform can become the tool of a vicious megalomania'.[15]

Historically, there were in fact important connections between 'Puritans' and 'occultists'. Robert Schuler observes 'the historical links between alchemy, Puritanism, and millenarianism'.[16] I suggest that the radical individualism represented, collectively, by these movements provide a potential for progressive masculine and feminine assertion barely contained by the play's conscious satire. Puritanism is admittedly a favourite target in Jonson's satires, not surprisingly considering the frequency of Puritan attacks on the stage. In *The Alchemist* this target includes not only the political and monetary desires of the Anabaptists, but also Mammon's dreams of a 'free state' (4.1.156) where he can enjoy, with Doll, the sensuous fruits of the philosopher's stone unmolested by princes jealous of his power. Thus, Jonson manages to ridicule both the killjoy repressive version of Puritanism represented by the Anabaptists and the carnivalesque grotesque Puritan that Mammon temporarily echoes.[17] Yet, underneath the ridicule lie serious psychological and social issues related to Jonson's 'disturbed awareness' (to reconsider Wayne's thesis) of his own personal implication in the satirized aspirations. Jonson wrote *The Alchemist* the same year he reconverted to Anglicanism, and evidently (in a rather oral-narcissistic fashion) downed the entire communion cup 'in token of true reconciliation'.[18] While I doubt there is much in the specific characters of the hypocritical Tribulation Wholesome and the more fanatical Ananias that Jonson even unconsciously approves of, I nevertheless suspect that his reconversion to Protestantism might have been accompanied by (psychological) considerations other than simply political expediency. Alchemy is literally a fraudulent art which constitutes a gross distortion of nature and the natural, but alchemy – with, in this historical context, decidedly protestant connotations – metaphorically comes to represent, through the agency of the 'venture tripartite', radically republican freedoms of self-determination that Jonson unconsciously identifies with.[19] While Mammon's 'occult' ambitions rapidly degenerate into narcissistic and self-indulgent desires, his aspirations initially are heroic and altruistic, and apparently catch the fancy of Subtle, who describes them in loving detail (1.4.11–29), and who is, after all, the eponymous character of Jonson's play, somehow central to its most vital creative dynamics and its deepest identifications.

The special affinity or respect that both Subtle and Mammon have for the (real or potential) partnership they share with Doll likely receives the playwright's conscious contempt for such weakening of 'masculine' dominion – just as we must laugh at Dapper when he is adjured to 'Kiss [the] departing part' (5.4.57) of the Queen of Fairy before he is dismissed. Mammon claims to Doll that he will soon possess the stone because he is 'master of the maistry' (4.1.122), but as he admits earlier to Surly, he does not require the piety or purity that 'are prerequisite to alchemical success'[20] because he simply 'buy[s] it' (2.2.100) – a good Jonsonian jab at nascent capitalist urges. Since the projected 'projection' is false, the con men must make Mammon fail through his attempted seduction of Doll – an easy ruse, considering Mammon's salaciousness – although the seduction turns out to be a remarkably liberal invitation for Doll to become *co-equal* in his fantastic 'perpetuity | Of life and lust' (4.1.165–6). The catastrophe is humorously construed as a kind of 'comic apocalypse' by the rogues, as Doll spews forth quotations from the puritan and rabbinical scholar Hugh Broughton at Mammon's mention of the 'fifth monarchy', the millenarian project he planned to 'erect' (4.5.26).[21] Doll thus cleverly *avoids* actual prostitution at this point, and her ability to perform Broughton renders her, I think, the intellectual equivalent of Subtle, with his (parodic) mastery of alchemical jargon. Ironically, the true role of prostitute in the play falls to Kastril's sister, the apparently brainless Dame Pliant, who becomes almost literally an alluring *object* that the majority of men in the play seek to possess.[22] Significantly, Subtle relinquishes his own interest in Dame Pliant with the remark to Face, 'Much good joy, and health to you, sir. | Marry a whore? [They are about to prostitute her to Surly as the Spanish count.] Fate, let me wed a witch first' (4.3.89–90). As a sorcerer or cunning man, Subtle 'is a kind of "witch" himself – Face in fact calls him one at [1.1.107] – and in a sense seeks his own here.'[23]

That Subtle's Achilles' heel is in essence his 'feminine' sympathies makes sense in terms of his 'profession', since the art of alchemy itself was often seen as analogous to human reproduction. Highly familiar with its technical details, Jonson repeatedly 'echoes the images of pregnancy and procreation so prominent in alchemical writings'.[24] Jonson conveys Subtle's subtle subordination to feminine power in intriguing ways. The alchemist presumes the grand powers of the magus in the opening scene, when he threatens Face: 'I'll thunder you in pieces. I will teach you | How to beware to tempt a fury again | That carries tempest in his hand and voice' (60–2). Jonson may allude here to Agrippa's belief that violent storms – which according to William Perkins can be raised by sorcerers or magicians with Satan's aid – could be allayed by the completely natural and *essential* power of women: 'if menstruous women shall walk naked . . . they are able to expel hail, tempests, and lightnings'.[25] Doll's ability to pacify her warring partners, and her warning to Subtle to 'gather . . . up' his 'menstrue' (116) after breaking his glass, are thus perhaps particularly significant. While the effeminization of Subtle may contribute to the play's satiric humour, the parallel between Subtle's and Jonson's essential *creativity* again raises the serious issue of unconscious identification. Critics have considered the possibility of 'womb envy' in male poets of the Renaissance.[26] In *The Alchemist*, it is certainly difficult to ignore the 'proximity of the "alchemical imagination" to the literary imagination'.[27] But alchemy's historical association with Protestantism also means it can be seen, according to the Weberian paradigm, as a proto-capitalist endeavour.

The Alchemist, appearing one year later than *Epicene*, contains similar (if potentially more subversive) disruptions of Jonsonian conservatism based on inherited, landed wealth. In both texts, 'an idealized and patriarchal version of natural time' – 'cyclical yet productive' – is disrupted by 'the wasteful and seemingly sterile pleasures of capitalism'. Both dramatize a 'consumer society . . . an effeminized, counterpatriarchal world in which art is a mode of consumption that abandons nature'.[28] Yet, *The Alchemist* comes closer, not of course to a full *realization*, but to an intimation that greater powers of self-determination, for both men and women of the lower classes, will depend on a radical social challenge to just such ideological configurations of nature. The proto-capitalist fantasies of *The Alchemist* are certainly haunted by sterility: as Subtle reveals in the opening scene, Face has been conversing with cobwebs since his 'mistress' death hath broke up house' (58); Lovewit's late wife has left no heirs. The conservative solution to this sterility, however, involves the emasculation of the entire venture tripartite. Lovewit's return, which follows the ruin of Mammon's hope for the millennium, in a sense repeats the pattern of 'comic apocalypse'. Like Overdo in *Bartholomew Fair*, Lovewit the patriarchal master of the house is a parodic god who in this case is indeed, as in the gospel parable, a bridegroom (for Pliant), and returns when least expected to reinstate order and end a world of fraud. Face's consequent loss of manliness could not be clearer: 'All my Captain's beard | Must off to make me appear smooth Jeremy [the butler]' (4.7.130–1). To save his skin, the butler's agency is now devoted to helping his master to the sexual prize to which he has himself previously aspired. This role as pander or pimp confirms the profession that Surly has linked Face with earlier, the supervision of a prostitution ring (2.3.300–6). But the role also associates the restoration of conservative social order with this same traffic in women; individual competition for Dame Pliant has simply been replaced by a more formal hierarchy of subordination and service.

Lovewit – with one of those Jonsonian names suggesting masculine competence, or at least authorial approval – has become a significant artistic and moral problem in criticism of the play. I suggest this problem directly reflects the conflicted nature of Jonson's evolving conceptions of masculinity. Lovewit's role in act 5 is brief, but quickly accumulates a series of disturbing ironies. Dressing up as the Spanish count himself, at the suggestion of his butler, Lovewit problematizes his own masculinity by indulging in the kind of performativity that, for Jonson, vitiates true manliness.[29] The fraudulence of the performance is particularly intense, if we accept Anne Barton's reading of its context:

> Spanish dress remains necessary because, although Surly has painstakingly informed Dame Pliant that Lovewit's house is a 'nest of villains' [4.6.2] out to cheat and despoil her, she remains so enamoured of their prediction that she will soon be transformed into a Spanish countess, hurried through the London streets with pages, ushers, footmen and eight coach-mares, that she cannot bear to relinquish it.[30]

Lovewit deliberately deceives his new wife, who perhaps deserves such loveless treatment insofar as she blindly embraces marriage as high-class prostitution. Lovewit himself is a kind of prostitute, since widow Pliant's greatest asset is her wealth. Lovewit proves a kind of thief, as he calmly appropriates booty accumulated by the venture tripartite, adroitly resisting any legal reclamation on the part of the gulls. And finally, Lovewit is a surprising bully, as he aggressively intimidates the 'angry boy' Kastril, who dares disapprove of his sister's marriage: 'Come, will you quarrel? I will feeze you, sirrah. | Why do you not buckle to your tools?' (5.5.131–2).

Lovewit's role is so tainted he seems almost a parody of the conservative, landed patriarchal social order – he has, after all, returned from his country estate, to which he fled for fear of the plague – that seeks to contain the excesses of the new (urban) individualism. Perhaps he embodies significant traces of a new man himself, who opportunistically imitates the older hierarchical self.[31] As he casts a shadow, there is a whiff of tragedy to his triumph, especially as it involves Face's ruthless betrayal of his confederates through the process of obsequiously re-embracing his social subordination. Jeremy's role-playing, though deft, is the kind that will establish itself anywhere, any time, for purposes of abject self-preservation. There remains something oddly poignant in the lost potential of the greater players, Subtle and Doll, and something distinctly paradoxical in the suggestion that the radical masculinity of the utterly disenfranchised Subtle emerges finally as (potentially) less chimerical than the conservative, hierarchical masculinity of Lovewit and Face, who, socially, have won the day. The tragedy of Subtle's defeat is that he has defined himself and his powers not in contradistinction to women and femininity, but through a co-operative dialectic that recognizes the (social) potential in other (talented or virtuous) individuals and hence enhances his own creativity.[32] Subtle's portrayal intimates that the most effective way to establish or promote an interiority that can effect social change is to recognize that same interiority or agency in those individuals, of either gender, with whom one interacts.[33] The suggestion is so revolutionary that the playwright, at the time of *The Alchemist*'s composition, still consciously resists it.

   Jonson, in the face of Subtle's heroic potential, portrays all three of the confederacy as rogues, and Face's betrayal is anticipated by Subtle (in reverse) when he remarks privately to Doll:

> Soon at night, my Dolly,
> When we are shipped and all our goods aboard
> Eastward for Ratcliffe, we will turn our course
> To Brentford, westward, if thou say'st the word,
> And take our leaves of this o'erweening rascal,
> This peremptory Face.
>
> (5.4.74–9)

With Subtle's endearment, 'My fine flittermouse, | My bird o'the night' (88–9), they fall to kissing, but their anticipation of Brentford, 'a famous rendezvous for lovers and fugitives outside London',[34] is shattered by Face's return and his announcement of their necessary (and penniless) retreat. Nevertheless Subtle and Doll show us something new in Jonson: a *rapprochement* between masculine and feminine, where the marginalized but resourceful man sees an equal partner – 'if thou say'st the word' – in the marginalized but resourceful woman, not an object to be exchanged or possessed. Doll foreshadows the more sensitive and comprehensive portrayal of women in Jonson's ensuing plays, such as Grace

Wellborn and even Ursula the pig woman in *Bartholomew Fair*, or Frances Fitzdottrel in *The Devil Is an Ass*. And *Bartholomew Fair*, with its exposure of the mania of its self-appointed censors, reveals Jonson's conscious recognition of the limits of an authoritarian satire, which he unconsciously anticipates in *The Alchemist*. At the risk of romanticizing Jonson, I suggest that *The Alchemist* reveals something even more profound. In the intimate 'billing' of Subtle and Doll before they fly the coop, we see something so much better than the competitive seizure of a wealthy widow. We see a reckless, daring, appealingly illicit love, which transcends the more typical early modern heterosexual union, delimited through homosocial and patriarchal constraints. Much subsequent literature, over the centuries, will follow this cue.

Performing Women in *The Alchemist*

Julie Sanders

Scholarship on *The Alchemist* takes as given that the play is deeply embedded in its own practices and conventions as a piece of early modern theatre. Written, as we have learned elsewhere in this volume, with the Blackfriars Theatre and its precinct in mind, the play draws attention to its own act of social and cartographical placement: Subtle makes a pointed reference in the opening scene to events unfolding in 'Your master's Worship's house, here, in the Friars' (1.1.17) and the play's 'Argument', a witty acrostic included in printed editions, further sketches the analogy between the house of the play world and the theatre house in which it was staged:[35]

> T he sickness hot, a master quit, for fear,
> H is house in town, and left one servant there.
> E ase him corrupted, and gave means to know
> A cheater and his punk, who, now brought low,
> L eaving their narrow practice, were become
> C ozeners at large; and, only wanting some

H ouse to set up, with him they here contract,
E ach for a share, and all begin to act.
M uch company they draw and much abuse
I n casting figures, telling fortunes, news,
S elling of flies, flat bawdry, with the stone,
T ill it and they and all in fume are gone.

                                                    (Argument.1–12)

The 'house' which the argument describes is, to all intents and purposes, a theatre. The servant it mentions, Jeremy – or 'Face' as he is referred to for the majority of the play – forms a company with his colleagues in crime, a 'cheater' (Subtle) and a 'punk' (Doll Common, the prostitute, to whom we will return). Their contract with one another deliberately resembles that which actors in the King's Men, who staged *The Alchemist* in its earliest performances in Oxford and London in 1610, would have recognized as akin to their own professional contracts which allotted them individual shares in a joint stock company. The performances of the 'venture tripartite' (1.1.135) of servant, cheater and punk draw another kind of 'company'; which is to say paying audiences, just like those who would have paid to see Jonson's play. This metatheatre is self-conscious and sustained throughout the play. Disguise and impersonation rest at the heart of the alchemical scam concocted by the team and the connections extend to the use of borrowed stage costumes, roles and even lines, in the course of the unfolding action.

What might paying attention in new ways to this sustained metatheatricality in the context of thinking about gender, and in particular Jonsonian representations of the female experience, mean for our understanding of the female roles of this play? In exploring this question here, I am thinking across time, attending to the particular situation of the boy actors who played those female parts in their original performances, but also projecting forwards to female actors of a more modern sensibility and training and what might strike them about Jonson's women when they are trying to recreate these roles anew on the contemporary stage.

It would be false to suggest that women actors have always praised Jonson's female characters or, indeed, the experience of playing them. The Royal Shakespeare Company actor Fiona Shaw notoriously declared her loathing of Jonsonian drama after she took the role of Lady Frances Frampul in John Caird's 1987 production of *The New Inn*: 'It's an old man's play about a young man's world. . . . The play should have explored the neurotic situation of Lady Frampul far more.'[36] Many performers speak anecdotally about feeling frustrated by the lack of lines their parts have or by the lack of agency they feel is accorded their characters. Bald statistics can, however, be misleading. The number of lines accorded to a character does not necessarily tell us everything about the impact or dynamic of a particular role in performance. Admittedly Shakespeare's Rosalind, from *As You Like It*, a much loved role for women actors, is also the most extensive female part in the Shakespearean canon in terms of lines and stage presence, famously even being accorded the last word of that play ('It is not the fashion to see the lady the epilogue'[37]) but lines alone do not reveal everything about stage time, presence or even agency, especially in the Jonsonian oeuvre. Respecting Jonson's self-assigned role as a social satirist, the lack of speech he sometimes accords his socially and physically constrained women may tell us as much about the way that society treats them as any self-confessional soliloquy; simply because Jonson writes female roles that enact these kinds of social constraints need not signify that he endorses the actions of wider society. Rather, it may evidence the inverse: that by inviting audiences to notice these largely silent or silenced women we pay attention to their plight.

Dame Pliant in *The Alchemist* is a fine working example of this last point. Only talked of in earlier segments of the play, she does not appear physically onstage until some way into the action at 4.2. And even then she remains largely mute, or at most reduced to unheard whispers (5.5.146 s.d.), her hotheaded and querulous brother Kastril doing much of the talking for her. The audience, however, is not necessarily unaware of Pliant's presence throughout as she is summarily subjected to verbal and physical definition by male characters, Subtle not least: '*He kisses her again.* | [*Aside*] 'Slight, she melts | Like a myrobalan!' (4.2.41–2). A myrobalan is a wild plum and this particular description, as well as having obvious sensory and sexual qualities, reduces Pliant to a fruit ripe for the picking much the same as the nubile and marriageable country daughters who are brought to the big house in 'To Penshurst':

> Some bring a capon, some a rural cake,
> Some nuts, some apples
> . . .
>   or else send
> By their ripe daughters, whom they would commend
> This way to husbands.
>
>   (51–5)[38]

In both cases, I would argue, the Jonsonian deployment of metaphor does more to reveal the problems inherent in a society that nurtures a marriage market in quite such explicit ways than it does to reveal deep misogyny in the playwright himself.

Admittedly, Doll Common herself has little good to say about her one female counterpart on the stage: Face asks her: 'And how do you like | The Lady Pliant?' and she replies with considerable acerbic bite: 'A good dull innocent' (5.4.66–7). Contemporary female actors in the role, struggling to find the spotlight on stage with their mere nine and a half spoken lines, might well share the sentiment.[39] Certainly, Pliant is easily impressed: 'Brother, | he calls me lady too' (4.2.54–5); she comes across as a person of unanswered questions and vehement exclamations with limited world experience other than in the relatively rarefied environment of her rural homestead. She is equipped with few of the skills to cope in the knowing confines of the city and yet she is undoubtedly crucial to the play and its plot-lines. Just because Jonson portrays or depicts patriarchal society's tendency to reduce women to sexual objects in the way that both Doll and Pliant are objectified in the course of *The Alchemist* does not mean this is an act of straightforward moral endorsement. The playwright turns a mirror on the problems of the age; Face tells us as much in his closing address to the audience: 'you, that are my country' (5.5.163), as he puts it. It is true that a male character gets the last word in this play but more notably, perhaps, these are the words of a jobbing actor, which return us not only to normative patriarchy but also to that self-conscious metatheatricality which I suggest is the keynote of this drama: '[*Addressing the audience*] My part a little fell in this last scene, | Yet 'twas decorum' (5.5.158–9). In the plays that Jonson went on to write in the wake of *The Alchemist*, the perils and inequities of the marriage market resurface as tropes in ways that lend credence to Ian McAdam's sense earlier in this chapter that, at least as far as women's parts go, this text is a hinge-play of sorts, prefiguring later more extended and explicit concerns with the fate of the female, married or unmarried.

Pliant, the 'soft buxom widow' (4.2.37) of this play, at least in Subtle's terms, is notably also an heiress and that makes her a desirable commodity in the fiscally driven world of *The Alchemist*. Initially, Subtle and Face vie for her attentions: 'She is a delicate dabchick! I must have her' (4.2.60), declares Face with some stridency. Pertinax Surly soon joins in on the act, feigning the part of an avenging hero, 'Lady, you see into what hands you are fall'n, | 'Mongst what a nest of villains!' (4.6.1–2), but in reality using and abusing Pliant as much as any of the other men. Pliant's heavy-handed brother insists on her compliance in all matters, threatening her with physical abuse if she declines. Ultimately, she is simply appropriated as part of the stolen booty of the venture tripartite requisitioned by Lovewit, the returning master. Pliant's silence in the final scene in which she appears in the play (5.6) might be understood in the light of these observations as a marker of Jonson's empathy for the young widow, constrained as she is by society's expectations and destined as she is to be handed around as an object of desire.

The reason why Lovewit can consider the flagrant act of wresting Pliant from the grasping hands of his aberrant servant and the fellow scamsters who have taken over his house is because he is himself a widower. Subtle informs us early on that the death

of Face's mistress 'hath broke up house' (1.1.58). We never learn
if Mistress Lovewit died of the same plague epidemic that has
seemingly prompted her husband's flight to the countryside in the
hot and dangerous summer months but it seems clear that she
was a woman of some standing, in her own household at least.[40]
There is one other fleeting but resonant moment in the play when
it gestures at the significance of an absent woman in her domestic
setting. In 5.1, several members of the Blackfriars neighbourhood
cluster around Lovewit's front door to inform him of the strange
comings and goings that have been witnessed at his residence during his absence:

LOVEWIT	Has there been such resort, say you?
FIRST NEIGHBOUR	Daily, sir.
SECOND NEIGHBOUR	And nightly, too.
THIRD NEIGHBOUR	Ay, some as brave as lords.
FOURTH NEIGHBOUR	Ladies and gentlewomen.
FIFTH NEIGHBOUR	Citizens' wives.
FIRST NEIGHBOUR	And knights.
SIXTH NEIGHBOUR	In coaches.
SECOND NEIGHBOUR	Yes, and oyster-women.
FIRST NEIGHBOUR	Beside other gallants.
THIRD NEIGHBOUR	Sailors' wives.
FOURTH NEIGHBOUR	Tobacco-men.

(5.1.1–5)

Once again, metatheatrical resonances are to the fore of this
exchange. The Blackfriars Theatre, as Andrew Gurr has demonstrated, was the subject of neighbourhood complaints about
disturbances (not least from coaches crowding down the narrow
alleyways of the precinct) when it became a commercial theatre
enterprise in the seventeenth century.[41] It is one of these complain-
ing neighbours in particular who interests me here. Neighbour six
informs Lovewit of particular nocturnal noises he has overheard
while quietly labouring at domestic duties at home: 'About |
Some three weeks since, I heard a doleful cry, | As I sat up a-mending

my wife's stockings' (5.1.32–4). The wife of neighbour six, albeit unseen and unheard on the stage of *The Alchemist*, makes her mark as a woman with domestic agency, strong enough to enlist her husband to mend her hosiery.[42]

Several scholars have begun more recently to redress an older critical tendency to dismiss Jonson as a misogynist by studying the elite female culture, a world of patrons and poetesses, movers and shakers, with whom he interacted and the print afterlife of *The Alchemist* has an important role to play in this regard.[43] The play is dedicated to Lady Mary Wroth, daughter of Sir Robert Sidney, brother of the courtier poet Sir Philip and owner of the aforementioned Penshurst estate in Kent. Mary would herself go on to be a writer of considerable note, producing an epic romance and a sonnet sequence among other works and Jonson praised her literary skills in one of his own rare forays into the sonnet form.[44] Rather than rest in the realm of the paratextual material of the print edition, in order to fully appreciate how Jonson genuinely pays attention and accords agency to women in *The Alchemist* we need to drill down to the impacts and effects of the play in performance. To do this I will turn for the remaining part of this chapter to the main female protagonist, Doll Common.

Doll is a Southwark prostitute but she is also much more than that label alone would suggest. As well as being one-third of the 'venture tripartite', she is an actor of impressive quick-change skills, performing the parts of both the Fairy Queen in a performance that puns on 'quean' meaning prostitute (to delude the hapless romantic, Dapper the clerk), and a learned Puritan lady (to appeal, in turn, to the voracious sexual appetite of Sir Epicure Mammon). While in one way we might see her performance of these roles as another form of prostitution, in actuality she studiously avoids sleeping with any of the clients. In this way, her acting skills liberate her from the trajectory of the play's opening scene, where Subtle and Face draw straws (or 'cuts') as to who will sleep with her that night: 'The longest cut at night | Shall draw thee for his Doll Particular' (1.1.178–9). Helen Ostovich has drawn attention to the promise and wonder Doll represents to the clients and the empowering effect of her role-play as a result.[45] Subtle compares her to a romance heroine: 'Royal Doll! Spoken like Claridiana, and thyself' (1.1.174–5). Claridiana was the female protagonist of *The Mirror of Knighthood*, a popular sixteenth-century Spanish romance by Diego Ortuñez de Calahorra; Doll is briefly assigned a starring role here and it is equally notable that when acknowledging her verbal dexterity Subtle plays tribute to her as an individual as well as to the power of the personae she assumes. What we begin to see, then, as the play unfolds, is that Doll is an agent. In the remarkable opening scene, to which I will return in a moment, it is she who watches the windows, responds to bells and knocks, announces all comers to the property and guards the doorway. In this way, her role is a feminized version of the Plautine witty servant and achieves real kinships with Mosca from Jonson's earlier stage comedy *Volpone*. At other times, Doll is co-actor and co-conspirator in the alchemical scam, a stage performer of considerable skill and effect. This account of her part in things seems at odds with the sense of abject females so often lazily associated with Jonson's plays.

What then might a close reading of Doll's role beyond just the roles she plays tell us? In their fine readings of the early modern practice of learning theatre roles as individual 'parts' – with actors provided often just with their own part and necessary cue lines in script form – Simon Palfrey and Tiffany Stern have given us fresh insight into how early modern plays were collaboratively produced by performance as well as the ways in which cues contribute to the creation of individual characters as part of a more complex whole.[46] At a very practical level, of course, this attention to cues gives us a sense of the early modern theatre at work: actors depending on each other to support the production of event and meaning, the cue serving as part of the forward dynamic of any play. There is always the chance that a cue might go wrong, be missed or indeed misdelivered; we witness in operation through the play's 'formal architecture' the dependency of actors on each other, and on teamwork.[47] Subtle and Face have often been described as a consummate comic 'double act'; they are highly dependent on each other for cue lines and prompts in the play's dramaturgy. Face even draws attention to this fact at 3.3 when he says to Subtle: 'Take but the cues I give you' (80).[48] Simon Palfrey asserts that speech-cues are 'a hinge-point where decisions are made, relationships are tested, and identities forged' and we can see this idea enacted in the *The Alchemist*'s opening scene.[49] Here Subtle and Face's exchange of invective relies on quick-fire provision of cues for comic and political effect and Doll's carefully timed interventions, themselves cued by the duo's exchanges, bring back into the visibility the world of the street and the law just outside the room where the conspirators argue. In this very practical version of theatre, the ensemble rather than individual characters proves to be the driving force and a woman, an articulate and active woman, is very much a part of that ensemble.

Though 1.1 of *The Alchemist* opens *in medias res*, in the middle of a raging argument between the highly competitive Subtle and Face, the opening two lines are in fact shared between the venture tripartite. Subtle and Face have to share the opening line, proving through the rhythmic structure and linguistics and poetic formalities that they *do* depend on each other despite the surface enmity of their words and, tellingly, Doll gets the whole of the second line:

FACE	Believe 't, I will.
SUBTLE	Thy worst. I fart at thee.
DOLL	Ha' you your wits? Why, gentlemen! For love –

                                                                        (1.1.1–2)

As well as being a voice of harmony rather than dissent, attempting to quell the 'civil war' (1.1.82) between the two men, Doll is also the character who is conscious of audiences (in the street, in the neighbourhood, and presumably in the theatre in which they are all performing – once again she is a crucial link to the metatheatrical core): 'Will you have | The neighbours hear you? Will you betray all?' (1.1.7–8). Her long and confident speech from line 125 onwards not only exhibits a genuine fear of the legal consequences of their criminal activity but also accuses the men of threatening the balance of the performing ensemble, a threat to theatre itself:

> [*To FACE*] You will accuse him? You will bring him in
> Within the statute? Who shall take your word?
> A whoreson upstart apocryphal captain,
> Whom not a puritan in Blackfriars will trust
> So much as for a feather! [*To subtle*] And you too
> Will give the cause, forsooth? You will insult
> And claim a primacy in the divisions?
> You must be chief? As if you only had
> The powder to project with? And the work
> Were not begun out of equality?
> The venture tripartite? All things in common?
> Without priority? 'Sdeath, you perpetual curs,
> Fall to your couples again and cozen kindly
> And heartily and lovingly, as you should,
> And lose not the beginning of a term,
> Or by this hand I shall grow factious too
> And take my part and quit you.

$$(1.1.125–41)$$

In a sentence that might have been crafted to describe the opening scene of *The Alchemist*, Palfrey observes that 'The cue is more than an exchange of batons or even a switch-point or hinge-point. It can also be conceived as a very real space, shared or fought between two [or more] players.'[50] Doll's threat to remove her 'part' in this way, then, is also a threat to remove her essential cues and contribution to the alchemical performance. In this respect Doll is well aware of her value in the theatrical transactions that constitute the play. She uses the discourse of 'parts' and the division of labour, 'common work' (1.1.156) as she terms it, throughout to describe the activities of the trio but also to gesture towards simpler theatrical conventions which mean that words associated with her name, profession and reputation will seem to hail her onto the stage and into the audience's view:

MAMMON   I urged that,
And cleared to him that Sisyphus was damned
To roll the ceaseless stone only because
He would have made ours common.
              DOLL *is seen.*

                                          Who is this?
                                          (2.3.207–10)

Doll is all too aware of herself as the 'res publica' or public thing
that is the prostitute: 'Have yet some care of me, o'your republic –'
(1.1.110) and, for that reason alone, I would not want to lose sight of
the fact that, for all their agency, all three of the 'venture tripartite'
are put back in their place, socially speaking, by the close of the play.
Face is restored to his servant's livery as Jeremy, attending to his
returned master's every need. For Subtle and Doll the trajectory is
even more of a downward one; they are summarily dispatched over a
back wall by Face, presumably to return to their former Southwark
haunts (5.4.132–3), carrying none of the spoils and only, in Doll's
case, letters of reference to notorious brothels (5.4.141–2). The
theatrical agency I am according Doll in *The Alchemist* should not,
then, be overdetermined. Both she and Pliant are effectively rendered mute by the end of the play; as Helen Ostovich notes, their
parts become virtually 'interchangeable'.[51] Nevertheless, in combination, they provide a forceful defence not only of Jonson's interest
in and considerable empathy for the female condition, but of his
intrinsic theatricality, a theatricality in which female roles definitely
have a part to play.

CHAPTER SIX

New Directions: *The Alchemist* and the Lower Bodily Stratum

BRUCE BOEHRER

Waste matters

The world of Ben Jonson's *The Alchemist* seems composed equally of gold and precious materials on one hand and of excrement and sewage on the other. Sir Epicure Mammon fixates on the precious substances, imagining that when he has acquired the philosopher's stone, his 'meat shall all come in in Indian shells, | Dishes of agate, set in gold and studded | With emeralds, sapphires, hyacinths, and rubies' (2.2.72–4). Dapper fantasizes that he will 'win ten thousand pound' at gambling (1.2.136). Drugger dreams of becoming 'a great distiller' and making his own 'assay . . . at the philosopher's stone' (1.3.78–80). The puritan Tribulation Wholesome aims to ply 'the civil magistrate' with drinkable gold – *aurum potabile* – as a sort of bribe or lobbyist's gift on behalf of the reformed faith (3.1.41–2). And so on.

Indeed, the obsession with gold and its surrogates may comprise the single most obvious feature of Jonson's comedy, providing the motive force behind virtually all its events. But *The Alchemist* attends equally to matters of a more fundamental nature, too. Its opening line ends with the phrase 'I fart at thee' (1.1.1) and serves as only the first of many such eruptions to afflict the play. Face recalls Subtle's appearance at their first meeting, 'at Pie Corner' where the alchemist walked 'Piteously costive', 'pinned up in the several rags | [He]'d raked and picked from dunghills', and shivering under 'a thin threaden cloak | That scarce would cover [his] no-buttocks' (1.1.28, 33–4, 36–7). For his part, Subtle describes

Face as a 'scarab', as 'vermin', a creature he has raised 'out of dung', the fit companion of 'brooms and dust and wat'ring pots' (1.1.59, 64, 67). Dapper spends the play's last two acts locked in 'Fortune's privy lodgings' (3.5.79) – the outhouse adjoining Face and Subtle's laboratory. And the laboratory's own explosion in act 4, scene 5 serves as a great and sour echo of act 1's 'I fart at thee.'

In fact, *The Alchemist* depicts excrement and gold as interchangeable. According to Subtle, the latter may be refined out of something very like the former – a liquid substance called Number One ('the one part') and a solid substance called Number Two ('th'other part'):

> It is, of the one part,
> A humid exhalation which we would call
> *Materia liquida*, or the unctuous water;
> On th'other part, a certain crass and viscous
> Portion of earth; both which, concorporate,
> Do make the elementary matter of gold[.]
>
> (2.3.142–7)

Thus the transformation of base matter to precious metal follows a logic already manifest in the cycle of nature:

> [W]ho doth not see in daily practice
> Art can beget bees, hornets, beetles, wasps
> Out of the carcasses and dung of creatures[?]
> . . .
> And these are living creatures, far more perfect
> And excellent than metals.
>
> (2.3.171–6)

But if Subtle presents sewage as unrefined gold, Surly sees alchemy as unalloyed sewage, an assemblage 'Of piss and egg-shells, women's terms, man's blood, | Hair o'the head, burnt clouts, chalk, merds, and clay' (2.3.194–5). These opposed points of view energize Jonson's comedy from beginning to end.

As it develops, *The Alchemist* draws its most basic social distinction between characters who recognize shit for what it is and those who mistake it for treasure. The former group consists of Subtle, Face and Doll Common – the play's premier purveyors of excrement – together with Lovewit and to a lesser degree Surly; the latter group includes Mammon, Dapper, Drugger, Kastril and the Puritans. Thus, it makes perfect sense that Dapper's sojourn in the privy should be presented as the climax of an elaborate ritual of cleansing whereby the clerk is to be 'bathed and fumigated' before being ushered into the presence of the Queen of Fairy (1.2.145; see also 3.5.80–1). When the noisome business concludes in a fraudulent interview with Doll Common in the guise of the Fairy Queen, Dapper stoops to 'Kiss her departing part' (5.4.57), still unable to distinguish between purity and filth.

Likewise, Mammon imagines himself in glory, made fabulously rich by the philosopher's stone and surrounded by admirers:

> my flatterers
> Shall be the pure and gravest of divines
> That I can get for money; my mere fools,
> Eloquent burgesses; and then my poets
> The same that writ so subtly of the fart,
> Whom I will entertain still for that subject.

>   (2.2.59–64)

The fart in question was introduced into the proceedings of the House of Commons on 4 March 1607 by Sir Henry Ludlow, in response to Sir John Croke's delivery of a message from the House of Lords on the subject of Scottish naturalization.[1] According to earwitness testimony, Ludlow's comment issued fittingly from 'the nether end of the House . . . whereat the Company laughing the Messenger was almost out of Countenance'.[2] Noting that Sir Henry's father, Sir Edward, had also distinguished himself by farting in Parliament, contemporaries excused the son's performance as the product of 'Infirmity Naturall, not Malice'.[3] But Sir Henry's emission migrated swiftly into the public sphere, where it became the subject of various literary productions. Hence, its reappearance in Mammon's fantasies to mark the acme of poetic expression, while at the same time signalling the debased quality of Mammon's own tastes and aspirations.

With Tribulation Wholesome and his band of true believers, the story remains much the same. On one hand, the Puritans' sense of spiritual election attaches itself naturally to the qualities of cleanliness and godliness; as Ananias insists, 'The sanctified cause | Should have a sanctified course' (3.1.13–14). But Tribulation offers a more nuanced and self-serving perspective. Drawing inspiration from a scripture passage popular among reformers – the Pauline declaration that 'Unto the pure all things are pure' (Titus 1.15) – he argues that 'The children of perdition are ofttimes | Made instruments even of the greatest works' (3.1.15–16). This logic permits the reformed brethren to mingle with such questionable figures as Subtle and Face, for such questionable purposes as the counterfeiting of coin. Taken to its limits, Tribulation's casuistry even enables him to imagine Subtle as a man of God:

> It may be so.
> Whenas the work is done, the stone is made,
> This heat of his may turn into a zeal
> And stand up for the beauteous discipline
> Against the menstruous cloth and rag of Rome.
>
> (3.1.29–33)

Thus Jonson excrementalizes each of his major gull-figures. But *The Alchemist*'s principal social distinction – as put above, that between shit-recognizers and shit-misrecognizers – conforms less to the dyad of virtue and vice than to that of knavery and folly. Fittingly, Jonson's figures of judgement acquire the same cloacal associations as do the gulls on whom they prey. A vocabulary that equates physical with spiritual pollution tars all the play's characters with the same brush, more or less. The parallel grows most obvious with Subtle and Face, whose dunghill origins we have already paused to consider. Doll Common, however, deserves equal notice as an emblem of what might be called the Feminine Excremental. When Dapper is not kissing her nether parts, Mammon – typically mistaking her for 'a great lady' (4.1.24) – prepares to court her in the aureate terms of classical myth:

> Now, Epicure,
> Heighten thyself. Talk to her all in gold;
> Rain her as many showers as Jove did drops
> Unto his Danaë: show the god a miser
> Compared with Mammon. What? The stone will do't.
> She shall feel gold, taste gold, hear gold, sleep gold,
> Nay, we will *concumbere* gold.
>
> (4.1.24–30)

But as Surly suggests elsewhere, Doll's choice of profession associates her with a different kind of golden shower entirely:

> Yes, when I see [alchemical projection work], I will [believe it].
> But if my eyes do cozen me so – and I
> Giving 'em no occasion – sure I'll have
> A whore shall piss 'em out next day.
>
> (2.1.42–5)

This passage remains one of the more inscrutable in *The Alchemist*. Editors seldom gloss it, and its specific meaning remains unclear. Gail Paster links it to a 'now-obscure semiotics of urine and whores' occasioned by 'urine's unreliability as a diagnostic tool', which quality allies it emblematically with the deceitfulness of harlots.[4] Yet, the exact relation between Surly's eyesight and the whore's urinary function remains uncertain for all that. It may involve the ravages of syphilis; thus Shakespeare's Pandarus in *Troilus and Cressida* imagines his auditors losing their eyesight as the lesions of tertiary syphilis eat away at their facial tissues: 'As many as be here of Pandars' hall, | Your eyes, half out, weep out at Pandar's fall.'[5] But even so, the corrosive effect of Surly's whore's urine – and more broadly, the mechanical relation of the whore's piss to the extinction of Surly's eyesight – calls for a better explanation than any yet advanced. On a general level, however, Surly's language trades on a traditional association of sex-workers with the lower bodily stratum, and this same association comes likewise into play when Doll Common conducts Dapper forth 'by the back way' (1.2.163) to his outhouse, or when Dapper kisses her 'departing part', or when Mammon refers to her as 'Madam Suppository' (5.5.13) – this last phrase glancing at her supposititious identity as 'a great lady' but equally at the medical consequences of keeping her company.

Indeed, *The Alchemist*'s various excremental associations extend even to the house in which Subtle, Face and Doll receive their guests. Not only is this structure replete with 'back way[s]' and 'privy lodgings', not only does it host a flatulent explosion of alchemical apparatus, but it is also full of foul smells and vapours. As Face laments after the explosion, 'All [our] works | Are flown *in fumo*' (4.5.58), and again 'All [is] flown, or stinks' (4.5.89). As Ananias declares later, 'Your stench, it is broke forth. Abomination | Is in the house' (5.4.45–6). Kastril threatens to turn the place over to the public sanitation authorities: 'Yes, I will fetch the scavenger and the constable' (5.4.48). And Lovewit's closing description of his home's interior further cements its association with various kinds of filth:

> Here I find
> The empty walls, worse than I left 'em, smoked,
> A few cracked pots and glasses, and a furnace,
> The ceiling filled with poesies of the candle,
> And madam with a dildo writ o'the walls.
>
> (5.5.38–42)

The phrase 'poesies of the candle' is usually taken to refer to smoke-stains caused by burning candles, but it has also been glossed as graffiti scrawled with charcoal or candle smoke.[6] As for the mysterious 'madam with a dildo', this might refer either to an obscene picture or to a lewd jingle.[7] In the latter vein, we might associate it with the most notorious pornographic poem of Elizabethan England, Thomas Nashe's 'The Choise of Valentines'.[8] Known to contemporaries as 'Nashe's Dildo', this erotic verse narrative reaches its climax, in at least two senses of the word, when its heroine impales herself on the aforementioned sex toy. But specific references aside, the general sense of Lovewit's remarks is clear: his house has been trashed both literally and figuratively, transformed into the equivalent of an urban rubbish dump.

In fact, as *The Alchemist* progresses we may gradually come to feel that for all the play's discriminatory zeal, its gold and its sewage remain intimately related. Jonson may insist that the translation of base matter to precious metal is a hoax – what we would now call bullshit – but his comedy takes real delight in the opposite gesture: that of reducing gold to excrement. Mammon's schemes, Tribulation's plans, the glittering hopes of Dapper and Drugger, all are eventually diminished to the humblest of materials. And if we may say this about the play's visions of worldly riches, we may say much the same thing about its treatment of spiritual wealth: the treasure of faith. That, at least, is the logic behind Surly's self-description as 'somewhat costive of belief' (2.3.26) – a phrase echoed in Face's reference to Surly as 'Yon costive cheater' (3.3.1). Such language would set Surly and Tribulation at the opposite extremes of a continuum of faith-troped-as-peristalsis, with Surly's constipation offset by the Puritan's credulity – his spiritual diarrhoea. The self-proclaimed sceptic and the self-announced man of God thus emerge as complementary figures presiding over an urban landscape whose only stable, enduring quality is its faeculence. *Inter faeces et urinam nascimur, as Saint Augustine's proverb affirms: we are born amidst urine and faeces.*

Jonsonian shit: The scholarly heritage

So whence this copromania? If we pose the question in strictly literary terms, the answer seems obvious: classical antiquity. Jonson earned distinction in his day as the foremost English exponent of a neoclassical literary order that saw itself as extending

Graeco-Roman tastes and preoccupations. Graeco-Roman writers, in turn, make frequent, flamboyant use of cloacal language and motifs, especially in the genres with which Jonson himself was most closely associated: satire and epigram. Martial's epigrams offer a useful case in point. Jonson knew them well and admired them enough to incorporate matter from three of them (5.78, 10.48 and 11.52) into his own Epigram 101 ('Inviting a Friend to Supper'); likewise three copies of different editions of Martial have survived from Jonson's own library, replete with marginalia in the later poet's hand.[9] And as it happens, these marginalia include a series of notes on specific passages in the Roman poet's work that conflate the functions of mouth and anus/genitals, passages associated with the motif of *os impurum* – 'the unclean mouth that supposedly results from oral intercourse'.[10] So in this specific case we have a record of Jonson's interest in Roman satirical language involving the lower bodily stratum, a record that has survived in Jonson's own handwriting. Even a cursory inspection of the poet's broader literary output will confirm that this interest is no isolated thing.

But there is something unsatisfying about viewing Jonson's fascination with the gutter as simply an extension of earlier literary practice, as if he only focused upon sewage because others had done so before him. In essence, this explanation just kicks the question of origins down the road a couple of millennia without directly addressing it, whereas various schools of theory – whether the psychoanalytic, Bakhtinian or post-structuralist – aim for a broader resolution of the problem. In the case of Jonson, psychoanalysis weighed in first, with Edmund Wilson describing the poet as 'an obvious example of a psychological type which has been described by Freud and designated with a technical name, *anal erotic*'.[11] Freud's description of anal eroticism, first advanced in 1908, leaves no doubt that he regarded the condition as a neurosis associated with – what else? – unresolved sexual issues:

The people I am about to describe are . . . especially *orderly*, *parsimonious*, and *obstinate*. Each of these words actually

covers a small group or series of interrelated character-traits.
'Orderly' covers the notion of bodily cleanliness, as well as
of conscientiousness in carrying out small duties and trust-
worthiness. . . . Parsimony may appear in the exaggerated
form of avarice; and obstinacy can go over into defiance, to
which rage and revengefulness are easily joined. . . . [S]uch
people are born with a sexual constitution in which the ero-
togenicity of the anal zone is exceptionally strong[,] . . . and
. . . the regularity with which this triad of properties is present in their character may be brought into relation with the
disappearance of anal erotism.[12]

In short, the anal-erotic personality develops as a product of sublimation, emerging when the kinds of sexual pleasure associated
with the anal region are energetically repressed. Thus Wilson's
anal-erotic portrait of Jonson tends to present him, too, as a sig-
nally damaged individual, with his work and personality both
marred by such 'glaring defects' as an obsession with hoarding
and cataloguing, a tendency to use excrement as an instrument
of shaming and aggression, and an inclination to meanness and
stinginess.[13] *The Alchemist*'s scatological moments would seem to
conform well with this diagnosis. Still, it seems most inadequate –
and in an all-too-typical psychoanalytic way – to dismiss one of
the triumphs of the early modern stage as a product of mental
maladjustment, as if it were the emotional equivalent of a kidney
stone or a plantar wart.

Bakhtinian theory approaches the matter from a different
angle, concentrating on what might be called the cultural or folk-
loric dimensions of excrement. Bakhtin conceptualizes these
through opposed models of body-image which he allies to more
broadly opposed social configurations: the grotesque and the classical. Thus 'the unique yet complex carnival experience of the
people' finds its somatic counterpart in a grotesque body that
'transgresses . . . its own limits', that 'swallows, devours, rends the
world apart, is enriched and grows at the world's expense', that
defies categories and reverses hierarchies such that 'the buttocks

[is] persistently trying to take the place of the head and the head that of the buttocks'.[14] By contrast, 'the literary and artistic canon of antiquity' asserts itself through a classical body that is 'isolated, alone, fenced off from other bodies', and that serves as a model for more figurative acts of fencing-off as these occur, for instance, in systems of social and professional precedence.[15]

Bakhtin develops his canons of the grotesque and the classical via critical engagement with the work of Rabelais – a French author of some importance for Jonson.[16] Moreover, Jonson's own work is manifestly preoccupied with various kinds of social distinction comparable to that between classical and popular cultures. But in Jonson, the relation between the classical and the popular proves far less stable than Bakhtin imagines it to be in the case of Rabelais. Mammon's fantasies of wealth and privilege dissolve into rubbish, while Jonson's own efforts to forge a laureate identity for himself repeatedly involve the staging of popular festive forms such as fairs and charivaris. Hence, the most celebrated application of Bakhtinian theory to Jonson's work – that of Peter Stallybrass and Allon White – presents the poet as deeply conflicted, drawn to fantasies of social advancement like those of a Mammon or a Dapper but equally obsessed by the humbler social forms from which he seeks to extricate himself:

> A recurrent pattern emerges: the 'top' attempts to reject and eliminate the 'bottom' for reasons of prestige and status, only to discover, not only that it is in some way frequently dependent upon that low-Other . . ., but also that the top *includes* that low symbolically, as a primary eroticized constituent of its own fantasy life. The result is a mobile, conflictual fusion of power, fear, and desire in the construction of subjectivity: a psychological dependence upon precisely those Others which are being rigorously opposed and excluded at the social level.[17]

In its emphasis upon 'psychological dependence', upon the erotic character of social fantasy, and upon the obsessive yet futile nature of efforts at social discrimination, this view of Jonson remains uncomfortably similar to Freud's medically condescending portrait of the anal-erotic.

More recently, scholars have sought to account for Jonson's excremental moments by approaching them through various kinds of post-modern or post-structuralist theory. Gail Paster has drawn on Pierre Bourdieu's sociological analysis of the habitus to place Jonson in a history of manners that constructs masculinity around various models of self-control to which moments of urinary and faecal incontinence may be invidiously contrasted.[18] I have invoked the work of Gilles Deleuze and Félix Guattari – especially their notion of becoming – to account for the instability that characterizes Jonson's language of praise and of satire.[19] Jonathan Gil Harris has employed the anthropological theory of Emile Durkheim, Clifford Geertz, and others to depict Jonson's tropes of bodily invasion and expulsion as metaphors for the social body or body politic more generally.[20] Whatever the merits or demerits of these various approaches to Jonson's excrementality, they all agree in deriving the poet's scatological tendencies from his mental constitution, as an expression of issues with body control, personal advancement, or the definition of social groups. For all of these commentators, from Freud to Harris, Jonsonian shit remains primarily and paradoxically a psychic phenomenon.

But it need not. We might also account for Jonson's fascination with excrement another way, not by viewing it as an expression of a distinctive (and usually morbid) literary personality but rather as a reasonable response to changing conditions in the poet's physical environment. This approach to the subject would align with current efforts in the literary profession to develop an environmentally responsible critical practice, an eco-criticism that shows proper respect for the natural world's changing role in the production of literary art. Such criticism would have the advantage of understanding that before shit can evolve into metaphor, or habitus, or reaction-formation, it must start out as shit, pure and simple. And an eco-critical approach to Jonsonian scatology would return the poet's literary practice to the material conditions of his life. In what remains of this essay, I shall therefore try to outline the general form that an eco-critical account of Jonson's fascination with excrement might take.

Places of excrement

In keeping with its derivation from the Greek *oikos*, or home, ecology is all about place: specifically, about the systemic relations between life forms and their surroundings in a single definable habitat. As it happens, Ben Jonson spent most of his life within such a habitat area: what we might now call the London-Westminster metroplex. And as it further happens, that area suffered far-reaching environmental change during the poet's lifetime. Jonson's work should thus prove amenable to eco-critical study, and his preoccupation with sewage provides a case in point.

Between the poet's birth in 1573 and his death in 1637, the population of London roughly doubled, from about 150,000 to about 300,000.[21] In 1610 – the year of *The Alchemist*'s first performance, and also the year in which the play's action is set – the number of the city's inhabitants hovered around a quarter of a million. This rate of growth was unprecedented both for Britain and for Europe as a whole, and it had risen steadily since 1500, when London was home to only some 50,000 people. While such figures seem puny from the twenty-first-century standpoint, they placed a grievous burden on the city's resources and infrastructure. They also mark the beginnings of London's modern population explosion, and to this extent they set the stage for cultural developments to come.

The environmental consequences of this growth cannot be fully enumerated in the space available here. On the most basic level, they involved a sharp increase in local demand for shelter, energy, foodstuffs and water; an equally sharp increase in various health risks related to urban overcrowding; and the beginnings of a set of modern pollution problems that continue to this day to affect the quality of the city's land, water and atmosphere. All these changes were visible to Jonson's contemporaries, at least some of whom regarded them with deep consternation. John Stow's *A Survey of*

London, the classic account of the city's growth during the early modern period, thus repeatedly laments the environmental degradation attendant upon runaway urban development. According to Stow, the ditch encircling the city walls since medieval times had by the early 1600s been 'forced either to a verie narrow, and the same a filthie channell, or altogither stopped up'; the city's streets were blighted with 'filthy passage[s]'; and the suburban liberties had devolved into 'a continuall building of tenements'.[22] As might be expected, in other words, London's growth was manifesting itself on the ecological level in part through an unprecedented accumulation of urban sewage and rubbish. The 300 per cent growth in the city's population that occurred 75 years prior to Jonson's birth entailed a comparable increase in the quantities of human waste deposited into its environs; likewise, the even steeper growth rates of the poet's own lifetime entailed even greater volumes of waste production. These increases, in turn, paralleled a comparable rise in the production of related rubbish such as the runoff from tanneries situated north of the city walls.

It would be a mistake to claim that London's waste management system was overwhelmed by this increase, because to say so would imply that something like a coherent system actually existed. In fact, the city's Metropolitan Commission of Sewers would not be established until 1848; in the meantime, Londoners continued to deal with their waste haphazardly, in ways developed during the previous centuries. Citizens lucky enough to reside alongside the Thames or another one of the local waterways deposited their filth straight into the river's estuary. Less fortunate Londoners dug privies into the ground, and as the solid matter contained in such repositories accumulated, the city's scavengers exhumed it and either dumped it in the local rivers or transported to laystalls outside the city walls. Admittedly, some adjustments were made, as when, during the reign of Henry VIII, the city's 'main streets were paved for the first time . . ., with runnels to permit sewage to escape more rapidly to the Fleet River and to the Thames'.[23] But by channelling runoff more efficiently into the local waterways, these conduits arguably did as much harm as good. In any case, Jonsonian London was settling bit by bit into a self-created morass of refuse and sludge.

As it happens, Jonson himself was unusually well placed to witness this development. As a child, he lived with his mother and stepfather in the suburban liberties west of London proper, in Hartshorn Lane, Westminster. Hartshorn Lane is now known as Northumberland Street, and it occupies a prime piece of Westminster real estate between Trafalgar Square and Charing Cross Station. In the late sixteenth century, however, it was a dodgy neighbourhood full of transients and recent arrivals to the city. According to biographer David Riggs, 'during Jonson's lifetime, Hartshorn Lane would become one of the major sewage canals in the greater London area'.[24] The cottage in which the poet grew up, moreover, was distinguished by 'the sewage ditch that ran along the premises' and upon which Jonson's stepfather constructed a 'little garden' like those that – to John Stow's dismay – were also obstructing the town ditch to the east.[25] So as a child, the poet already found himself in intimate conjunction with the city's waste, which ran in substantial quantities through his backyard and whose chemical components – if his cottage garden grew vegetables and herbs – would have made their way through his alimentary tract as well.

Beyond Hartshorn Lane, London's liberties more generally provided the breeding ground for much of the city's growing environmental blight. It was to the liberties that the area's steady stream of immigrants relocated, many of them settling into haphazard tenements that had been erected on suburban property expropriated from the church during Henry VIII's dissolution of the monasteries. Likewise, it was to extramural laystalls in the liberties that the city's scavengers conveyed much of London's own sewage and other refuse. *The Alchemist* was of course first acted by the King's Men at the Globe, which was of course located in the Bankside liberty of Southwark, and to this extent the play's scatology seems appropriate not only to its author's childhood circumstances but also to the space of its own initial performance.

In fact, the same could be said with equal justice of *The Alchemist*'s setting. The play's action occurs within Lovewit's house 'here in the Friars' (1.1.17), in the intramural liberty of Blackfriars, more or less directly across the Thames from the Globe. As a space free from the Corporation of London's supervision, the Blackfriars liberty would have proven naturally hospitable to the schemes of Subtle, Face and Doll. Moreover, this area was at least equally known for its nonhuman trash, for it was through the Blackfriars liberty that London's most notorious sewer, the Fleet River, found its way to the Thames. One chronicler of the Fleet has described its history as 'a decline from a river to a brook, from a brook to a ditch, and from a ditch to a drain'.[26] Nowadays it is almost invisible, having been completely bricked over in the eighteenth century; at low tide, however, passersby can still glimpse it entering the Thames through a sewer-like concrete aperture underneath Blackfriars Bridge. In Jacobean times, this waterway's decline was already well advanced, and no one would document its condition more memorably than Jonson himself, in the last of his *Epigrams*:

> Here several ghosts did flit
> About the shore, of farts but late departed,
> White, black, blue, green,
> . . .
> [Meanwhile, turds] languishing stuck upon the wall,
> Or were precipitated down the jakes,
> And, after, swam abroad in ample flakes[.][27]

William Slights has claimed that Fleet Ditch was 'as large a part of the symbolic geography of Jonson's London as Mary Le Bow, or St Paul's'.[28] Certainly, its repeated appearance in the poet's work attests to the intensity of his imaginative engagement with it. And with good reason: Jonson not only grew up amidst London's accumulating sewage, but also spent his adult life surrounded by it as well. He himself lived in Saint Anne's parish, Blackfriars, and it was 'From [his] house in the Blackfriars' that he composed the prefatory epistle to *Volpone* in 1607, three years before the first performance of *The Alchemist*.[29] Likewise, he seems to have spent 1604–5, as well as the five years from 1613 to 1618, residing with his patron Esmé Stuart, Seigneur d'Aubigny and third Duke of Lennox, at the young nobleman's town house 'near Playhouse Yard next to the Blackfriars Theatre'.[30] So in composing *The Alchemist*, Jonson set the play not only in his own city, but even in his own neighbourhood. If the play exhibits an unusual interest in sewers and privies, excrement and rubbish, we need not explain this interest via the poet's own supposed psychic maladjustment. Instead, we need only do what Jonson himself obviously did while writing: we need only consider his surroundings.

The backside of progress

Finally, we should note one more thing about how Jonson presents those surroundings. He does not focus upon sewage alone, and he seems to regard it more as process than as product. As observed at the outset of this essay, *The Alchemist*'s scatology occurs in tandem with its avarice, so much so that excrement and gold form something like the comedy's controlling conceptual binary, its terms at once superficially opposed and yet deeply interdependent. This relationship, in turn, comprises the play's signal proto-ecological insight, rendered all the more striking for the intuitive manner in which it is presented.

   In short, Jonson understood that London had become a city rich in shit, but also understood that it was becoming rich, pure and simple, and that the shit and the wealth were interrelated. To put the matter differently, early modern London's exorbitant growth not only produced environmental problems such as pollution, overcrowding and epidemic disease, it also led to some of the glories of Western civilization. Under the Tudor and early Stuart monarchs, the city refurbished itself in ways of lasting importance for urban history, art history, architectural history and social history. The improvements in question defy summary here, but consider some examples. The city gates at Ludgate, Aldgate and Aldersgate were rebuilt in 1586, 1608 and 1617, respectively; Ludgate prison was rebuilt in 1585; and Bridewell workhouse was founded in 1553.[31] During the sixteenth and seventeenth centuries a whole series of cisterns and water-conduits was introduced, including, in 1582, the city's first indoor plumbing system.[32] Gresham's Royal Exchange, built in Cornhill between 1566 and 1568, heralded London's coming of age as a modern commercial centre. Inigo Jones's royal banqueting house, constructed at Whitehall roughly a decade after *The Alchemist*'s first performance, brought Palladianism to London. By the 1630s, the first of London's great city squares appeared at Lincoln's Inn Fields and Covent Garden. This programme of re-edification took place on an increasing scale throughout the city, in ways that both derived from and contributed to the capital's growing environmental problems. In effect, London was pitching its mansions in the place of excrement.

For their part, Jonson's characters in *The Alchemist* – like Jonson himself – are keenly sensitive to the city's increasing vitality. As a result, parts of the play read almost like an urban visitors' guide, packed with references to local tourist attractions and places of interest. Face schedules a rendezvous with Surly 'i'the Temple Church' (2.3.289), within walking distance of Blackfriars between the Fleet and the Thames. Urging Dame Pliant to receive the advances of a Spanish grandee (actually Surly in disguise), Subtle and Face tempt her with fantasies of life in London's smart set:

SUBTLE   What, when she comes to taste
          The pleasures of a countess! To be courted –
          . . .
FACE   And has her pages, ushers,
          Footmen, and coaches –
SUBTLE   Her six mares –
FACE   Nay, eight!
SUBTLE   To hurry her through London, to th'Exchange,
          Bedlam, the China-houses –

                                             (4.4.39–40, 45–8)

Confronting an irate mob outside his house, Lovewit exclaims, 'The world's turned Bedlam', to which Face responds, 'These are all broke loose | Out of Saint Katherine's, where they use to keep | The better sort of mad-folks' (5.4.53–6). Lamenting the failure of Mammon's plans for the philosopher's stone, Face ironically details his client's intended acts of charity:

> [H]e would ha' built
> The city new, and made a ditch about it
> Of silver, should have run with cream from Hoxton,
> That every Sunday in Moorfields the younkers,
> And tits and tomboys should have fed on, gratis.
>
> (5.5.76–80)

The ditch of silver in this scenario may be read as an ironic counterpart to the fetid trench that actually encircled London in Jonson's day, and whose deterioration Stow had lamented in his *Survey*. Likewise, the artificial conveyance of potable liquids into the city was an idea whose time had come by the early 1600s. London had been steadily outgrowing and befouling its local sources of drinking water, with the result that by the end of Queen Elizabeth's reign a group of entrepreneurs began planning an aqueduct project known as the New River, designed to convey drinking water into the city from 36 miles away in Hertfordshire.[33] In 1609, when Jonson was composing *The Alchemist*, this undertaking had lain dormant for some time, but that year it was re-energized under the leadership of Sir Hugh Myddelton, construction work began on it in earnest, and in 1613 the New River would finally be opened to London's thirsty inhabitants. So when Face torments Mammon with the idea of a civic lacteduct built of silver, his vision speaks directly to then-current environmental developments. Nor does *The Alchemist*'s interest in ditches and conduits end here. Face also twits Drugger for his stinginess by claiming that he fell ill 'for being 'sessed at eighteen pence, | For the waterwork' (3.4.123–4), and the waterwork in question might conceivably be any one of three for-profit water-utility projects operating in London by 1610: either the New River project, or the tidal water-wheel installed near London Bridge in 1582 by the Dutch engineer Peter Moryce, or the horse-drawn water-pump erected at Broken Wharf in 1594 by Bevis Bulmar.[34] Whichever one of these projects Jonson meant, it – or one of its fellows – also appears earlier in the play, when Mammon indulges in typically grandiose fantasies about piping medicine into the city's houses, only to have his ambitions ridiculed by Surly:

> MAMMON   I'll give away so much unto my man
> Shall serve th' whole city with preservative
> Weekly, each house his dose, and at the rate –
> SURLY   As he that built the waterwork does with water?
>   (2.1.73–6)

In fact, Mammon, the most vainglorious of Jonson's dupes in *The Alchemist*, emerges from his play as something like a grand parody of the impulse to urban development. Thus, he insists to Subtle that his desire for the philosopher's stone derives from deep-seated philanthropic aspirations:

> I assure you,
> I shall employ it all in pious uses:
> Founding of colleges and grammar schools,
> Marrying young virgins, building hospitals,
> And now and then a church.
>   (2.3.48–52)

And Subtle, a far more accomplished bullshit-artist than Mammon will ever be, mocks these same virtuous pretensions in conversation with Face:

> Methinks I see him entering ordinaries
> Dispensing for the pox, and plaguy-houses,
> Reaching his dose, walking Moorfields for lepers,
> And offering citizens' wives pomander bracelets

As his preservative, made of the elixir,
Searching the spital to make old bawds young
And the highways for beggars to make rich.
I see no end of his labours.

(1.4.18–25)

Ironically, Subtle himself sets the play's standard for faux philanthropy when warning Mammon against the sin of covetousness:

[M]y labours
. . .
Have looked no way but unto public good,
To pious uses and dear charity,
Now grown a prodigy with men. Wherein
If you, my son, should now prevaricate,
And to your own particular lusts employ
So great and catholic a bliss, be sure
A curse will follow[.]

(2.3.11, 16–22)

Since neither Mammon nor Subtle possesses any genuine charitable instinct, these lines take on a strangely prophetic quality,
anticipating the misfortunes that await both characters and casting
their eventual difficulties in the form of poetic justice.

Thus, *The Alchemist* forces the rhetoric of urban development
and social improvement to occupy the same conceptual space as
the language of scatology and execration. This gesture, in turn,
seems also appropriate to the civic space within which Jonson set
his play, a locale equally distinguished by the close juxtaposition
of pious works and the shit they produce. And in broader terms,
Jonson remained suspicious of improvement schemes throughout
his career, especially when they were coupled with scientific jargon
and eleemosynary pretensions. In *Volpone*, Sir Politic Would-Be
conceives an idiotic device to test whether incoming ships are
infected with the plague. In *The Devil Is an Ass*, Merecraft urges
Fitzdottrel into a half-witted project for wetland reclamation.

In *The Staple of News*, the London newspaper industry develops as a second-order promotional scam, marketing accounts of other half-baked marvels as a pretended service to the city's inhabitants.

This sceptical view of science and progress has been associated with recent developments in environmentalist philosophy and practice – how justly the reader may decide for herself.[35] In the short-to-middle-run, however, it placed Jonson on the wrong side of history. The infant news industry he mocked in *The Staple of News* has grown and prospered on Fleet Street, whereas the sewage-choked river for which that street is named has receded into invisibility. To judge by all the usual metrics – population, life expectancy, standard of living, incidence of disease, and so on – modern London is far larger, healthier, wealthier and cleaner than the city of Jonson's day, and its good fortune has largely derived from the efforts of people who may be viewed as the heirs of Subtle, Mammon and Tribulation: scientists, civic entrepreneurs, enterprising men of the cloth, and so forth. Nor would it be right to describe Jonson as a conservationist *avant la lettre*. His is a distinctly urban sensibility, endlessly fascinated by the city's doings, with little appreciation for the beauties of nature, little interest in rural matters and no real awareness that the natural world might be in need of protection from human interference. But Jonson did share certain broad convictions with many modern environmentalists: that progress only comes at a price; that the price in question can only be known in retrospect and may well be unaffordable; that self-interest is seldom compatible with the public good, however much self-serving individuals might try to confuse the two; and that the filth we produce in service of our dreams generally endures longer than the dreams themselves. To this limited extent, we might credit him with a mode of proto-ecological awareness.

CHAPTER SEVEN

New Directions: Waiting for the End?
Alchemy and Apocalypse in *The Alchemist*

MARK HOULAHAN

Waiting for the end, boys, waiting for the end.
What is there to be or do?
What's become of me or you?
Are we kind or are we true?
Sitting two and two, boys, waiting for the end.
Shall I build a tower, boys, knowing it will rend
Crack upon the hour, boys, waiting for the end?
Shall I pluck a flower, boys, shall I save or spend?
All turns sour, boys, waiting for the end.[1]

In the winter of 1979, I played the part of Dapper in an Auckland University production of *The Alchemist*. As publicist for the show, I found Jonson's brilliant farce a harder commodity to shift in the market than our company's annual outdoor Shakespeare, which always sold out. Few people came to the Jonson show, and fewer still had any real grasp of what it was about – doubtless this was more our fault than Jonson's. We did however attract one very keen audience member, a self-proclaimed local alchemist. This was the end of the 1970s, and such flaky remnants of the 1960s' 'Age of Aquarius' still floated about. He was very disappointed in our production, not because the acting was unconvincing or the direction uncertain, but rather because our publicity had misled him into thinking the play would demonstrate and celebrate the arts of alchemy. Instead, we clearly used Jonson's script to disrespect the practice of alchemy. Moreover, we demonstrated no alchemy at all on stage.

Now this production had made a virtue of necessity. It was far easier to use modern dress and a bare stage than to simulate on a tiny budget Lovewit's substantial Jacobean townhouse in the Blackfriars, with its TARDIS-like capacity to suggest so many more rooms and hiding spaces than we see on stage. The trio of tricksters, Doll, Face and Subtle, were likewise very low-rent. Throughout, the stage was littered not with allusions to alchemy, but rather with the detritus of modern life. Aptly enough for the mostly student audience, the stage resembled an unruly student flat, with empty takeout boxes (pizza, fried chicken) strewn everywhere.

In this respect, at least, the production design was responsive to Jonson's original published text of the play, where only two places indicate any evidence of alchemy as specifically called for. In the first scene (1.1.115.1), Doll resorts to violence to bring Face and Subtle to heel, and to do so, according to the stage directions in the 1616 Folio, '*She catcheth out Face his sword, and breakes Subtle's glass*'.[2] The 'glass' here would be something like a modern test tube, borne out of the back room from whence the quarrel erupts as the play begins, and containing most likely some kind of weirdly viscous liquid, with which Subtle earlier in the scene threatens Face to 'gum your silks | With good strong water, an you come' (1.1.6–7). The only other direct evidence of 'alchemy' comes at the end of act 4, when we hear '*A great crack and noise within*' (4.5.55.1),[3] the simulated sound of the non-existent alchemical still falling apart. This is the climax of a sequence not only essential, of course, for the unravelling of the elaborate cons of the earlier acts of the play, but also for grasping the force of apocalypse as a term for a play ostensibly preoccupied with alchemy; accordingly, this chapter will return to this scene in detail later. In the meantime, it is enough to note that, to stage this scene effectively, all you would need is a really loud clanging noise (very easily managed in even the poorest of theatres). One of the many layers of irony in the play, then, is that it persuades us that more 'alchemy' is more present than is in fact the case. The sense in which alchemy pervades the play would have eluded the literal reading of the

Auckland alchemist who attended our production a generation ago. Pepys famously sneered that Shakespeare's *Twelfth Night* was a 'silly play' having nothing at all to do with the 'name or the day' (the 'Twelfth-night feast' of Epiphany on 6 January). Likewise, the Auckland alchemist discovered that, on first viewing, Jonson's play had really nothing much to do with alchemy either.

Most likely those encountering the play for the first time do so in the context of undergraduate surveys of Renaissance drama, especially those which emphasize non-Shakespearean material.[4] Students might well access the play by turning to terms more normally invoked for the formalist 'close' reading of poetry, 'the "tenor" (or the "general drift", the underlying idea which the metaphor expresses) and the "vehicle" (the basic analogy which is used to embody or carry the tenor)'.[5] In these terms, they readily grasp the tenor or general drift of the play perceiving the alchemy scam as a precursor to internet-based frauds, alert to the energetic greed of the fraudsters and the stupefying yet hilarious gullibility of their prey. You can perceive the 'tenor' of the play then (as you can with Jonson's earlier Venetian farce *Volpone*) while more or less ignoring the context of alchemy. The minimal alchemical requirements Jonson's stagecraft calls for assists this ignorance. And yet the main contention of this chapter will be to show that to neglect the context of alchemy and apocalypse in the play is to miss crucial ways in which Jonson speaks through the play to his own culture. Moreover, alchemy and apocalypse are inextricably linked: if apocalypse proposes a form of alchemical morphing of the world to some higher state, so too the fulfilment of the alchemical project would result in the apocalyptic transformation of the world. I will review the range of meanings these terms might have for Renaissance audiences and readers, and then show how these terms resonate through the play. The resulting 'reading' or interpretation would be not a New Historicist interpretation but rather a newly invigorated historical approach to the text.

In the 1980s and 1990s, Jonson's plays were perhaps less attended to than his poems and masques. Those decades were the peak of 'New Historicism' as a school of interpretation which promoted a vigorously political 'interrogation' of literary texts, showing how they (and their authors) were implicated by the politics of the Renaissance. Renaissance writers were often then seen to be complicit in the projects of the Renaissance state. In these terms, Jonson's country house poem 'To Penshurst' and his masques for the court of James I showed him a willing and anxious servant, all too ready to service a proto-absolutist, elitist ideology. Plays like *The Alchemist*, written for public performance, were less easily interpreted as offering commentary on the actions of the monarch and his courtiers. When Face announces in his epilogue speech that 'I put myself | On you, that are my country' (5.5.162–3), he clearly suggests a wider audience than the court of James itself. Then too the placement of these lines suggests we might take him as a spokesperson for Jonson. The term 'country' might of course be interpreted in a political sense, but not, I think, in terms of encouraging any communal kind of movement. Rather, viewing the play through the perspectives of alchemy and apoca- lypse shows how much Jonson valued the individual; alchemy and apocalypse are represented as follies each of us ought best to avoid.

Alchemy

Alchemy is an ancient practice, one of the many practices from classical times reinvigorated in the late medieval and Renaissance Europe. Alchemical lore derived partly from ancient Greece and, in particular, ancient Egypt, for the longevity of Egyptian society commanded great respect throughout Europe. Although the skill of actually reading Egyptian hieroglyphs was not unlocked until the early nineteenth century, many were taken with the thought of comprehending the universe through hieroglyphic figures. The writings of Hermes Trismegistus (an apocryphal figure) were thought especially fertile in this regard, and were crucial for the dissemination of alchemical concepts. Though alchemy is in fact a pseudo-science (as its assumptions about the nature of matter have been discredited since the middle of the seventeenth century), its adepts behaved as if they were what we would think of as 'scientists', what in the seventeenth century would be thought a 'natural philosopher'. The surface activity in an alchemist's cell, at first glance, would resemble the goings-on in a chemical or biological laboratory. The term 'adept' is appropriate for followers of alchemy, because alchemical tracts are swathed in a mystical, gnomic, quasi-religious language. You could not achieve perfection as an alchemist unless you yourself were pure in spirit. If alchemy were to work (though of course it never could), you would be refined without and within. H. J. Sheppard explains that:

> Alchemy is the art of liberating parts of the Cosmos from temporal existence and achieving perfection, which, for metals is gold, and for man, longevity, then immortality and, finally, redemption. Material perfection was sought through the action of a preparation (Philosopher's Stone for metals; Elixir of Life for humans), while spiritual ennoblement resulted from some form of inner revelation or other enlightenment.[6]

Friar Bacon, the famous twelfth-century Franciscan, puts it his way in his *Mirrour of Alchemy*, in a translation published in 1597 (and which very likely Jonson consulted while drafting *The Alchemist*):

> *Alchimy* is a Science, teaching how to transforme any kind of mettall into another: and that by a proper medicine, as it appeareth by many Philsophers Bookes. *Alchimy* therefore is a science teaching how to make and compound a certain medicine, which is called *Elixir*, the which, when it is cast upon metals or imperfect bodies, doth fully perfect them in the verie projection.[7]

All matter, alchemy assumed, was compounded from the four fundamental elements: earth, water, air and fire. Under certain conditions the compound of any metal could be remingled with the addition of the vital fifth element, the stone. Paradoxically, this stone came in liquid form, like mercury, a viscous element much discussed in alchemical tracts and frequently deployed in alchemical experiments, as was also sulphur, since its power to corrode objects rapidly was helpful for simulating the appearance of alchemical transformation. The morphing ideally worked through 12 phases (which Bacon's *Mirror* delineates), climaxing with the act of 'projection'. Here the 'philosopher's stone' would be introduced in its liquid state to baser metals. The result would be the most perfect of all metals, gold. Nature was assumed to be generative, literally a fertile 'matrix'. The application of the alchemist's art would lead to the breeding of a more perfect nature than the one provided in the Genesis account of the creation of the world, for alchemists were driven by the certain knowledge that

> metals were living substances, that natural gold was the end result of long 'gestation' within earth's womb; and, adopting the metaphor of human and divine sexual differentiation and conjunction, that sulphur and mercury were the 'reproductive fluids' from which metals arose.[8]

Friar Bacon's *Mirror* synthesized a heritage of Egyptian, Greek and Arabic alchemical learning which was available in manuscript and then printed books throughout Europe from the twelfth century onwards. The print revolution meant that the small minority, at least, who could read Latin and Greek, as well as the larger group who could read books in their native tongues, could gain the secrets of the philosophers. In England, the interest in such publications climaxed in the period during and immediately after the English civil wars, for more 'books on alchemy were published in England between 1650 and 1680 than before or afterwards'.[9] As modern histories of science have shown, not coincidentally, this same period sees the rise of the Royal Society and the beginning of true modern science based on accurate recording of experimentation, enabling the real understanding of the fundamental elements of which our cosmos is constructed. If you experimented using alchemical methods in the same way, as most famously, Sir Isaac Newton did, you would discover experimentally what Jonson had theatrically shown earlier: that alchemy was a fraud.

In the late sixteenth century, however, alchemy's grandest claims could still be maintained and in certain circles, more illustrious by far than even those Sir Epicure Mammon might wish to frequent, were given a great deal of credibility and support. John Dee, perhaps the greatest polymath of sixteenth-century England, published an alchemical tract, the *Monas Hieroglyphica* in 1564. The extraordinary library collection Dee assembled was steeped in hermetic lore and consulted by many; through the support of influential nobles at the court, his views gained the attention of Elizabeth herself.[10] A thousand miles from London, the court of Rudolph II in Prague became the seat of magical, hermetical, Rosicrucian and alchemical speculation. Dee was a noted figure there also, as was the famous Edward Kelley, an outright charlatan. With his mordant ear for the current and the popular, Jonson's packed text assimilates both Dee and Kelley within its alchemical patina. Compared to such figures, Face, Subtle and Doll are small-town crooks. If you could harness the wealth of an entire kingdom, what could you not achieve? Turning such wealth 'As fits a king's remembrance' (as Gertrude puts it[11]) into gold would satisfy even Epicure Mammon's avaricious desire to magic up the entire wealth of South America's gold and silver mines in the course of a single day.

Jonson, like Chaucer before him, clearly loved, perversely, the alchemy his play teaches us to despise. His views are clearer in the text of his 1615 masque, *Mercury Vindicated*, where alchemy is the bogus 'art' and mercury the voice of the truth of nature in its unaltered state. Jonson was not alone in his interest; in his 1605 collaboration with Marston and Chapman, *Eastward Ho!*, the 'names of the principal characters are derived from alchemy',[12] and frame the wealth and wife-hunting quests which dominate their desires. A host of Renaissance writers used alchemy as a metaphorical frame, not because they thought it would truly transform the external world but rather, as Stanton J. Linden shows in *Dark*

Hieroglyphicks, because it was a powerful way of evoking the poetic transforming of the inner self. Shakespeare, Marvell, Vaughan and Milton use the jargon for this purpose.[13] It is the inner transformation the would-be adepts on the day of *The Alchemist* seek, and which they conspicuously fail to achieve.

Jonson then capitalizes on two other key attributes of the alchemical tracts. First, on one climactic day of 'projection', the process of 'golding' the world would be complete. The process of projection is to finish on the day the play unfolds, and thus aligns seamlessly with Jonson's remorseless application of the Aristotelian unities of time, place and action. Second, the system of alchemy projects a fundamentally gendered view of the world: for the chemical wedding would bring together the great male and female capacities of the universe. Jonson draws on this wittily (sometimes saucily) throughout the play as he freely samples from his range of alchemical readings. In terms of genre, the wedding of 'male' and 'female' is a brilliant vehicle for the satirical version of the marriage comedy Jonson constructs. Destabilizing the alchemy in act 4 occurs at the precise point in the play where male and female relations are starting to unravel. That unravelling fits perfectly also the strain of apocalypse imagery which is a marked feature of the play. To see how alchemy and apocalypse coalesce together, we need to review the background of apocalypse that underpins the play, before returning to act 4.

Apocalypse now and then

Whereas the principles underpinning alchemy have long since been discredited, a cultural process to which Jonson's play contributed, the prophetic assumptions around ideas of apocalypse have maintained a force. In 2012, the trendiest version of this process will be speculations focused on the Mayan apocalypse, and the assumption that the Mayan calendar, properly decoded, indicates that 2012 will see a series of world-ending events unfold. In the years before the year 2000, pre-millennial anxieties swept the world, notably the fear that, on the stroke of midnight of 31 December 1999, all computer systems would crash.[14] Jonson could not have known anything about Mayan civilization, nor of the notorious Y2K bug, but in his culture it was not uncommon to assume that the end of the world might be imminent and that England, fighting of course on the side of the forces of righteousness, would prevail when evil was finally defeated. For such ideas, in Renaissance England, you would turn to the prophetic texts of scripture, most notably the book of Daniel, from the Old Testament, and the book of Revelation, the last book in the New Testament. The term 'revelation' is the Englished version of that book's title in Greek (in which it was composed) and Latin: 'apocalypsis'. Literally this means the revelation or unveiling. On the Greek island of Patmos, John reports a series of visions. He is taken up to heaven, and sees the whole of the earth. With the gift of prophecy, he grasps what will happen as our world ends and a new heaven and a new earth, perfected now by God's handiwork, comes into being. The vision is political – he sees the passing away of a whole series of kingdoms, and temporal – he provides a time sequence for the events leading to the end of this world. The Revelation, in these terms, recasts images from the book of Daniel, where Daniel decodes a series of visions dreamt by the Babylonian ruler Nebuchadnezzar. Like John of Patmos, Daniel foresees the downfall of earthly kingdoms, followed by a perfected, sanctified kingdom.[15]

This kind of prophetic apocalypse flourished in the ancient near east from around 700 BC, not just in ancient Jewish culture but in those surrounding, for Jewish and Christian apocalypses have links to Babylonian, Chaldean, and Zoroastrian beliefs and texts.[16] Through the Old and New Testaments of the Christian Bible, as well as through the so-called apocryphal books, such as the book of Esdras and Bel and the Dragon, the peoples of Christian Europe inherited these traditions. Throughout the Middle Ages, the interpretation of these books was dominated in Catholic theology by the writings of St Augustine. It was not for humankind, according to Augustine, to understand the timing of the events Daniel and Revelation predicted. Rather, we should understand that in the fullness of time, according to a timetable God himself would dictate, the world would achieve perfection. In the meantime, the task of humankind was to wait on these events.

During the Reformation in the sixteenth century, protestant thinkers throughout northern Europe advanced a radically different interpretation of these prophetic books. These new ideas were explored by such key protestant theologians as Calvin and Luther. In England, these ideas acquired mainstream respectability. The new interpretation was encoded in the 1560 Geneva Bible, the English translation used in English churches, and the version of scripture which Jonson and Shakespeare knew well. In parish churches, many could read and also visually absorb the many powerful illustrations from John's Foxe's famous *Book of Martyrs*, or in the fulsome and richly informative title it was first published under, his

> Actes and Monuments of matters most speciall and memorable, happenyng in the Church, with an Universall history of the same, wherein is set forth at large the whole race and course of the Church, from the primitive age to these latter tymes of ours, with the bloudy times, horrible troubles, and great persecutions against the true Martyrs of Christ, fought and wrought by Heathen Emperours, as nowe lately practised by Romish Priests, specially in this Realme of England.[17]

I have quoted this evocative title at such length because it is such a useful epitome of the Protestant approach to apocalypse which feeds in to the texture of the play.

Nebuchadnezzar dreamed of a strange beast, with parts comprised of iron, clay, brass, silver and gold. These elements, Daniel informed him, indicated the rise and fall of four kingdoms to be followed by a sanctified fifth: 'and his kingdom *that* which shall not be destroyed' (Dan. 7.14). In the Revelation, John describes an even stranger composite beast, with seven heads and ten horns, and on each horn a crown. These two described in prophetic form a political, chronological process: 'And there are seven kings: five are fallen, and one is, *and* the other is not yet come' (Rev. 17.10). The fallen kingdoms John sees as the realm of the beast, the Antichrist linked with the notorious number 666. This is the realm of the female figure crucial to Doll's role-playing: the 'woman . . . arrayed in purple and scarlet colour, and decked with gold and precious stones. . . . And upon her forehead *was* a name written, MYSTERY, BABYLON THE GREAT, THE MOTHER OF HARLOTS AND ABOMINATIONS OF THE EARTH' (Rev. 17.3–5). John sees the fall of this woman and the city over which she presides as central to the final defeat of the Antichrist.

But when would these events take place? In the 'time of the end', Daniel assures us, 'many shall run to and fro, and knowledge shall be increased' (Dan. 12.4). Those who read the Geneva version of Daniel and Revelation or Foxe's history of Christian martyrdom could learn that that time might be soon at hand, that they were living through the latter days of this world. This perspective was expanded in overwhelming detail in sermons and tracts which proliferated in the late sixteenth and early seventeenth centuries. There had been four earthly kingdoms: the Chaldean, Persian, Greek and Roman Empires. The rule of Pagan Rome extended into the rule of the Catholic church, linked in so much protestant imagery with Revelation's scarlet woman, the whore of Babylon. Rome was a city of seven hills, like 'the seven mountains, on which the woman sitteth' (Rev. 17.9). Protestant churches were now set against the Catholic church, and might thus have a key role in the events of the 'latter days'. Chronicles such as Foxe's sketched the key events in this long history and forecast the possible timetable. Daniel and Revelation were rich in symbols for sacred time: 1,260 days, three and a half weeks, an hour in heaven, and the millennial (thousand year) period during which the Antichrist would be chained up. If you decoded these correctly, in terms of human time, you would know the timetable for the end of the world. After the millennium of being chained, the Antichrist would be let loose, but then would come the final degradation of evil. If you fought on the side of the saints, you could anticipate the ecstasy of entering the new kingdom at the end of times. In Jonson's lifetime, many were confident they could so decode prophetic texts but, as they assumed they would be on the winning side, the apocalypse held out not fear for them but ecstatic joy as they awaited the second coming.

The idea that these prophecies were the literal truth of the history of the world has had a continuing influence from Jonson's time to ours. Oral Roberts, a famous twentieth-century American evangelical preacher, puts it this way in his commentary on Revelation:

> I love the thought of Christ's Second Coming. My heart is thrilled when I think that this may be the year our Lord returns for his own. . . . The drama of the end-time is unfolding. The clouds are lifting. The dawn is breaking.[18]

Roberts's joyful expectation of apocalypse links back to the Reformation readings of prophecy I have quickly sketched here. In modern times, this joyous understanding of apocalypse has been pushed aside by the many uses of apocalypse in the popular imagination, where the term apocalypse indicates 'a disaster resulting in drastic, irreversible damage to human society or the environment, esp. on a global scale'.[19] We see this most clearly perhaps in Hollywood films, from *Apocalypse Now* to *Armageddon*; in the early twenty-first-century big-screen eco-thrillers have frequently depicted global environmental collapse. In these scenarios, whatever apocalypse portends, it won't be nice.

The dupes in Jonson's play hope otherwise. In their fevered imaginations alchemy and apocalypse are deeply linked in material ways. The transformation of base matter into gold would require an apocalyptic rearrangement of the world. This fifth element, newly formed from the dregs of the previous four, would be a metallic version of the fifth kingdom itself. The result, however, would be earthly, not heavenly joy. If you could control the process of alchemy you could certainly know the day and the hour when the transformation would be complete, and be primed to take advantage of it. This would be a day of ultimate promise – precisely of

course what Subtle, Doll and Face have been promising their cli-
entele. Culturally, the scenario plays upon the assumption, common to apocalyptic and alchemical thinking, that there would be
a single joyous day when all hopes were fulfilled. Dramaturgically,
of course, this expectation sets up the scenario played out on stage,
the singular day when all dreams of avarice will come true. It thus
seems no accident that alchemy and apocalypse are interlinked
precisely at the point in the play when those dreams are at their
height and when they must be shattered so entertainingly.

The Reformation's concept of apocalypse enters the play
through the two Anabaptist evangelists: Ananias and Tribulation.
Their plan is clear: the profits from projection will be devoted, as
Subtle puts it, to 'rooting out the bishops | Or th'antichristian
hierarchy' (2.5.82–3); and as Tribulation agrees the money will
enable them to 'stand up for the beauteous discipline | Against
the menstruous cloth and rag of Rome' (3.1.32–3). To such puritans as these, the activities of the conservative Anglican church
increasingly came to resemble those of the Pope in Rome. Ananias,
the junior, is ever vigilant for signs of the Antichrist in the world,
perceiving that Subtle 'bears | The visible mark of the beast in
his forehead' (3.1.7–8). All Roman Catholic countries, from this
perspective, would look suspect. Thus, to Ananias, Surly in his
Spanish heiress-hunting disguise, 'look'st like Antichrist in that
lewd hat' (4.7.55). Both Ananias and Tribulation are well read
in scripture, and can readily quote from prophecy. 'The place
[Lovewit's house]', says Ananias, 'is become a cage of unclean
birds' (5.3.46–7), recalling the fallen satanic city of Babylon, the
'cage of every unclean and hateful bird' (Rev. 18.2); the house he
claims as the domain also of 'Locusts | Of the foul pit' (5.5.13–14),
arising out of the 'bottomless pit' whence 'there came out of the
smoke locusts upon the earth' (Rev. 9.2–3). Aptly in this scene
Pastor Tribulation makes the more erudite prophetic allusion, to
the apocrypha, describing the house as 'Profane as Bel, and the
dragon' (5.5.14). The wit of quoting scripture, of course, is not
quite enough for them to triumph. Jonson shows their motivation to be as degradedly base as anyone else's in his scheme. The

money they 'invest' in alchemy is lost to them, remaining (like everything else in the house) in Lovewit's hands. They cannot contrive a Fifth, sacred Monarchy by these means.

They are a lively pair on stage, and a good dress rehearsal for the figure of Zeal-of-the-Land Busy in *Bartholomew Fair*; yet, they do not seem to have excited Jonson's satiric inventiveness as much as Sir Epicure Mammon, who pursues with apocalyptic fervour a lavishly material golden age. He is the chief victim, the target of a ten-month 'long con'. His desire for a golden age is anchored in utopian beneficence. 'If his dream last', Subtle tells us, 'he'll turn the age to gold' (1.4.29); he will use his power to heal the sick, 'Dispensing for the pox . . . walking Moorfields for lepers' (19–20). Mammon endorses this projection of his virtue: 'I shall employ it all in pious uses: | Founding of colleges and grammar schools, | Marrying young virgins, building hospitals, | And now and then a church' (2.3.49–53). In the light of Jonson's proto-Dickensian knack for capturing the qualities of his charac- ters in their name,[20] it is not surprising to discover that Epicure Mammon is not planning to lead a Christian republic of virtue but rather to use the infinite wealth and eternal youth the 'stone' will grant to indulge a lifestyle that would exceed even the worst legends of the feats of Roman emperors:

> We'll therefore go with all, my girl, and live
> In a free state, where we will eat our mullets,
> Soused in high-country wines, sup pheasants' eggs,
> And have our cockles boiled in silver shells,
> Our shrimps to swim again, as when they lived,
> In a rare butter made of dolphins' milk.
>
> . . .
> And so enjoy a perpetuity
> Of life and lust[.]
>
> (4.1.155–66)

There may be scant 'alchemy' staged during the play, but such passages are vivid support for Anne Barton's claim that the key transformations in the play happen through its language, as here so densely and sickeningly material.[21] Epicure disappears, as it were, into the substances in which he takes pleasure but which for the audience become disgusting. There is an additional frisson for us now, as our own emotive responses to dolphins (promoted by eco-tourism and 'swimming with dolphins' excursions) render the thought of dolphin's butter more repellent, perhaps, than even Jonson initially intended. The metaphors evoke the paradoxical state of Mammon's desires. On the one hand, he seeks here to melt his flesh into all manner of other soft, luxurious substances. On the other, like King Midas he will, if he can, literally turn everything to gold, imagining a fortune that will exceed that of the mines of Solomon and fabled mines of the Spanish Americas combined: 'I'll change | All that is metal in thy house to gold' (2.1.29–30).[22] In his metallic paradise, he will eat off 'Dishes of agate, set in gold and studded | With emeralds, sapphires, hyacinths, and rubies' (2.2.73–4). In personal terms, he imagines a state like the holy city of New Jerusalem: 'and the city *was* pure gold, like unto clear glass. And the foundations of the wall of the city *were* garnished with all manner of precious stones' (Rev. 21.18–19). Revelation uses metals from our world to evoke the splendour of the new heaven and earth, after our world has passed away. Epicure has no such spiritual aim in mind. Rather in his own dreamed-of '*novo orbe*' (2.1.2) or fifth kingdom, he will get to spend the fifth element the final projection will create for him. He will not wait for the world-to-come to claim his reward; and it is the vehement claiming of his reward that proves his downfall. The enacting of this fuses alchemy, apocalypse and the genre of comedy.

Each of the dupes requires enticement to keep them in circulation: a little piece of what they most desire while they await the final outcome. Face and Doll assume whatever role is necessary to mirror back to the clients their inner desires. The stakes are highest in their traffic with Mammon: he expects the greatest reward, and so, over the preceding ten months, they have milked him the most in advance. Dapper achieves an audience with the Queen of the Fairies, a scenario played out with contempt for its

ludicrousness and the baffling stupidity of anyone who would fall
for it. Mammon instead is baited with the deranged sister of a
lord; she comes equipped with prophetic accessories:

> She is a most rare scholar,
> And is gone mad with studying Broughton's works.
> If you but name a word touching the Hebrew,
> She falls into her fit and will discourse
> So learnedly of genealogies
> As you would run mad too to hear her, sir.

> (2.3.237–42)

As editors of the play frequently note, the author referred to here
is Hugh Broughton, a Puritan minster and theologian, whose
Revelation of the Holy Apocalyps was published the same year the
play was first performed. Jonson may have read it, along with
Broughton's 1590 *Concent of Scripture*, which he samples generously in 4.5. Here Doll in role as the aristocratic prophetess lapses
(as Subtle foretells in 2.3) into apocalyptic madness in order to
forestall Mammon's advances. He wants his golden age, with its
accompanying wanton pleasures, now. Inadvertently, he uses pro-
phetic trigger words, sufficient to set Doll off: 'Alas I talked | Of
a fifth monarchy I would erect | With the philosopher's stone,
by chance, and she | Falls on the other four straight' (4.5.25–8).
Here, at the climax of the play, is the quintessence of its commin-
gling of alchemy and apocalypse.

Mammon's fifth monarchy would be founded on the successful and perpetual recreation of the fifth element, gold. His vision
of a fifth kingdom provokes from Doll a stream of prophetic language narrating the chronology of the four earthly kingdoms that,
in Renaissance schemes (like Broughton's and John Foxe's) based
both on Daniel and Revelation, would precede the final fifth. As
many of his fellow commentators did, Broughton set out a divine
chronology of the world, which Doll excerpts for her prophetic

rant. Jonson would have had other options for illustrating Doll's madness, as volubly crazed women were stereotypical figures on the Jacobean stage. Then too he could have shown her with the babble of glossolalia, speaking in unknown tongues as if moved to do so by the Holy Spirit. The recourse to Broughton is clearly deliberate.

Alchemy and apocalypse share a common gendered language. They envision the unity of the world, and all its matter, as a coming together of the female and male powers that animate the world. When male and female were sacredly conjoined, according to alchemical lore, then you would have the miraculously all-powerful stone. The book of Revelation also forecasts a sacred marriage. The downfall of the whore of Babylon would be succeeded by the marriage of Christ with his church, the New Jerusalem linked forever to her husband/messiah. Jonson upends these sacred longings, using the rhetoric of apocalypse to adorn the farce of sex. The Mammon we see in act 2, with his dreams of world domination, is reduced to begging Doll for sexual favours. 'There was no unchaste purpose' (4.5.37), he assures Subtle. We see no impurity on stage, for it is an important part of the overall con-game that none of the gulls be given what they want, but there is no doubt that Mammon's purposes with Doll are specifically unchaste. Her stream of prophesying, it seems, is triggered at the point when Mammon presses his claims too ardently. The complexities of Doll's chantings become a kind of prophetic foreplay: '*and the fourth Beast.* | *That was Gog-north, and Egypt-south, which after* | *Was called Gog Iron-leg, and South Iron-leg*' (4.5.4–6). All he can do is stumble after, desperate to interject: 'Lady . . . Dear lady' (4.5.7, 14). To no avail. The baseness of his desire has been exposed; and the apocalypse scenario is flourished to bring about his comeuppance. The trio use this moment to bring their 'great work' crashing down, purporting that Mammon's impure desires have impeded it fatally: 'It has stood still this half hour' (4.5.42), admonishes Subtle. Purity of intention was crucial for

the success of alchemy; only a morally upright adept could prevail; purity too was required for those aiming to survive the end
times and enter the New Jerusalem: 'be thou faithful unto death,
and I will give thee a crown of life' (Rev. 2.10). Mammon's actions
will 'retard | The work a month at least' (4.5.51–2). Moments
later, the whole bogus experiment totters, with the '*great crack and
noise within*', which Face interprets for us: 'Every glass is burst,
| Furnace and all rent down, as if a bolt | Of thunder had been
driven through the house!' (4.5.58–60). The 'bolt of thunder' is a
nice touch, for it suggests some divine judgement has been passed
on Mammon. Face, of course, is simulating verbally the signs
of divine providence to cover this climactic stage of their scam.
Their intertwining of the discourses of alchemy and apocalypse
is entirely opportunistic, based on their shrewd grasp of what the
credulous, in 1610, might think possible. On the public Jacobean
stage, no such direct divine judgement would be shown. Jonson
reserved epiphanies of gods, in classical disguise, for his more eso-
terically contrived court masques. Here the chance for divinely
ordained metamorphosis vanishes in this great '*crack*'; in its wake
the returning Lovewit can only find

> empty walls, worse than I left 'em, smoked,
> A few cracked pots and glasses, and a furnace,
> The ceiling filled with poesies of the candle,
> And madam with a dildo writ o'the walls.

(5.5.39–42)

What then becomes of apocalypse amidst this fifth-act detritus?
Empson's poem, quoted as the outset of this chapter, provides
a perspective: 'Waiting for the end, boys, waiting for the end. |
What is there to be or do?' Prophesying the apocalypse or projecting alchemy would both be ways of hastening the end. From
the perspective of the victorious, in the end times, or the lucky
inheritors of alchemy's unlimited wealth, the result would be a

form of divine comedy, as Dante more spiritually describes it in his famous *Paradiso*, but this is not the kind of comedy produced on the Jacobean stage, nor is our fate beyond the end of this world something with which Jonson is concerned. Rather for him the question, while waiting for the end, is 'what is there to be or do?' Here the issue is not whether Jonson personally believed in either alchemy or a coming apocalypse; it is that he uses these tropes to reflect on London life. What Helen Ostovich claims of his break-out humours comedy *Every Man Out of His Humour* seems true of *The Alchemist*, written ten years later: 'In this array of human folly, Jonson musters a mad variety of perspectives that may render the viewers sane.'[23] To the chagrin of all the dupes in the play, no alchemy takes place. Rather, in the fifth act, we see a sordid series of asset transfers. First, Face claims all the treasure the trio have been given; then Lovewit claims all these, as the owner of the house, and refuses to acknowledge any other claims of ownership. No fifth kingdom, evidently, is at hand. In the kingdom of James I, in 1610, Lovewit and his sidekick Face will continue to flourish.

All the victims of the scam desperately desire to transform. That applies to the scammers too. Through alchemy they aspire to a higher state. None succeed. The victims cannot transcend their humour; Subtle and Doll are despatched, neither wealthier nor wiser. Face changes back to being the butler Jeremy, reverting to his subservient role, content, yet trapped within Lovewit's house. In his epilogue, Face turns out to us, the imagined audience: 'I put myself | On you, that are my country, and this pelf | . . . rests | To feast you often, and invite new guests' (5.5.162–5). If we let him, he will scam us again. The task is given to us to complete. The puppet-like characters seem incapable of change; hence their desperation to invoke the magic of external assistance to transform. Jonson hopes more for the audience's power to change than his characters show. For most students of the play, the promises of alchemy or apocalypse will no longer seem credible. Yet, the promise of great wealth and power shimmers still before us, the inducement behind so many contemporary scams. It is important to reflect on the historical and cultural context in which the play was written, as this chapter has shown. But Jonson's greatest plays remain more than quaint curiosities, no matter how crammed they are with the curious lore of his age. The regularity with which, in our world, people still succumb to schemes which will get you rich quicker than could ever be possible is still a world in which *The Alchemist*'s scenarios retain a moral force.

CHAPTER EIGHT

Pedagogical Strategies and Web Resources

ERIN JULIAN AND HELEN OSTOVICH

Students used only to Shakespeare can find Jonson a hard sell. He has a different sound, a different theatrical consciousness, a whole different dramaturgy depending on different blocking, a different concept of space and place, a different approach to complex character and action. Jonson, like the pedagogy we might use in teaching *The Alchemist*, expects – demands, really – collaborative investment in the play. That means recognizing that the play is not a movie, a novel, an essay or a poem (despite Jonson's own preference for calling his works poems); that its ideas shoot out through satirically biting comedy, that Jonsonian comedy is not merely facile entertainment, but instead serious food for thought; that Jonson's plays have concrete and readable appeals to all the senses and, through those senses, to the imagination and intelligence of his audience. Active imagination is a key ingredient when actors work on a bare stage, with limited props and special effects, using entrances and exits from one of two or maybe three doors in the tiring-house wall, with possible use of traps or upper stage. Many students have never been to a theatre, never felt the rapport that actors and audiences generate as a shared involvement in a staged fiction that both is and is not 'reality'. There is no Jonson film industry or theatre festival where students might learn why Jonson, not Shakespeare, was the model for seventeenth-century playwrights.[1] They may not understand that audiences come to the theatre prepared to believe (almost anything) and that actors want to deliver. The meaning they produce together may be different for every participant, but it arises from a complex intersection of roles, sounds, sights, spaces and assumptions about places, and provokes a virtual tactility or visceral response to the embodied script, in one way compelling the actor to vary or test what he does in each show, and in another way affecting the spectator who sees the play once but remembers or reads it later. Plays are not rigid or fixed. The collaboration between page and stage, rehearsal and performance, actors' parts and actors' bodies, actors and props or costumes, actors and audiences – all of this collaboration constantly feeds the show. If all the students do is read the play, they nibble at it, but miss the feast. Perhaps they never develop a real appetite for Jonsonian theatre at all.

Learning through performance: Practical investigations

Students who engage closely with Jonson can derive a rich understanding of the theatrical alternatives in early modern London, especially if they have a reason to move from solitary reading of the play, to lectures on the play's setting and ideas, to tutorial discussion of their own essays on how or why a scene works, to a smaller group engaged in actually preparing and performing a scene that should shed light on the whole play. That is, the assignment of scene research and performance as the major project of a course compels students to work hard at understanding what a complex thing a play is and how theatre makes meaning through collaboration.[2] This project teaches them to read other plays with more theatrical awareness, it helps them develop skills and vocabularies for expressing their ideas, and lets them apply their practical experience and acquired sensitivity to seeing and interpreting other performances. Their final research/performance essays, individually written, analyse and synthesize the collaborative experience of rehearsing and performing – including research, acknowledgement of how ideas develop in a group, assessment of the contributions of each member to the whole, and presentation of a vivid thesis that relies on bodies, minds and emotional energy to project a shared vision to their audience.

Students at McMaster who performed *The Alchemist* 5.4 in spring 2008 as part of the English 2B06 class on the development of early drama were terrified of Jonson by reputation and even by mere reading of the play. The play as a whole seemed to them to place formidable demands on amateur actors. But as they engaged with the text, learning lines and walking through the scene experimenting with the blocking, they discovered two vitally important things: that Jonson supplies all the direction actors need in the text, either stated or implied; and that understanding one scene in depth helped them see the whole play in keen perspective. Many of their performance choices were based on a complete absence of budget: costumes, as a result, began as basic black, with a few add-ons. The eclectic result was actually helpful and funny for their audience: 'Captain' Face, for example, was dressed as a pirate, in basic black, plus Halloween pirate hat and black eye-patch; the actor felt that the disguise was 'ironically illuminating'. Doll wore black fishnet tights (ripped) and heels, under a kimono, which she draped over her camisole and quickly pulled-on stiff crinolines to play the Fairy Queen. Her 'tough' trademark was the cigar she was apparently smoking throughout. For the blindfolded Dapper, however, kissing her 'departing part' felt right, as he grovelled and stroked the 'gown'. The terrified Subtle, at first in a lab coat, and then quick-changing into a black star-studded magician's gown with astronomically inclined cap (another Halloween costume), gained confidence as Dapper succumbed to fears that his 'aunt' might reject him. The fact that none of the costumes seemed necessary, because Dapper remained blindfolded throughout the scene, added to the audience's hilarity. Once Dapper makes his stumbling exit, the quarrel explodes the 'venter tripartite', neatly set up by the giggling and snogging of Subtle and Doll, certain they could put one over on Face. But Face then coolly reveals what one student called his 'complex interiority' and coincidentally ends their revolt by revealing that the returned Lovewit has forgiven him. Therefore, 'my smock-rampant' and the 'Doctor' must quit the house before the officers arrive. The Dapper-actor played all the officers offstage, hammering on the door and shouting, speeding the exit of the two losers, who hurled stage-whispered threats as they went. What this group managed to achieve was remarkable: insight into the play as text and as script – insight into performance that transparently stage-manages, quick-changes and mediates between backstage and onstage business to reflect the power struggle inherent in the plot. This double-dynamic also made them recognize Jonson's demonstration that role-playing is an everyday reality, both sinister and comical in revealing deceit (especially self-deceit) as a staple of life, no matter how we label it or dress it up. The audience, in their reviews of this perfor-mance, especially enjoyed the climax of the scene when Face drew his pirate dagger and kicked the others out. As they commented, 'Even criminals cannot tell whom to trust'. They liked the way Face demonstrated his authority in the scene by using direct address, the only actor on stage to 'see' and play up to the audience; they also noted that his pirate theme set off the complex criminality of the plot: 'No honour among thieves!', as one student wrote. Another, delighted, wrote about 'the magic of trickery' in creating the confusion of the scene. Neither the actors nor the audience would have learned any of this interpretative data so vividly if they had not participated in scene performance.

Preparation for this kind of major project on a scene from *The Alchemist* may involve other hands-on cultural studies. One stun-ningly informative task students can do is simply to search *Early English Books Online* (*EEBO*) for anything published in 1610, the year the play was written and performed: they will turn up 411 records that reveal intense interest in sermons and biblical explication; prognostications and almanacs (sometimes includ-ing mathematics instruction); memorials dedicated to the defeat of the Gunpowder Plot on 5 November 1605; bibles; musical scores; ballads and verse-tales; anti-Jesuit attacks; 'news' from Europe, Virginia, and elsewhere; romances; plays; children's books; oaths taken by freemen of the City; parliamentary peti-tions and announcements, including notice of the creation of the Prince of Wales; puritan writings – many of them reprinted mul-tiple times, such as Calvin, Becon's *The Sick Man's Salve*, and, most importantly, Hugh Broughton's *A Revelation of the Holy Apocalyps*; moral philosophy (Should a widow remarry? Is divorce acceptable? What of remarriage after divorce?); history and geographical description; medical texts (especially plague preventatives); picture books and emblems; poetry; heraldry; and domestic texts (Dod and Cleaver's *Household Management*). The titles are informative in themselves; students can select one item to browse through and report on, particularly constructing a discussion of how such a publication would affect their understanding of events or characters in *The Alchemist*.

Another useful independent search on the internet might provide information about plague between 1590–1615, especially if the students discover the Bills of Mortality for specific years, medical efforts to combat plague, prayers and sermons of comfort, and City edicts from the common council. Some of this information is on *EEBO*, but the topic requires a broader search. A search on alchemy and the philosopher's stone might include such famous figures as Roger Bacon, Paracelsus, John Dee and Edward Kelley, whose biographies reveal fascinating data on cultural assumptions and impacts. Another good online search might be the history of Blackfriars, the liberty (What is a liberty? Who lived there? What are silenced ministers?) and the theatre itself (What company performed there? Who owned the playhouse? What other plays were performed at that site before 1610? What other cities in England enjoyed theatre on tour?). *Internet Shakespeare Editions* (http://internetshakespeare.uvic.ca) is a good starting point for the basic information about the Blackfriars theatre in particular and private theatres in general. Alternatively, students might try an advanced search on *British History Online* (www.british-history.ac.uk) for 'Blackfriars District' or 'Blackfriars Theatre' (restricting searches to the London area will help narrow results productively) to find early modern accounts of the locale. Further readable, concise and easily obtainable critical sources on the audiences, owners, companies and physical conditions of the Blackfriars theatre are Andrew Gurr's well-known work on playing and performance conditions in *Playgoing in Shakespeare's London* and *The Shakespearean Stage 1574–1642*.

Even more entertaining, a search for information on Anabaptists might lead them to surprising histories inside and outside of England. Since the internet content available on Anabaptists can be overwhelming, it may be useful to suggest *GAMEO*: the *Global Anabaptist Mennonite Encyclopedia Online* (www.gameo.org) as a reliable starting point for students. This site has brief but thorough articles on a variety of Anabaptist figures, events and concepts, with bibliographies for every page. Students can read about the Münster Rebellion, and its associated figures Berndt Knipperdolling and Jan van Leydon (whom Ananias and Tribulation parody in *The Alchemist*). *GAMEO* also has an Anabaptist-related bibliography that updates frequently, and a library of translated historical documents (such as catechisms, and confessions and articles of faith). Another dynamic contextual resource on Anabaptists is 'The Siege of Münster', an episode of Melvyn Bragg's BBC Radio 4 show *In Our Time* from 2009, which remains available for download in the *In Our Time* 'History' archive online.[3] The main page for the episode also provides a brief bibliography related to the discussion, including works by the speakers and Norman Cohn's *The Pursuit of the Millennium: Revolutionary Millenarians and Mystical Anarchists of the Middle Ages* – placing the historical event in the context of the millenarian tradition (as Mark Houlahan discusses in his chapter in this volume).

Similarly, information on thieves and rogues in the decades leading up to 1610 might lead students to cony-catching tales, canting language or incidents of tricksterism at the inns of court. (Below we offer both print sources relating to tricksterism that can be paired with *The Alchemist* on the syllabus, and web resources available to enable students to explore independently. Both types of resources will help bring London's criminal world to life in entertaining and thought-provoking ways.) Students may introduce research on these topics into lectures or tutorial meetings, as well as to their own performance group. Pedagogically, whatever excites independent involvement in and discussion of the course materials in relation to bizarre or arcane discoveries generally improves the level of interaction with the plays and with their peers, not to mention with their professor and/or teaching assistant. Often students who get used to sharing ideas within a small intensely focused performance group will want to maintain that high level of community by continuing to read and discuss plays together for the remainder of the academic year, even after they have completed their own performance project. Performing is a bonding experience and the collaboration required for good performance produces a desire for more collaborative work. In effect, students learn to appreciate and trust one another's judgement by discovering, testing and arguing meanings just for the fun of it.

The Alchemist in the syllabus: Plays, poems and pamphlets

This play works well in combination with others, depending on the focus you want to place on its interpretation. One useful starter is Chapman, Jonson and Marston's *Eastward Ho!* which introduces students to the basic ingredients of alchemy as well as to the tools of the goldsmith (helpful if they want to research 'clipping' and 'coining'): touchstone, gold and quicksilver. Although this play does not focus on alchemy as a scam, it does illustrate metaphorically the principles by which it is supposed to work. The metal (the gold in 'Golding') needs contact with mercury (Quicksilver) and 'salt' (or wit, imagination, intelligence) in order to effect any change into quintessence; and Touchstone is the test for the purity of the result. If students read the play and discuss the impact of Quicksilver on various characters (Gertrude, Wolf, Golding, Touchstone), especially in act 5, the alchemical metaphor explains the conversions of the happy ending, as well as the surprising behaviour and performative choice of Golding as the instigator of the reprieves. The research can expand into readings about John Dee, Edward Kelley and Paracelsus. If the focus is instead on magicians, there are many texts to choose from: Greene's *Friar Bacon and Friar Bungay*; Shakespeare's *The Tempest*; Marlowe's *Doctor Faustus*; Peele's *The Old Wives Tale*; and the anonymous *The Puritan, or the Widow of Watling Street*. All of them question the role of the magus, the impact of his 'magic', its usefulness to the state, if not to the individual, and the importance of recognizing the limits of such esoteric outreach. Students might pursue such fascinating questions as: How far can we assume a parallel between Bacon's brazen head and Subtle's offstage laboratory, Faustus's books and Sacrapant's light?

If the focus is genre, on city comedies that stress playfulness and theatricality, again the list of plays is entertaining and informative about early modern urban life: Beaumont's *The Knight of the Burning Pestle*; Barry's *Ram Alley*; Middleton's *The Roaring Girl*, or *A Chaste Maid in Cheapside*; Dekker's *The Shoemaker's Holiday*. All of them stress location, location, location, as well as the joys of cross-dressing – whether crossing lines of class, profession or gender. For colourful examples of London's crowdedness, economic competition and everyday performances in Jonson's own city comedies, one might also use the Paul's Walk scene in *Every Man Out of His Humour*, or especially *Epicene* 1.1 – when Truewit, Clerimont and Clerimont's boy name all the social and commercial noises of London that Morose wants to avoid. For a short contextual support, Jonson's epigram 'On the Famous Voyage' further catalogues the sights and smells of the city revealing both its grim reality and the way that a comical spirit might be a way of resisting or making that reality tolerable (a common feature of city comedies – especially Jonson's *The Alchemist*).

A study of urban space should include a focus on neighbourhoods, and, as we suggested above, especially Blackfriars. Many good sources can help students create maps and discover the histories and implication of place and space: the still-developing *Map of Early Modern London* is a good place to start (http://mapoflondon.uvic.ca) – it also has a page on 'Teaching' with sample syllabi and other resources, as does the REED-affiliated *Early Modern London Theatres* (*EMLoT*) (www.emlot.kcl.ac.uk), also with a 'Learning Zone'; to which you can add readings from John Stow's *Survey of London* (some of which is on the *Map of London* site, but Stow is readily available in libraries and online as updated by John Strype at www.hrionline.ac.uk/strype as well as on *EEBO*), Edward H.

Sugden's *A Topographical Dictionary to the Works of Shakespeare and his Fellow Dramatists*, and Fran Chalfant's *Ben Jonson's London*. Significant work on the London orientation appears in such critical volumes as James D. Mardock's *Our Scene Is London: Ben Jonson's City and the Space of the Author* (2008), Jean Howard's *Theater of a City: The Places of London Comedy: 1598–1642*, Mathew Martin's *Between Theatre and Philosophy: Skepticism in the Major City Comedies of Ben Jonson and Thomas Middleton* (2001), Gail Kern Paster's *The Idea of the City in the Age of Shakespeare* (1985), Lawrence Manley's *Literature and Culture in Early Modern London* (1995; rpt. 2005), and Susan Wells's 'Jacobean City Comedy and the Ideology of the City', *English Literary History* 48 (1981), 37–60. On city comedy and Jonson, of course the first reference is Brian Gibbons's *Jacobean City Comedy: A Study of Satiric Plays by Jonson, Marston and Middleton* (1968); but anyone's list should include a range of texts that help to position Jonson's work: Steven Mullaney's *The Place of the Stage: License, Play, and Power in Renaissance England* (1988); W. David Kay, *Ben Jonson, A Literary Life* (1995); Richard Cave, Elizabeth Schafer and Brian Woolland, *Ben Jonson and Theatre: Performance, Practice and Theory* (1999); James Loxley, *The Complete Critical Guide to Ben Jonson* (2002); Brian Woolland (ed.), *Jonsonians: Living Traditions* (2003); Dieter Mehl, Angela Stock and Anne-Julia Zwietlein (eds), *Plotting Early Modern London* (2004); A. D. Cousins and Alison V. Scott (eds), *Ben Jonson and the Politics of Genre* (2009); Julie Sanders (ed.) *Ben Jonson in Context* (2010); and Mark Bayer's *Theatre, Community, and Civic Engagement in Jacobean London* (2011).

To approach Jonson from another angle, try examining the structure of his play from the point of view of the Aristophanic satiric fantasy of personal empowerment and civic reformation. Start with a good modern translation of Aristophanes' *The Clouds* (the figure of the dotty professor and his adherents) or *The Birds* (how to keep your customers flocking in). Ask to what degree various characters look only for money, or only for the excitement of acquisition, or only for the political and personal power that can come with the acquisition of wealth. Like Aristophanes, Jonson built his plays to develop towards a full scene, with the entire cast plus extras on stage at a key explosive moment: how does the script manage the stage in such scenes? Why are all the neighbours staged in act 5 of *The Alchemist*? Does large-scale fraud ever change? Compare the con-games in the play to news events and interviews with people bilked by modern scammers like Bernard Madoff (see articles on Wikipedia). Helpful early modern resources on popular crime include Robert Greene's cony-catching pamphlets, or other rogue tales/thieves' cant sources, especially Thomas Harman's *Caveat for Common Cursitors* (1566), Thomas Middleton's *The Black Book* (1604), and Thomas Dekker's *The Bellman of London* (1608), *Lantern and Candlelight* (1608) and *The Gull's Hornbook* (1609). Do you have to be dishonest yourself in order to be scammed by a con-artist? Of particular interest to students in the context of Jonson's play might also be *The Brideling, Sadling and Ryding of a Rich Churle in Hampshire* (1595) which recounts two tales of Judith Philips.[4] In the first story, Philips steals the linens from the home of Pope (the wealthy title churl) and his wife, as the couple themselves are 'grovelling on [their] bellies' outside their home while they wait the arrival of the Queen of Fairies who will bless them with wealth.[5] Can we feel any sympathy for characters like these (or like Dapper) who are not only greedy, but also astoundingly gullible? A passage from 'Shaving' or 'Cruelty' of Dekker's *The Seven Deadly Sins of London* might provide an idea of how common con-artists (in all professions) were thought to be in the city, or how unpleasant and hopeless the city might have felt in times of plague: so much so that a sick or fearful resident might have considered consulting even a shady alchemist or cunning man for protection and hope against the disease. Again, one might also send students to *EEBO* to see how many cony-catching pamphlets they can find, or better yet to the *English Broadside Ballad Archive* (http://ebba.english.ucsb. edu); crime was clearly a regular-enough event in early modern London that it became a source of common jokes and songs. Does being scammed, then, automatically mean moral or intellectual failing? Or is it just part of the everyday life for London's citizens? You can remind students that even the clever Subtle and Doll are the victims of a scam at the end of *The Alchemist*. How is anyone to avoid becoming a victim of con-artistry when criminals are seemingly everywhere?

Jonson opens his targets to include spiritual criminals as well as financial ones. Is it fair of Jonson to equate thieves' cant with puritan cant? Use *EEBO* to locate puritan rants like Broughton's *A Revelation of the Holy Apocalyps*, or Philip Stubbes's *Anatomy of Abuses* (1583, available online as a full text), or histories and anecdotes of Anabaptist activities in London, Amsterdam and Munich. And again direct students to have a look at the historical documents on the *GAMEO* site to contrast the sort of language Anabaptists actually used and that which Ananias and Tribulation use.

Finally, what can this play tell us about Jonson's concept of female characters as games-players? Dame Pliant and the fish-wives who come to the door may represent some women as superstitious or solely sexual, but Doll Common is a woman of many parts – lady, scholar, madwoman, puritan, prostitute, Fairy Queen, whatever men desire, certainly far more than a simple sex object. In the alchemical metaphor that generates the energy of the play, she is mercury, the highly volatile substance that interacts with metal to achieve some gold at least, before the experiment blows up and scatters most of the potential profit. She is certainly not a Shakespearean heroine; she has more in common with the feisty women in Middleton's plays (more on this comparison below), and here students might do well to remember that early modern female characters were played by boys. What has Jonson done with Doll to make her both playable and (for the audience, at least) transparently a boy actor as well as 'a woman'? A good prelude for understanding Jonson's staging of women is *Epicene; or the Silent Woman*, his controversial play of the year before (1609), censored off the stage. This intellectual farce is no-holds-barred theatre, in which satire is no respecter of gender or class. And yet students would do well to remember that *The Alchemist* was dedicated to Lady Mary Wroth, lady-in-waiting, poet, and resilient victim of family and court politics. She is a good target for student research: what kind of woman was she, and why did Jonson think she would appreciate the play?

Further online resources: The spaces of London

In addition to the textual pairings and critical and online resources listed above, there are a number of further web resources to bring the city and its inhabitants to life for your students in ways that are relevant to *The Alchemist*, and which can work alongside the primary texts and critical sources already listed. For example, you might use Jean Howard's *Theater of a City* as a guideline for discussing the landscape of economic and social concerns that Jonson's rogues, gulls and theatre audience might have had. Howard divides her discussion of 'The Places of London Comedy' into four institutions: the Royal Exchange, debtors' prisons, bawdy-houses, and the ballrooms and academies. All of these appear one way or another in *The Alchemist*, and many have related online resources. You can do something as simple as directing students to the website of the contemporary Royal Exchange (www.theroyalexchange.co.uk). This site includes a brief history (with pictures) of the Exchange since 1565, but also images of its architecture in its contemporary context. Though rebuilt twice since Jonson's time, and refurbished and remodelled twice more in recent years, the building remains an impressive sixteenth century-esque edifice, that the website itself reads as a continuation of 'Thomas Gresham's . . . unique vision for the Royal Exchange': its impressiveness should remind students of the London trade and commerce that is in many ways the driving energy of *The Alchemist* and all city comedies.[6] The modern Exchange's advertisements for high-class products and parties certainly continue to show how economic desires and the dream of a high-class life (the very angle that the rogues work on Kastril) still appeals today. The gulls' weaknesses are not as distant as contemporary students might like to think!

The second of Howard's city spaces, the prisons, haunts *The Alchemist*, from the prison with which Doll threatens Mammon (and all who dabble in alchemy) in 4.4.152–4: ('beware, sir! You may come to end | The remnant of your days in a loathed prison | By speaking of it [the philosopher's stone]'), to a debtors' prison like Bridewell that Subtle alludes to when he mentions one of its inmates, 'Deaf John' (1.1.85),[7] and where the vulnerable like poor widows and orphans, unskilful gamblers like Dapper, and former vagabonds like Subtle might find themselves. The *London Lives 1690–1800* website (www.londonlives.org), though its focus is temporally after the period of Jonson's play, yet contains relevant information relating to Bridewell Prison and Hospital (starting from 1553) in its 'Criminal Justice' subsection of the 'Historical Backgrounds' area of the site. More usefully, this section provides a brief bibliography of preliminary resources for students interested in reading about Bridewell Prison or other crimes. For a more lively and entertaining representation of Bridewell from a seventeenth-century voice, students might also try searching for 'Bridewell' or 'prison' in the *English Broadside Ballad Archive*; here they can find 'Whipping Cheare. | Or the wofull lamentations of the three Sisters in the Spittle | when they were in new Bride-Well' (1625).

When Subtle and Face try to convince Kastril to marry his sister to the Spanish Don, they promise she will have 'Footmen and coaches . . . six mares . . . | To hurry her through London to th'Exchange, | Bedlam, the China-houses' (4.4.46–8), reminding us of another space of containment in London: Bethlehem Hospital, more familiarly known as 'Bedlam'. Here students can again visit the contemporary site of *Bethlehem Royal Hospital's Archive and Museum Service* (www.bethlemheritage.org.uk). Particularly interesting material on this site includes the 'Visiting Bethlem in the long eighteenth century' online exhibit. As with the *London Lives* project, this exhibit is slightly beyond the time of *The Alchemist's* Bedlam (the exhibit begins in 1676 when the hospital moved to its current location), but is still useful in understanding how early modern people might have considered bodies like the ill and the mad: not just as potentially dangerous or contagious and needing confinement and cure, but also a source of entertainment. One of the short videos, 'what did visitors to Bethlem want to see' suggests that early modern and restoration culture saw the inmates as kinds of performances. Students can follow up on this connection between the madhouse and performance with the *Internet Shakespeare Editions* entry on Bethlehem – here students can learn about stage plays that represented madhouses, as well as other hospitals and prisons.

Both of these latter bodies we've looked at – the poor and the ill – share in common the property of being socially disruptive, if not outright criminal, and in need of containment. They are also both potential sources of entertainment (entirely in keeping with Jonson's play where we as the audience enjoy the suffering of the unfortunate gulls). Female bodies, belonging (in Howard's model) to the space of the brothel, also share these qualities. The sheer number of popular pamphlets on female criminals attests to the entertainment value of scandals around female bodies.[8] Contemporary critical consensus is that female sexuality is a real social anxiety: prostitution, then, seems the most likely type of criminal act for the female body. As we have suggested above, however, in Jonson's play Doll is an integral and irreplaceable part of the con-artistry and stage management of the 'venture tripartite': not only is her body essential to the final 'act' of the group's theatrical explosion of Mammon, and the final act of the Fairy Queen scheme against Dapper, but also her shrewd thinking, her clever wit and her ability to perform. Doll is an excellent example of the ways that all criminals, but especially female criminals, are complex in the early modern imagination. The Bryn Mawr college exhibit, 'Pointing Fingers: Women, Sin, Crime, and Guilt', captures this complexity nicely (www.brynmawr.edu/library/exhibits/PointingFingers/guide.html). According to this exhibit's guide, women's criminal activities took many forms, including witchcraft, prostitution, scam artistry, divorce and adultery. Often women were criminals for more reasons than one. The infamous Moll Cutpurse is an excellent example – and a good essay question on city comedy's treatment of criminality and female criminals in particular might involve a comparison between Doll Common and Middleton's portrayal of Moll Frith in *The Roaring Girl*. In thinking of this contrast, students can download an account of Moll in the Bryn Mawr exhibit's link to Arthur Vincent's 1897 *Lives of Twelve Bad Women: Illustrations and Reviews of Feminine Turpitude Set Forth by Impartial Hands*), and well as the *Newgate Calendar*'s page on 'Mary Frith Otherwise Moll Cutpurse'. As a popular and public figure, Moll's sexuality is also perceived as public, whether in Vincent's denial that the landlord at the Globe Tavern objected to Moll on the basis of 'any scruples as to her moral character',[9] or in the *Newgate Calendar*'s assertion that:

> she was troubled with none of those longings which poor maidens are subject to. She had the power and strength to command her own pleasure of any person who had reasonable ability of body; and therefore she needed not to whine for it, as she was able to beat a fellow to compliance, without the unnecessary trouble of entreaties.[10]

Moll is also a social and legal problem because of her readiness to flout social conventions: she breaks sartorial rules, duels, attends bear-baiting and sits on the stage at the theatre. Moreover, as her name reminds us, she is a notorious cutpurse. In Middleton's city comedy, Moll defends her sexuality, drawing distinctions between acts of wearing of transvestite clothes and attending theatre, and unruly villains who are humourless, stupid, actually unchaste, and predatory or parasitical. Middleton tries to draw a clear distinction between those who are 'criminals' and those who are not – and in Middletonian fashion, the likeably transgressive and feisty Moll ends up the most chaste, and the most socially ordered body in the play. But there is no doubt that the real Moll was a criminal: prose accounts of her may celebrate her comic spirit, but make no denial that this spirit was both criminal and socially disruptive. This is the type of woman – indeed, the type of characters generally – that we find in Jonson's play: the charismatic figures are often the criminals (while the gulls are not always sympathetic!). And Doll, one of the most desired bodies in the play, is also one of the most criminal. Her expulsion from the house and back to the brothel at the end of the play and Dame Pliant's chaste replacement of her, is perhaps, as a few of the authors in this volume have surmised, a cause of regret, rather than for celebration of a restored patriarchal order. Students might be interested in discussing these issues in the context of a larger question of whether the ending is a conventionally 'happy' one.

Further online resources: Alchemy, science and knowledge

No discussion of web resources for *The Alchemist* would be complete without a few on alchemy. Here you can again start by directing students to try a general search for alchemy – how many fraudulent websites do they find (and which ones do they consider credible)? Pointing to the alchemy website (www.levity.com/alchemy) is a good way of showing how difficult it might be to discern between what they might consider sound and unsound knowledge. You can ask students to think about the aspects of the site about which they are most sceptical, and (before they scoff too loudly) ask them to consider what these less credible aspects of the site are offering visitors. How is our culture driven by the same desires as the rogues and gulls in Jonson's play? Certainly, the site leads students to historical documents about alchemy and provides images (along with their source texts) which may be helpful for students who wish to get a clearer grasp on the theatrics of alchemy, how its language sounded, and what its place was in early modern culture – if alchemy is so clearly a target for satire why were alchemical discourses so prevalent, and why were alchemists tolerated at all? You can also direct them to *Epact: Scientific Instruments of Medieval and Renaissance Europe* (www.mhs.ox.ac.uk/epact), run by the Museum of the History of Science, Oxford, the British Museum, London, the Museum of the History of Science, Florence, and the Museum Boerhaave, Leiden. *Epact* collects images and descriptions of the early scientific instruments including astrolabes, astronomical clocks and compendiums, armillary spheres, compasses and dials, gunner's instruments, mining instruments nocturnals, measuring rules, and wind vanes. The site could facilitate the beginning of a discussion on the value of truth and knowledge in the context of the theatricalism, criminality or city life of Jonson's play. You might present pictures from this site alongside images of instruments that students might find on the covers of alchemical treatises. Alternatively, you could begin by asking them to consider why alchemy is not listed in *Epact*'s brief essay detailing legitimate and ancient mathematics and sciences – which do include astronomy, geometry, navigation, cartography and time-telling. Yet, John Dee also produced *A playne discourse and humble advice . . . as concerning the needful reformation of the vulgar kalendar* and the *General and Rare Memorials pertayning to the Perfect Arte of Navigation* (knowledges which the site does consider legitimate). You can even point them to the detailed articles on the instruments, perhaps asking students to compare the languages of science as we see it here and the alchemical jargon in Jonson's play: many of the descriptions mention natural philosophers like Ptolemy (see *The Alchemist* 4.5.3), and employ the Latin and Greek (and Hebrew and Arabic words) which similarly riddle Subtle and Doll's recitations. How distinct are the languages of 'real' science and the alchemists' pseudo-science in the play? Does it matter which is real if neither is comprehensible? At what point does language (even scientific language) become a fashion, and what is its connection to 'truth' and 'knowledge' at this point?

Students who are able to get sense of the prevalence of early modern tricksterism and crime, the slipperiness of language, and the difficulty of distinguishing between 'true' knowledge and false may be more disposed to understand how the rogues are able to deceive their gulls so successfully. Subtle, Face and Doll are able to perform the language of alchemy and its promised rewards with a breathtaking comic energy that leaves their gulls baffled and delighted (and hopefully a performance group composed of students who have come to learn these lessons will be able to persuade their audience to give themselves up entirely to the onstage performers). Enjoyment, rather than discerning between truth and fiction correctly, is finally the point of *The Alchemist*. Surly might see through all the disguises, but his refusal to use the Don's costume for anything other than telling the truth of the situation to Dame Pliant means he loses out on an opportunity to get the girl.

As many chapters in this volume observe, crime was a real problem in early modern London, and in the cultural documents like cony-catching pamphlets and ballads we have discussed, crime seems to be everywhere – as it is in *The Alchemist*. But crime is also a source of entertainment in Jonson's play, as it is in early modern culture. Listen to the amateur singer of 'Dice, Wine and Women | OR | The unfortunate Gallant gull'd at London' (again on the *English Broadside Ballad Archive* (*EBBA*)): it's difficult not to laugh at the refrain, 'The causes why I am so poore, | Are Dice, Strong-waters, and whore', every time. An attentive audience should find it similarly difficult not to laugh at Jonson's play. And if students are initially having difficulty 'getting' the jokes because of their unfamiliarity with the rhythms of Jonson's language, take the time to reread the scene (aloud) of Dapper in the privy, or of Surly's defeat (this exercise works extremely well in a smaller tutorial or seminar setting). Ask them to paraphrase the scene. Can they think of modern entertainment equivalents? Students usually won't get through the exercise without a few giggles. Laughter, we must all agree, is really the point of the play.

Locating images

A final way you can help students access the world of *The Alchemist* is by providing them with image resources, and there are lots of excellent ones. Students should be encouraged to explore any online art databases to which their library subscribes (this suggestion may seem obvious, but undergraduates might not know such resources are available to go searching for). *ARTstor* is one such image database, and is a wonderful resource, with the one real drawback being that it can be slow in loading searches if they return many results (students may want to narrow their searches by location and date). As with *EEBO*, you can direct the students to do a broad search for materials from 1610 (or perhaps 1600–10), just to see which artists are active (they will find Rubens and El Greco, as well as Nicholas Hilliard), and very generally the kinds of subjects and styles that early modern artists were producing: as well as lots of portraits and religious pictures, they will find examples of early modern urban and court architecture, and arte-facts like purses, swords, armour and clothing (all of which may be helpful if they are doing a performance and interested in creat-ing a 'period' feel – but also if they are reading the play and want to get a sense of the period very quickly). Even more usefully, students can try keyword searches for concepts, ideas and prac-tices that we find in *The Alchemist*. A search on alchemy turns up, among other results, prints from Domenico Beccafumi's *Scenes from the Practice of Alchemy* (c. sixteenth century), a page from Thomas Norton's *Ordinal [of Alchemy]* – complete with a recipe for an elixir! (sixteenth and seventeenth century) – an anonymous fifteenth-century image of *The Antichrist Learning the Arts of Alchemy and Sorcery* (c.1482), and many images of emblems, forges (Breugel's 1558 *Alchemist*), and processes (the seventeenth-century *Copulation in the Alchemical Bottle, Symbolizing Putrefaction*). A search for the word 'fool' produces Albrecht Durer's 1507 and 1511 woodcut series of different types of fools (encourage students to see if they can find any of Jonson's gulls), as well as Bosch's images of extraction of the fool's stone (another stone that quack surgeons might have promised to find for the unwitting – in their own heads), and Leyden's 1508–10 *The Fortune Teller with a Fool* (which shows a woman taking money for a horoscope from a man who might be as gullible as Abel Drugger). A search for 'criminal' turns up Hans Schäufelein's sixteenth-century *A Fool Working for a Criminal Instead of a Virtuous Man* (n.d.).

Other productive search words include 'bear baiting', 'drug-ger' (which turns up Johann Zoffany's 1791 engraving of *David Garrick as Abel Drugger in 'The Alchemist'*), John Dee (which brings up his *A Playne Discourse and Humble Advise . . . as Concerning the*

Needfull Reformation of the Vulgar Kalendar (sixteenth century) and a reprint of his *General and Rare Memorials Pertayning to the Perfect Arte of Navigation* (1577) – complete with a drawing of Ptolemy's system, and Elias Ashmole's *Theatrum Chemicum Brittanicum, Vol. 2*, with a 'horoscope cast of Edward Kelley, erected by Dr. John Dee' (c.1650–99), as well as brothel, laboratory, tobacco, gambling, magician, conjurer and witch.

If your institution does not have access to a database like *ARTstor*, you can direct students to sites like *British Printed Images to 1600* (http://bpi1700.org.uk/jsp). The site can load slowly, and does not always produce results for search terms – in fact you may find it more productive to browse the site by subject rather than searching by keyword at all – but it can yield good results. In the context of *The Alchemist* you may want to browse especially the images in the 'society' subcategories, as well as the 'crime and punishment' section. The science and medicine categories also have treatises, some with images of labs and medical instruments, and the 'knights' subcategory also contains an image of a 'Spanish nobleman'.

Another potentially overlooked resource is the online content of art galleries and museums. The National Gallery in London, for example, has a 1661 image of an alchemist at his forge,[11] while the National Portrait Gallery (www.npg.org.uk) contains images of alchemists like John Dee and Hugh Broughton, as well as images of women like Mary Frith. The Bodleian library has several printed and manuscript book images in its 'Special Collections Images' (http://digital.bodleian.ox.ac.uk/index) – including books on apocalypse, medieval science, and Ashmole's *Theatrum Chemicum Brittanicum*. Searching for 'alchemy" in the 'Medieval and Renaissance Manuscripts' collection produces many wonderfully high-resolution images of alchemical texts and pictures.

NOTES

Introduction

1. *Informations to William Drummond of Hawthornden*, ed. Ian Donaldson, in *The Cambridge Edition of the Works of Ben Jonson* (hereafter *CWBJ*), gen. eds David Bevington, Martin Butler and Ian Donaldson, 7 volumes (Cambridge: Cambridge University Press, 2012), vol. 5, 367, lines 234–8. All Jonson quotations throughout this book are drawn from the Cambridge edition (*CWBJ*).

2. *Epicene, or The Silent Woman*, ed. David Bevington, *CWBJ*, vol. 3.

3. *Volpone*, ed. Richard Dutton, *CWBJ*, vol. 3. See also Subtle's boast of the '*magisterium*, our great work', *The Alchemist*, ed. Peter Holland and William Sherman, *CWBJ*, vol. 3, 1.4.14.

4. Epigram 133: 'On the Famous Voyage', *Epigrams*, ed. Colin Burrow, *CWBJ*, vol. 5.

5. *Mercury Vindicated from the Alchemists at Court*, ed. Martin Butler, *CWBJ*, vol. 4.

6. *The Underwood*, ed. Colin Burrow, *CWBJ*, vol. 7.

7. We have modernized this quotation from British Library, Harley Manuscript 6055, f25v, transcribed by Dr Emily Ross for her doctoral dissertation, 'The Current of Events: Gossip About the Controversial Marriages of Lady Arbella Stuart and Frances Coke in Jacobean England, 1610–1620', Otago University, 2009. See her comments on this case, 169–70. We are grateful to Dr Ross for sharing this allusion with us.

8. This pamphlet is printed in Barbara Rosen (ed.), *Witchcraft in England, 1558–1618* (Amherst: University of Massachusetts Press, 1991), 214–18.

9. The Front de Libération de Quebec (FLQ) was a militant political party in Canada active in the 1960s. Its history of violent action in pursuit of a separate Québécois nation culminated in 1970 with the October Crisis: the kidnapping of several oppositional political figures, the murder of Quebec's vice-premier Pierre Laporte, and the unlawful confinement of James Cross, the British diplomat, who was released after eight weeks. Prime Minister Pierre Trudeau invoked the War Measures Act, placing the province under strict police and military control.

1: The Critical Backstory

1. *The Table Talk and Omniana of Samuel Taylor Coleridge* (London: Oxford University Press, 1917), 312; qtd in Algernon Charles Swinburne, *A Study of Ben Jonson* (first published 1899; later edition, New York: Haskell House Publishers, 1968), 40.
2. Samuel Taylor Coleridge, *Coleridge's Miscellaneous Criticism*, ed. Thomas Middleton Raysor (Cambridge, MA, 1936), 46, 52 and 49; qtd in D. H. Craig (ed.), *Ben Jonson: The Critical Heritage, 1599–1798* (London and New York: Routledge, 1990), 33.
3. John Milton, *L'Allegro* (1631–2); qtd in Craig (ed.), *Critical Heritage*, 8.
4. Defence of the Epilogue appended to Dryden's *The Conquest of Granada by the Spaniards*, in two parts, acted at the Theatre Royal (London: printed for H. Herringman, 1672).
5. John Dryden, *An Essay of Dramatic Poesy* (London: printed for H. Herringman, 1684); qtd in Craig (ed.), *Critical Heritage*, 11.
6. Samuel Butler, *Prose Observations*, ed. and with an introduction by Hugh De Quehen (Oxford, 1979); qtd in Craig (ed.), *Critical Heritage*, 244–5.
7. Thomas Fuller, *History of the Worthies of England*, 1662; qtd in Craig (ed.), *Critical Heritage*, 237.
8. Aphra Behn, Preface to *The Dutch Lover*, 1673; qtd in Craig (ed.), *Critical Heritage*, 305.
9. Samuel Johnson, 'Prologue Spoken by Mr. Garrick' (1747), in *Prologue and Epilogue Spoken at the Opening of the Theatre in Drury-Lane*; qtd in Craig (ed.), *Critical Heritage*, 414.
10. Dryden, *An Essay of Dramatic Poesy*; qtd in Craig (ed.), *Critical Heritage*, 335.
11. Dryden, in Nicolas Boileau, *L'Art Poétique* (*The Art of Poetry*), made into English by Sir William Soame; since revised by John Dryden, Esq. (London, 1683); qtd in Craig (ed.), *Critical Heritage*, 320.
12. James Shirley, 'A Prologue to *The Alchemist* Acted There', for a performance of *The Alchemist*, probably in Dublin, some time between 1637 and 1640, printed in Shirley's *Poems* (1646); qtd in Craig (ed.), *Critical Heritage*, 179–80.
13. Sir John Suckling, *A Session of the Poets*, 1637; qtd in Craig (ed.), *Critical Heritage*, 178.
14. James Howell, 'To My Father, Mr. Ben Jonson' (c.1632); qtd in Craig (ed.), *Critical Heritage*, 171.
15. Qtd in Craig (ed.), *Critical Heritage*, 227.
16. *The Diary of Samuel Pepys*, ed. Robert Latham and William Matthews (1970–83) 5.232; qtd in Craig (ed.), *Critical Heritage*, 264.
17. Ibid., 269–70.

18. Edward Phillips, *Theatrum Poetarum* (1675); qtd in Craig (ed.), *Critical Heritage*, 308.

19. Gerald Eades Bentley, *Shakespeare and Jonson: Their Reputations in the Seventeenth Century Compared* (Chicago: University of Chicago Press, 1945); Jesse Franklin Bradley and Joseph Quincy Adams, *The Jonson Allusion-Book* (New Haven: Yale University Press, 1922); and C. B. Graham, 'Jonson Allusions in Restoration Comedy', *Review of English Studies* 15 (1939): 200–4.

20. Aphra Behn, 'An Epistle to the Reader', *The Dutch Lover* (1673), sig. a1'; qtd in Bentley, *Shakespeare and Jonson*, 159.

21. Richard Brome, *A Critical Edition of Brome's 'The Weeding of Covent Garden' and 'The Asparagus Garden'*, ed. Donald S. McClure (New York: Garland, 1980).

22. William Cavendish, Duke of Newcastle, *The Country Captain* and *The Variety* (London: printed for H. Robinson and H. Hoseley, 1649).

23. See Bentley, *Shakespeare and Jonson*, 2.94.

24. *Plays, Written by the Thrice Noble, Illustrious, and Excellent Princess, the Lady Marchioness of Newcastle* (London: printed for J. Martyn et al., 1662); qtd in Craig (ed.), *Critical Heritage*, 233–4.

25. Sir John Suckling, *A Session of the Poets*, written in 1637 and sung to King Charles during a hunting expedition. Reprinted in Bradley and Adams, *Jonson Allusion-Book*, 196.

26. Thomas Carew, 'To Ben Jonson upon Occasion of His Ode to Himself', *Poems*, 1640; qtd in Craig (ed.), *Critical Heritage*, 149.

27. William Burnaby, *Letters of Wit, Politicks and Morality*, 1701; qtd in Craig (ed.), *Critical Heritage*, 353–4.

28. Richard Steele, *The Tatler*, 10–12 May 1709; qtd in Craig (ed.), *Critical Heritage*, 359–60.

29. John Dennis, 'Epistle Dedicatory', *The Comical Gallant* (1702); qtd in Craig (ed.), *Critical Heritage*, 372.

30. Charles Gildon, *The Laws of Poetry* (1721), qtd in Craig (ed.), *Critical Heritage*, 374–5.

31. Theophilus Cibber and Robert Shiells, *The Lives of the Poets of Great Britain and Ireland* (1753); qtd in Craig (ed.), *Critical Heritage*, 438.

32. Richard Hurd, *Ars Poetica* (1753–7); qtd in Craig (ed.), *Critical Heritage*, 441.

33. David E. Baker, *Biographia dramatica, or a Companion to the Playhouse* (1764); qtd in Craig (ed.), *Critical Heritage*, 494.

34. David Garrick, qtd in Craig (ed.), *Critical Heritage*, 19.

35. Horace Walpole, *Anecdotes of Painting in England*, 3 vols (London: H. G. Bohn, 1862), vol. 2.

36. George Colman, *Anecdotes of Painting in England*, vol. 2, 1762–71; qtd in Craig (ed.), *Critical Heritage*, 534.

37. Charles Lamb (ed.), *Specimens of English Dramatic Poets Who Lived about the Time of Shakespeare* (London: printed for John Bumpus, 1813), 56; and William Hazlitt, *Lectures on the English Comic Writers* (1819), in *The Complete Works of William Hazlitt*, ed. P. P. Howe, 21 vols (London and Toronto: J. M. Dent, 1930–4), 6.38–9.

38. Swinburne, *A Study of Ben Jonson*, 35. All subsequent references from 35–8.

39. John Addington Symonds, *Ben Jonson* (London: Longmans, Green & Co., 1886), 97–104.

40. C. H. Herford and Percy and Evelyn Simpson (eds), *Ben Jonson*, 11 vols (Oxford: Clarendon Press, 1925–52); and F. H. Mares (ed.), *The Alchemist*, The Revels Plays (London: Methuen, 1967).

41. Edward Arber (ed.), *A Transcript of the Registers of the Company of Stationers of London, 1554–1640 A.D.* 5 vols (Gloucester, MA: P. Smith, 1967), 3.445.

42. Peter Whalley (ed.), *The Works of Ben Jonson.* Collated with all the former editions, and corr. With notes critical and explanatory, 7 vols (London: D. Midwinter [etc.] 1756).

43. David Garrick, *The Alchymist: A Comedy*, as altered from Ben Jonson. As performed at the Theatre Royal in Drury Lane (London: for John Bell, 1763, 1777).

44. Francis Gentleman, *The Tobacconist, a Comedy of Two Acts: Altered from Ben Johnson. Acted at the Theatres Royal in the Hay-Market and Edinburgh.* (*With Universal Applause*) (London: J. Bell [etc.]; and York: C. Etherington [etc.], 1771).

45. William Gifford (ed.), *The Works of Ben Jonson*, with notes, critical and explanatory, 9 vols (London: Nicol, 1816).

46. Early and mid-twentieth-century editions include: C. M. Hathaway (ed.), *The Alchemist*, Yale Studies in English (New Haven: Yale University Press, 1903); F. E. Schelling (ed.), *The Alchemist*, Belles-Lettres series 18 (Boston and London: D. C. Heath, 1904); G. A. Smithson's edition for Charles Mills Gayley's *Representative English Comedies* (New York: Macmillan, 1907). Mid-century editions include: G. E. Bentley (ed.), *The Alchemist* (New York: Appleton-Century-Crofts [c1947]); Douglas Brown (ed.), *The Alchemist* (London: Benn, 1966); J. B. Bamborough (ed.), *The Alchemist* (London: Macmillan, 1967); J. B. Steane (ed.), *The Alchemist* (Cambridge: Cambridge University Press, 1967); S. Musgrove (ed.), *The Alchemist* (Berkeley: University of California Press, 1968); Alvin B. Kernan (ed.), *The Alchemist* (New Haven: Yale University Press, 1974).

47. Helen Ostovich (ed.), *The Alchemist*, in *Ben Jonson: Four Comedies*, Longman Annotated Texts (London: Longman, 1997).

48. Herford and Simpson (eds), *Ben Jonson*.
49. Fredson Bowers, 'Greg's "Rationale of Copy Text" Revisited', *Studies in Bibliography* 31 (1978), 114.
50. F. H. Mares, Introduction, *The Alchemist*, lxxii–lxxiii.
51. Elizabeth Woodbridge Morris, *Studies in Jonson's Comedy* (Boston and New York: Lamson, Wolffe, 1898).
52. Eleanor Patience Lumley, *The Influence of Plautus on the Comedies of Ben Jonson* (New York: Knickerbocker Press, 1901).
53. Alfred Remy, 'Some Spanish Words in the Works of Ben Jonson', *Modern Language Notes* 21.3 (1906), 84–6.
54. Felix Emmanuel Schelling, 'William Lilly and *The Alchemist*', *Modern Language Notes* 26.2 (1911), 62–3.
55. C. R. Baskervill, *English Elements in Jonson's Early Comedy* (Austin: University of Texas, 1911).
56. Mina Kerr, *The Influence of Ben Jonson on English Comedy, 1598–1642* (Philadelphia: University of Pennsylvania Press; New York: Appleton, 1912).
57. G. Gregory Smith, *Ben Jonson* (London: Macmillan, 1919).
58. Byron Steel, *O Rare Ben Jonson* (New York: Knopf, 1928).
59. Huntington Brown, 'Ben Jonson and Rabelais', *Modern Language Notes* 44.1 (1929), 6–13.
60. See Mary Farrell, 'The Alchemy of Rabelais's Marrow Bone', *Modern Language Studies* 13.2 (1983), 97–104.
61. Anne Lake Prescott, 'Jonson's Rabelais', in James Hirsch (ed.), *New Perspectives on Ben Jonson* (Madison, NJ: Farleigh Dickinson University Press; London: Associated University Presses, 1997), 35–54.
62. Eric Linklater, *Ben Jonson and King James: Biography and Portrait* (London: J. Cape, 1931), 189–92.
63. John Palmer, *Ben Jonson* (New York: Viking, 1934), esp. 184.
64. L. C. Knights, *Drama and Society in the Age of Jonson* (London: Chatto & Windus, 1937); and 'Ben Jonson: Public Attitudes and Social Poetry', in William Blissett, Julian Patrick and R. W. Van Fossen (eds), *A Celebration of Ben Jonson* (Toronto: University of Toronto Press, 1973), 167–87.
65. Harry Levin, 'Jonson's Metempsychosis', *Philological Quarterly* 22 (1943), 239.
66. Alexander H. Sackton, *Rhetoric as a Dramatic Language in Ben Jonson* (New York: Columbia University Press, 1948), 148–67.
67. Charles Francis Wheeler, *Classical Mythology in the Plays, Masques, and Poems of Jonson* (Princeton: Princeton University Press, 1938), esp. 5–11.
68. Clifford Leech, 'Caroline Echoes of *The Alchemist*', *Review of English Studies* 16.64 (1940), 432–8.

69. Edgar Hill Duncan, 'Jonson's *Alchemist* and the Literature of Alchemy', *Publications of the Modern Language Association of America* 61.3 (1946), 699–710.

70. Johnstone Parr, 'Non-Alchemical Pseudo-Sciences in *The Alchemist*', *Philological Quarterly* 24 (1945), 85–9.

71. John Read, *The Alchemist in Life, Literature, and Art* (London and New York: T. Nelson, 1947).

72. Freda L. Townshend, *Apologie for Bartholomew Fayre: The Art of Jonson's Comedies* (New York: Modern Language Association of America, 1947), 82–103.

73. Lu Emily Pearson, 'Elizabethan Widows', in Hardin Craig (ed.), *Stanford Studies in Language and Literature* (Stanford: Stanford University Press, 1941), 124–42.

74. C. J. Sisson, 'A Topical Reference in *The Alchemist*', in James G. McManaway, Giles E. Dawson and Edwin E. Willoughby (eds), *Joseph Quincy Adams Memorial Studies* (Washington, DC: Folger Library, 1948), 739–41.

75. Joseph T. McCullen, Jr, 'Conference with the Queen of Fairies: A Study of Jonson's Workmanship in *The Alchemist*', *Studia Neophilologica* 23.2 (1951), 87–95; and Franklin B. Williams, Jr, 'Thomas Rogers as Ben Jonson's Dapper', *Yearbook of English Studies* 2 (1972), 73–7.

76. Richard Levin, 'Another "Source" for *The Alchemist* and Another Look at Source Studies', *English Literary Renaissance* 28.2 (1998), 210–30.

77. M. A. Shaaber, 'The "Vncleane Birds" in *The Alchemist*', *Modern Language Notes* 65.2 (1950), 106–9; and Malcolm H. South, 'The "Vncleane Birds, in Seuenty-Seuen": *The Alchemist*', *Studies in English Literature* 13.2 (1973), 331–43.

78. Paul Goodman, 'Comic Plots: *The Alchemist*', *The Structure of Literature* (Chicago: University of Chicago Press, 1954), 82–103.

79. Marchette Chute, *Ben Jonson of Westminster* (New York: Dutton, 1953).

80. John J. Enck, *Jonson and the Comic Truth* (Madison: University of Wisconsin Press, 1957), 152, 159.

81. Maurice Hussey, 'Ananias the Deacon: A Study of Religion in Jonson's *The Alchemist*', *English* 9.54 (1953), 207–12.

82. Edward B. Partridge, *The Broken Compass: A Study of the Major Comedies of Ben Jonson* (New York: Columbia University Press; London: Chatto & Windus, 1958), 158.

83. William Empson, '*The Alchemist*', *Hudson Review* 22.4 (1969–70), 596–7.

84. C. G. Thayer, 'The Middle Comedies', in *Ben Jonson: Studies in the Plays* (Norman: University of Oklahoma Press, 1963), 85, 110.

85. Gabriele Bernhard Jackson, *Vision and Judgment in Ben Jonson's Drama* (New Haven: Yale University Press, 1968), 93; 116.

86. Robert Knoll, *Ben Jonson's Plays: An Introduction* (Lincoln: University of Nebraska Press, 1964), 134–5.

87. Myrddin Jones, 'Sir Epicure Mammon: A Study in "Spiritual Fornication"', *Renaissance Quarterly* 22.3 (1969), 242.

88. William Blissett, 'The Venter Tripartite in *The Alchemist*', *Studies in English Literature* 8.2 (1968), 333.

89. *Volpone*, ed. Richard Dutton, *CWBJ*, vol. 4, Epistle, lines 89–92.

90. Brian Gibbons, *Jacobean City Comedy: A Study of Satiric Plays by Jonson, Marston, and Middleton* (Cambridge, MA: Harvard University Press, 1968); Jonathan Haynes, 'Representing the Underworld: *The Alchemist*', *Studies in Philology* 86.1 (1989), 18–41; and William R. Dynes, 'The Trickster Figure in Jacobean City Comedy', *Studies in English Literature* 33.2 (1993), 365–84.

91. Arnold Judd, 'Lovewit's Triumph and Jonsonian Morality: A Reading of *The Alchemist*', *Criticism* 11.2 (1969), 151–66.

92. Alan Dessen, '*The Alchemist*: Jonson's "Estates" Play', *Renaissance Drama* 7 (1964), 38–9. Dessen pursues this contention in his *Jonson's Moral Comedy* (Evanston, IL: Northwestern University Press, 1971).

93. L. A. Beaurline, *Jonson and Elizabethan Comedy: Essays in Dramatic Rhetoric* (San Marino, CA: Huntington Library, 1978), 201.

94. L. A. Beaurline, 'Ben Jonson and the Illusion of Completeness', *Publications of the Modern Language Association* 84.1 (1969), 54.

95. Jonas Barish, *Ben Jonson and the Language of Prose Comedy* (Cambridge, MA: Harvard University Press, 1960), 92.

96. Jonas Barish, 'Feasting and Judging in Jonsonian Comedy', *Renaissance Drama* n.s. 5 (1972), 25.

97. Ibid., 28.

98. Thomas M. Greene, 'Ben Jonson and the Centered Self', *Studies in English Literature* 10.2 (1970), 325.

99. Ibid., 346.

100. Michael Flachmann, 'Ben Jonson and the Alchemy of Satire', *Studies in English Literature* 17.2 (1977), 260.

101. Alvin Kernan, 'Alchemy and Acting: The Major Plays of Ben Jonson', *Studies in the Literary Imagination* 6.1 (1973), 4–6.

102. Ibid., 15–16.

103. James Shapiro, *Rival Playwrights: Marlowe, Jonson, Shakespeare* (New York: Columbia University Press, 1991), 66.

104. Richard Levin, '"No Laughing Matter": Some New Readings of *The Alchemist*', *Studies in the Literary Imagination* 6.1 (1973), 85–9.

105. Donald Gertmenian, 'Comic Experience in *Volpone* and *The Alchemist*', *Studies in English Literature* 17.2 (1977), 248.

106. Ian Donaldson, 'Language, Noise and Nonsense: *The Alchemist*', in Earl Miner (ed.), *Seventeenth-Century Imagery: Essays on Uses of Figurative Language from Donne to Farquhar* (Berkeley: University of California Press, 1971), 69–82.

107. Richard Dutton, '*Volpone* and *The Alchemist*: A Comparison in Satiric Techniques', *Renaissance and Modern Studies* 18 (1974), 60.

108. Douglas Duncan, *Ben Jonson and the Lucianic Tradition* (Cambridge and New York: Cambridge University Press, 1979), 191, 194.

109. Aliki Lafkidou Dick, *Paedeia through Laughter: Jonson's Aristophanic Appeal to Human Intelligence*, Studies in English Literature 76 (The Hague: Mouton, 1974), 63.

110. Robertson Davies, 'Ben Jonson and Alchemy', *Stratford Papers 1968–9*, ed. B. A. W. Jackson (Hamilton, ON: McMaster University Press, 1972), 42.

111. Leah S. Marcus, *The Politics of Mirth: Jonson, Herrick, Milton, Marvell, and the Defense of Old Holiday Pastimes* (Chicago: University of Chicago Press, 1986).

112. Anne Barton, '*The Alchemist*', in *Ben Jonson: Dramatist* (Cambridge and New York: Cambridge University Press, 1984), 136–7.

113. Ibid., 142.

114. Wayne Rebhorn, 'Jonson's "Jovy Boy": Lovewit and the Dupes in *The Alchemist*', *Journal of English and German Philology* 79.3 (1980), 355–6.

115. Gordon Sweeney, *Jonson and the Psychology of Public Theater* (Princeton: Princeton University Press, 1985), 125. All subsequent references are to pages 125–32.

116. R. L. Smallwood, '"Here, in the Friars": Immediacy and Theatricality in *The Alchemist*', *Review of English Studies* 32.126 (1981), 142–60.

117. William Armstrong, 'Ben Jonson and Jacobean Stagecraft', in John Russell Brown and Bernard Harris (eds), *Jacobean Theatre*, Stratford-upon-Avon Studies 9 (London: Arnold, 1966), 56.

118. Smallwood, '"Here, in the Friars"', 148.

119. Cheryl Lynn Ross, 'The Plague of *The Alchemist*', *Renaissance Quarterly* 41.3 (1988), 439–58. See also F. P. Wilson, *The Plague in Shakespeare's London* (Oxford: Oxford University Press, 1927).

120. Andrew Gurr, 'Prologue: Who Is Lovewit: What Is He?', in Richard Cave, Elizabeth Schafer and Brian Woolland (eds), *Ben Jonson and Theatre: Performance, Practice, and Theory* (London and New York: Routledge, 1999), 17.

121. W. David Kay, *Ben Jonson: A Literary Life* (Houndmills, Basingstoke: Macmillan; New York: St Martin's Press, 1995), 108–13.

122. Katharine Eisaman Maus, *Ben Jonson and the Roman Frame of Mind* (Princeton: Princeton University Press, 1984), 59–64.

123. Ibid., 83.

124. William Slights, 'The New Face of Secrecy in *The Alchemist*', in *Ben Jonson and the Art of Secrecy* (Toronto: University of Toronto Press, 1984), 106.

125. Maus, *Ben Jonson and the Roman Frame of Mind*, 84–7.

126. Ibid., 147.

127. Julie Sanders, 'Republicanism and Theatre', in *Ben Jonson's Theatrical Republics* (Houndmills: Macmillan; New York: St Martin's Press, 1998), 68–9.

128. Stanton J. Linden, *Darke Hieroglifphicks: Alchemy in English Literature from Chaucer to the Restoration* (Lexington: University Press of Kentucky, 1996), 128.

129. Richmond Barbour, '"When I Acted Young Antinous": Boy Actors and the Erotics of Jonsonian Theater', *Publications of the Modern Language Association* 110.5 (1995), 1006 and 1015.

2: *The Alchemist* on the Stage: Performance, Collaboration and Deviation

1. *The Alchemist*, with its vibrant performance history, particularly suffers from the decision by the Cambridge general editors to banish performance history from their magisterial new print edition of 2012. While the online version of the Jonson edition will include a stage history of *The Alchemist* by Lucy Munro, the implication that performance history can be dispensed with in the print edition is political and anti-theatrical in its prejudice.

2. Richard Cave, *Ben Jonson* (Houndmills: Macmillan, 1991), 84.

3. Robert Gale Noyes, *Ben Jonson on the English Stage 1660–1776* (New York and London: Benjamin Blom, 1935). For a discussion of survey approaches to the performance history of *The Alchemist* see Elizabeth Schafer, 'Troublesome Histories: Performance and Early Modern Drama', in Ton Hoenslaars (ed.), *The Cambridge Companion to Shakespeare and Contemporary Dramatists* (Cambridge: Cambridge University Press, 2012).

4. Noyes, *Ben Jonson on the English Stage*, 153.

5. Ejner J. Jensen, *Ben Jonson's Comedies on the Modern Stage* (Ann Arbor: UMI Research Press, 1985), 113, 114.

6. Lois Potter, 'The Swan Song of the Stage Historian', in Martin Butler (ed.), *Re-Presenting Ben Jonson: Text, History, Performance* (Houndmills: Macmillan, 1999), 193–209.

7. 'Prologue to the Reviv'd Alchemist', in C. H. Wilkinson, *Proceedings and Papers of the Oxford Bibliographical Society*, vol. 1, 281–2; qtd in C. H. Herford, Percy Simpson and Evelyn Simpson (eds), *Ben Jonson*, 11 vols (Oxford: Clarendon Press, 1925–52), 9.228.

8. Geoffrey Tillotson, *Times Literary Supplement*, 20 July 1933.

9. See T.W. Baldwin, *The Organisation and Personnel of the Shakespearean Company* (Princeton: Princeton University Press, 1927), 437.

10. Richard Cave, 'Script and Performance', in Cave, Schafer and Woolland, *Ben Jonson and Theatre*, 23–32.
11. Ibid., 26.
12. Ibid., 24, 26.
13. Particular thanks are due to Francesca Marini at the Stratford, Ontario archive; John Goodfellow and archivist Stella Lowe at the Royal Exchange; Helen Hargest at the Shakespeare Birthplace Trust; Jane May and Gabrielle Bonney at Belvoir St Theatre; and Matt Bartlett at Bell Shakespeare Company.
14. Francis Kirkman, *The Wits; or, Sport upon Sport* (London, 1662).
15. David Garrick, 'An Essay on Acting: In Which Will Be Consider'd The Mimical Behaviour of a Certain Fashionable Faulty Actor, and the Laudableness of Such Unmannerly, as Well as Inhumane Proceedings' (London, 1744), 7–8, reproduced in full in Michael Caines (ed.), *Lives of Shakespearian Actors 1*, vol. 1, 'David Garrick' (London: Pickering and Chatto, 2008), 23–50, 30–1.
16. Thomas Wilkes, *A General View of the Stage* (London: J. Coote, 1759), 257–8.
17. See Noyes, *Ben Jonson on the English Stage*, 127.
18. Ivor Brown, *The Guardian*, 3 August 1932.
19. Kenneth Tynan, *He That Plays the King; A View of the Theatre* (London: Longmans, 1950), 92–4.
20. Michael Allen, *Michigan Daily*, 26 March 1969.
21. Lawrence DeVine, *Detroit Free Press*, 27 March 1969.
22. Frank Morris, *Winnipeg Tribune*, 11 June 1969.
23. Lewis Funke, *New York Times*, 12 June 1969.
24. Jim Vanderlip, *Ontarion*, 10 October 1969.
25. Stewart Brown, *Spectator*, 11 June 1969.
26. Herbert Whittaker, *Globe and Mail*, 11 June 1969.
27. Audrey M. Ashley, *Ottawa Citizen*, 10 April 1969.
28. Jay Carr, *Detroit News*, 26 March 1969.
29. Roger Dettmer, *Chicago's American*, 5 March 1969.
30. That Gascon reshaped the text is indicated by the creative team credits including 'textual revisions' by Gascon. In this he was aided by Jack Ludwig (David Nicolette, *The Grand Rapids Press*, 11 June 1969; Nathan Cohen, *Toronto Daily Star*, 11 June 1969).
31. Ralph Hicklin, *Toronto Telegram*, 5 March 1969.
32. Kevin Kelly, *Boston Globe*, 12 June 1969.
33. Martin Gottfried, *Women's Wear Daily*, 13 June 1969.
34. Christopher Dafoe, *Vancouver Sun*, 8 July 1969.
35. Kevin Kelly, *Boston Globe*, 12 June 1969.
36. Morris, *Winnipeg Tribune*, 11 June 1969.
37. Hicklin, *Toronto Telegram*, 5 March 1969.

38. Carr, *Detroit News*, 26 March 1969.

39. See, for example, the discussion by Robert Pollak in the *Hyde Park Herald*, Chicago, 19 March 1969. See also the discussion of theatre space in David Nicolette, *The Grand Rapids Press*, 11 June 1969 and William Leonard, the *Chicago Tribune*, 6 March 1969.

40. Performance analysis of Hersov's production is based on memories of the matinee performance on 23 May, on tour at the Bedford Arts Centre.

41. For the replicating of the Royal Exchange stage see *The Guardian*, 20 March 1987.

42. Martin Hoyle, *Financial Times*, 23 February 1987.

43. Joan Seddon, *Manchester Evening News*, 20 February 1987.

44. Timothy Ramsden, *Times Educational Supplement*, 6 March 1987.

45. Simon Warner, *Evening Courier*, 23 February 1987.

46. Kenny Everett (1944–95) was a British comedian famous for manic and mad-cap character comedy.

47. Jeremy Kingston, *The Times*, 21 February 1987.

48. See, for example, Brown, *The Spectator*, 11 June 1969.

49. Ron Lawson, *Bolton Evening News*, 20 February 1987.

50. Programme supplement, tour.

51. Anton Wahlberg, *Tribune*, 13 March 1987.

52. See the prompt copy in the archive of the Manchester Royal Exchange Theatre.

53. Performance analysis of Mendes's production is based on memories of a performance at the Swan in 1991 and a viewing of the archival video of a 1992 performance at the Barbican.

54. Michael Coveney, *Observer*, 1 September 1991.

55. Paul Taylor, *Independent*, 29 August 1991.

56. Kenneth Hurren, *Mail on Sunday*, 1 September 1991.

57. Kirsty Milne, *Sunday Telegraph*, 1 September 1991.

58. Charles Spencer, *Telegraph*, 29 August 1991.

59. Malcolm Rutherford, *Financial Times*, 21 April 1992.

60. Taylor, *Independent*, 29 August 1991.

61. John Peter, *Sunday Times*, 1 September 1991.

62. Rex Gibson, *Times Educational Supplement*, 13 September 1991.

63. 'Interlude I; Sam Mendes talks to Brian Woolland', in Cave, Schafer and Woolland, *Ben Jonson and Theatre*, 79–85, 81.

64. Ibid., 83.

65. Ibid., 80.

66. Ibid., 81.

67. Sheridan Morley, *Herald Tribune*, 29 April 1992; Sarah Hemming, *The Independent*, 17 April 1992; and Keith Stanfield, *City Limits*, 23 April 1992 also invoked Mamet.

68. Spencer, *Telegraph*, 29 August 1991.
69. Ibid.
70. Taylor, *Independent*, 29 August 1991.
71. Michael Quinn, *What's On*, 4 September 1991.
72. Hemming, *Independent*, 17 April 1992.
73. 'Interlude I; Sam Mendes talks to Brian Woolland', 83.
74. Spencer, *Telegraph*, 29 August 1991.
75. Nicholas de Jongh, *Evening Standard*, 16 April 1992.
76. Taylor, *Independent*, 29 August 1991.
77. See Jensen, *Ben Jonson's Comedies on the Modern Stage*, 94–7. Guthrie first updated *The Alchemist* for the Vic-Wells in 1944.
78. Barry Edelstein, *New York Times*, 13 February 2000.
79. Performance analysis of Armfield's production is based on an archival video recording filmed on 24 September 1996, as well as memories of a live performance.
80. Joyce Morgan, *Australian*, 23 August 1996.
81. References to *Glengarry Glen Ross* and *Reservoir Dogs* appeared in Belvoir's media releases and in reviews.
82. James Waites, *Sydney Morning Herald*, 29 August 1996.
83. Morgan, *Australian*, 23 August 1996.
84. Paul Fraser, *Mosman Daily*, 5 September 1996.
85. John McCallum, *Australian*, 29 August 1996.
86. Melissa Bellanta, *Life Matters*, ABC Radio National, June 2011, http:// mpegmedia.abc.net.au/rn/podcast/2011/06/lms_20110609_0943.mp3. Bellanta's book, *Larrikins: A History*, will be published by University of Queensland Press in 2012.
87. Penny Gay, 'Recent Australian *Shrews*: The "Larrikin Element"', in Jonathan Bate, Jill L. Levenson and Dieter Mehl (eds), *Shakespeare and the Twentieth Century: The Selected Proceedings of the International Shakespeare Association World Congress, Los Angeles, 1996* (Cranbury, NJ, London and Mississauga, Ontario: Associated University Press, 1998), 170.
88. Rush emphasizes the deep formative influence of pantomime and vaudeville acts in the travelling tent shows that enthralled him as a child in Queensland in the 1950s, when this performance tradition was on the cusp of being eclipsed as popular entertainment by television. Geoffrey Rush, interviewed by Emma Cox, Melbourne, 23 July 2011.
89. Rush points out that the acrostic Argument, spoken by Lovewit with Face, Subtle and Doll in a freeze, was added after opening night. He explains: 'That helped enormously; it gave the audience a chance to look at the room, look at who we were and theatrically it . . . opened the play out instantly; somebody came up and spoke to the audience – whereas the fight is so inward.' Schafer, 'Jonson Down Under: An Australian *Alchemist*', in Cave, Schafer and Woolland, *Ben Jonson and Theatre*, 195.

90. Steve McLeod, *Sydney Star Observer*, 12 September 1996.

91. Waites, *Sydney Morning Herald*, 29 August 1996.

92. McCallum, *Australian*, 29 August 1996.

93. Pamela Payne, *Sun-Herald*, 1 September 1996.

94. Waites, *Sydney Morning Herald*, 29 August 1996.

95. Susan Mooney, *Wentworth Courier*, 4 September 1996.

96. Paul LePetit, *Sunday Telegraph*, 1 September 1996.

97. See Rob Pensalfini, 'Not in Our Own Voices: Accent and Identity in Contemporary Australian Shakespeare Performance', *Australasian Drama Studies* 54 (2009), 142–58.

98. McLeod, *Sydney Star Observer*, 12 September 1996.

99. Geoffrey Milne notes (in an observation made prior to Belvoir St Theatre's renovation in 2005–6), 'the space is too small and technologically ill-equipped (as a matter of deliberate house style) to be anything but an actors' space: the close proximity and cramped confines force almost all of our attention onto the actor and the text'. 'Geoffrey Rush: Manic Genius or Team Player?', *Contemporary Theatre Review* 14.3 (2004), 26.

100. An Iced VoVo is a sweet biscuit made by the Australian-based (and formerly owned) company Arnott's.

101. Fraser, *Mosman Daily*, 5 September 1996. Armfield maintains that the preview audiences were receptive, that they 'just took the play full-in-the-face', in contrast to the media- and industry-peopled audience on opening night, in front of whom, he observes, 'the actors certainly felt they were being assessed'. McLeod, *Sydney Star Observer*, 12 September 1996.

102. Performance analysis of Bell's production is based on an archival DVD recording filmed on 24 March 2009 at the Sydney Opera House Playhouse.

103. 'John Bell Talks about *The Alchemist* (2009)', www.youtube.com/watch?v=rdINQO17MrA.

104. Aaron Ridgway, *Canberra Times*, 2 May 2009.

105. Nicholas Pickard, *Sun-Herald*, 29 March 2009.

106. *Daily Telegraph*, 25 March 2009.

107. Sue Gough, *Courier Mail*, 27 February 2009.

108. Diana Simmonds, *Stage Noise*, 21 March 2009.

109. 'John Bell Talks about *The Alchemist* (2009)'.

110. Katie Stewart, 'Performance Notes for Educators', *The Alchemist*, Queensland Government (Education Queensland) and Queensland Theatre Company, 2009, 14.

111. Stewart, 'Performance Notes for Educators', 14–15.

112. Ridgway, *Canberra Times*, 2 May 2009.

113. Melissa Bellanta, 'The Larrikin Girl', *Journal of Australian Studies* 34.4 (2010), 499–512. While Jonson's Doll is not presented as enjoying the female friendships that would support the case for her as a 'larrikin girl' in Bellanta's terms, Doll's relative autonomy as far as Symes's

characterization was concerned distinguished her from the position of subservience (and vulnerability) to male power that would relegate her merely as a larrikin's 'moll'.

3: The State of the Art

1. Charles Nicholl, '*Ben Jonson: A Life* by Ian Donaldson – Review', *The Guardian*, 14 October 2011.

2. Peter Holland and William Sherman (eds), *The Alchemist* in Bevington, Butler and Ian (gen. eds), *CWBJ*, vol. 3.

3. Cited from the LION transcription, http://lion.chadwyck.co.uk

4. Felix E. Schelling (ed.), *The Alchemist*, cited from the Project Gutenberg e-text at www.gutenberg.org/ebooks/4081

5. Matthew Steggle, '"Knowledge Will Be Multiplied": Digital Literary Studies and Early Modern Literature', in Raymond G. Siemens and Susan Schreibman (eds), *A Companion to Digital Literary Studies* (Oxford: Blackwell, 2007), 90.

6. Jonson, *The Alchemist*, ed. Clark Holloway, http://hollowaypages.com/jonson1692alchemist.htm

7. Jonson, *The Works of Ben Jonson, Volume 3*, ed. Peter Whalley (1756), http://books.google.co.uk/ebooks?id=VjgJAAAAQAAJ

8. Jonson, *The Works of Ben Jonson, Volume 4*, ed. William Gifford (1816), http://books.google.co.uk/books?id=UT4UAAAAYAAJ

9. In *Bell's British Theatre*, Volume 17 (1780), www.archive.org/details/bellsbritishthe19bellgoog

10. David Bevington, 'The Major Comedies', in Richard Harp and Stanley Stewart (eds), *The Cambridge Companion to Ben Jonson* (Cambridge: Cambridge University Press, 2000), 81.

11. Ibid., 84.

12. Ian Donaldson, *Ben Jonson: A Life* (Oxford: Clarendon Press, 2012), 248.

13. Ibid., 254.

14. Derek B. Alwes, 'Service as Mastery in *The Alchemist*', *Ben Jonson Journal* 17.1 (2010), 38–59.

15. Russell West, *Spatial Representations and the Jacobean Stage: From Shakespeare to Webster* (Basingstoke: Palgrave, 2002), 43.

16. Ibid., 57.

17. Andrew Hiscock, *The Uses of This World: Thinking Space in Shakespeare, Marlowe, Cary and Jonson* (Cardiff: University of Wales Press, 2004), 16.

18. Shona McIntosh, 'Space, Place and Transformation in *Eastward Ho!* and *The Alchemist*', in Joan Fitzpatrick and John Martin (eds), *The Idea of the*

    City: Early-Modern, Modern and Post-Modern Locations and Communities (Newcastle upon Tyne: Cambridge Scholars, 2009), 66.

19. James Mardock, *Our Scene Is London: Ben Jonson's City and the Space of the Author* (London: Routledge, 2008).

20. James Loxley, *The Complete Critical Guide to Ben Jonson* (London: Routledge, 2002), 84.

21. Sean McEvoy, *Ben Jonson, Renaissance Dramatist* (Edinburgh: Edinburgh University Press, 2008).

22. Ibid., 101.

23. Ibid., 102.

24. Ian Donaldson, 'Clockwork Comedy: Time and *The Alchemist*', in *Jonson's Magic Houses: Essays in Interpretation* (Oxford: Oxford University Press, 1997), 102.

25. Anthony J. Ouellette, '*The Alchemist* and the Emerging Adult Private Playhouse', *Studies in English Literature, 1500–1900* 45 (2005), 375–99.

26. Melissa D. Aaron, '"Beware at What Hands Thou Receiv'st Thy Commodity": *The Alchemist* and the King's Men Fleece the Customers, 1610', in Paul Menzer (ed.), *Inside Shakespeare: Essays on the Blackfriars Stage* (Selinsgrove, PA: Susquehanna University Press, 2006), 75.

27. Ibid., 72.

28. David Lucking, 'Carrying Tempest in His Hand and Voice: The Figure of the Magician in Jonson and Shakespeare', *English Studies: A Journal of English Language and Literature* 85.4 (2004), 297–310.

29. Arlene Oseman, 'Going Round in Circles with Jonson and Shakespeare', *Shakespeare in Southern Africa: Journal of the Shakespeare Society of Southern Africa* 15 (2003), 71.

30. Melissa Smith, 'The Playhouse as Plaguehouse in Early Modern Revenge Tragedy', *Journal of the Washington Academy of Science* 89.1/2 (Spring/Summer 2003), 77–86.

31. Patrick Phillips, '"You Need Not Fear the House": The Absence of Plague in *The Alchemist*', *Ben Jonson Journal* 13 (2006), 43–62.

32. Julie Sanders, Kate Chedgzoy and Susan Wiseman, 'Introduction', in Julie Sanders, Kate Chedgzoy and Susan Wiseman (eds), *Refashioning Ben Jonson: Gender, Politics, and the Jonsonian Canon* (Basingstoke: Palgrave Macmillan, 1998), 1–27, esp. 15.

33. Ian McAdam, 'The Repudiation of the Marvelous: Jonson's *The Alchemist* and the Limits of Satire', *Quidditas* 21 (2000), 74.

34. Ibid., 67.

35. Ibid., 74–5.

36. Lynn S. Meskill, 'Jonson and the Alchemical Economy of Desire: Creation, Defacement and Castration in *The Alchemist*', *Cahiers élisabéthains* 62 (2002), 62.

37. Ibid., 51.
38. Ibid., 62.
39. Caroline McManus, 'Queen Elizabeth, Dol Common, and the Performance of the Royal Maundy', *English Literary Renaissance* 32 (2002), 189–213.
40. Regina Buccola, *Fairies, Fractious Women, and the Old Faith; Fairy Lore in Early Modern British Drama and Culture* (Selinsgrove, PA: Susquehanna University Press, 2006), 112.
41. Mark Albert Johnston, 'Prosthetic Absence in Ben Jonson's *Epicoene, The Alchemist*, and *Bartholomew Fair*', *English Literary Renaissance* 37.3 (2007), 403.
42. Ibid., 413.
43. Lois Potter, 'How Quick Was a Quick Change? *The Alchemist* and Blackfriars Staging', in Peter Kanelos and Matt Kozusko (eds), *Thunder at a Playhouse: Essaying Shakespeare and the Early Modern Stage* (Selinsgrove, PA: Susquehanna University Press, 2010), 203.
44. Ibid., 208.
45. Jennifer A. Low, *Manhood and the Duel: Masculinity in Early Modern Drama and Culture* (London: Palgrave Macmillan, 2003).
46. Anthony Ellis, 'Senescence in Jonson's *Alchemist*: Magic, Mortality, and the Debasement of (the Golden) Age', *Ben Jonson Journal* 12 (2005), 23–44.
47. Anthony Ellis, *Old Age, Masculinity, and Early Modern Drama: Comic Elders on the Italian and Shakespearean Stage* (Aldershot: Ashgate, 2009).
48. Katherine Eggert, '*The Alchemist* and Science', in Garrett A. Sullivan, Patrick Cheney and Andrew Hadfield (eds), *Early Modern English Drama: A Critical Companion* (Oxford: Oxford University Press, 2006), 200–12.
49. Anthony Miller, 'Ben Jonson and "the Proper Passion of Mettalls"', *Parergon: Journal of the Australian and New Zealand Association for Medieval and Early Modern Studies* 23.2 (2006), 57–72; 'Ben Jonson and "the Proper Passion of Mettalls"', in Andrew Lynch and Anne M. Scott (eds), *Renaissance Poetry and Drama in Context: Essays for Christopher Wortham* (Newcastle upon Tyne: Cambridge Scholars, 2008), 145–57. Page references here are to the *Parergon* version.
50. Ibid., 57.
51. John Shanahan, 'Ben Jonson's *Alchemist* and Early Modern Laboratory Space', *Journal for Early Modern Cultural Studies* 8.1 (2008), 37.
52. Ibid., 38.
53. Henry S. Turner, *The English Renaissance Stage: Geometry, Poetics, and the Practical Spatial Arts 1580–1630* (Oxford: Oxford University Press, 2006), 265.
54. Richard Levin, 'Occult Interior Design in Jonson's Day and Ours, and a New Source for *The Alchemist*', *Research Opportunities in Renaissance Drama* 46 (2007), 116–18.

55. Jonathan Haynes, 'Representing the Underworld: *The Alchemist*', *Studies in Philology* 86 (1989), 18–41.

56. Peggy A. Knapp, 'The Work of Alchemy', *Journal of Medieval and Early Modern Studies* 30.3 (2000), 575.

57. Ibid., 586.

58. Ibid., 594.

59. Eric Wilson, 'Abel Drugger's Sign and the Fetishes of Material Culture', in Carla Mazzio and Douglas Trevor (eds), *Historicism, Psychoanalysis, and Early Modern Culture* (New York: Routledge, 2000), 110–34.

60. Stephanie Boluk and Wylie Lenz, 'Infection, Media, and Capitalism: From Early Modern Plagues to Postmodern Zombies', *Journal for Early Modern Cultural Studies* 10.2 (June 2010), 127.

61. Ceri Sullivan, *The Rhetoric of Credit: Merchants in Early Modern Writing* (Teaneck: Farleigh Dickinson University Press, 2002), 110.

62. Ibid., 108.

63. Elizabeth Rivlin, 'The Rogues' Paradox: Redefining Work in *The Alchemist*', in Natasha Korda and Michelle Dowd (eds), *Working Subjects in Early Modern Drama* (Aldershot: Ashgate, 2011), 123.

64. Mathew Martin, 'Play and Plague in Ben Jonson's *The Alchemist*', *English Studies in Canada* 26.4 (2000), 393.

65. Ibid., 400.

66. Mary Thomas Crane, 'What Was Performance?' *Criticism: A Quarterly for Literature and the Arts* 43.2 (Spring 2001), 169.

67. Ibid., 184.

68. Sean McEvoy, 'Hieronimo's Old Cloak: Theatricality and Representation in Ben Jonson's Middle Comedies', *Ben Jonson Journal* 11 (2004), 82.

69. Rick Bowers, *Radical Comedy in Early Modern England* (Aldershot: Ashgate, 2008), 101.

70. Ibid.

71. Ibid., 102.

72. Ibid., 97.

73. Raphael Shargel, 'The Devolution of *The Alchemist*: Garrick, Gentleman, and "Genteel Comedy"', *Restoration and 18th Century Theatre Research* 19.2 (2004), 5.

74. Ibid., 13.

75. Donald Beecher, 'Suspense Is Believing: The Reality of Ben Jonson's *The Alchemist*', *Theta* 8 (2009), 3–14, www.cesr.univ-tours.fr/Publications/Theta8

76. Sir Philip Sidney, *The Defence of Poesy* in *Sir Philip Sidney*, ed. Katherine Duncan-Jones (Oxford: Oxford University Press, 1989), 230.

77. Julie Sanders, '"Powdered with Golden Rain": The Myth of Danae in Early Modern Drama', *Early Modern Literary Studies* 8.2 (September 2002), 1.1–23, http://purl.oclc.org/emls/08–2/sanddane.htm

78. Duncan Salkeld, 'Literary Traces in Bridewell and Bethlem, 1602–1624', *Review of English Studies* 56 (2005), 379–85.

79. Amra Raza, 'Dynamic Linguistic and Artistic Patterns in Jonson's *The Alchemist*', *Journal of Research (Humanities)* 42–5 (2006), 37–70.

80. Nicholas McDowell, 'Early Modern Stereotypes and the Rise of English: Jonson, Dryden, Arnold, Eliot', *Critical Quarterly* 48.3 (2006), 25–34.

4: New Directions: Space, Plague and Satire in Ben Jonson's *The Alchemist*

1. Steven Rappaport, *Worlds within Worlds: Structures of Life in Sixteenth-Century London* (Cambridge: Cambridge University Press, 1989), 18.

2. Ibid., 182–3.

3. I. W. Archer, *The Pursuit of Stability: Social Relations in Elizabethan London* (Cambridge: Cambridge University Press, 1991), 74.

4. Ibid., 215.

5. Paul Slack, *Poverty and Policy in Tudor and Stuart England* (London: Longman, 1988), 26.

6. L. H. Yungblut, *Strangers Settled Here Amongst Us: Policies, Perceptions and the Presence of Aliens in Elizabethan England* (London: Routledge, 1996), 29.

7. Steven Mullaney, *The Place of the Stage: License, Play, and Power in Renaissance England* (Chicago: University of Chicago Press, 1988), 42–5.

8. Paul Griffiths, *Lost Londons: Change, Crime, and Control in the Capital City, 1550–1660* (Cambridge: Cambridge University Press, 2008), 1.

9. Ibid.

10. Yungblut, *Strangers Settled Here Amongst Us*, 29.

11. Griffiths, *Lost Londons*, 47–55.

12. Ibid., 81–2.

13. Mullaney, *The Place of the Stage*, 21–2.

14. Andrew Gurr, *The Shakespearean Stage, 1574–1642* (Cambridge: Cambridge University Press, 1992), 154–6.

15. Qtd in ibid., 155.

16. Qtd in ibid., 155–6.

17. James Knowles, 'Jonson's *Entertainment at Britain's Burse*', in Martin Butler (ed.), *Re-Presenting Ben Jonson: Text, History, Performance* (Houndmills, Basingstoke: Macmillan, 1999), 115.

18. John Stow, *A Survey of London by John Stow, Reprinted from the Text of 1603*, ed. Charles Lethbridge Kingsford, 2 vols (Oxford: Clarendon, 1908), 1.xcviii. For easy access, see the Kingsford edition of Stow on *British History Online*, www.british-history.ac.uk/source.aspx?pubid=593

19. Ibid., 2.199.

20. Ibid., 1.84–5.

21. Patrick Collinson, 'John Stow and Nostalgic Antiquarianism', in J. F. Merritt (ed.), *Imagining Early Modern London: Perceptions and Portrayals of the City from Stow to Strype, 1596–1720* (Cambridge: Cambridge University Press, 2001), 27.
22. Stow, *Survey of London*, 2.202.
23. Ibid., 2.214.
24. Lawrence Manley, *Literature and Culture in Early Modern London* (Cambridge: Cambridge University Press, 1995), 127.
25. Jean Howard, *Theatre of a City: The Places of London Comedy, 1598–1642* (Philadelphia: University of Pennsylvania Press, 2007), 13.
26. Ibid., 59.
27. Thomas Dekker and John Webster, *Westward Hoe* (London, 1607), *Early English Books Online*, http://gateway.proquest.com/openurl?ctx_ver=Z39.88–2003&res_id=xri:eebo&rft_id=xri:eebo:citation:99845201
28. Thomas Middleton, *A Chaste Maid in Cheapside*, ed. Linda Woodbridge, in Gary Taylor and John Lavagnino (eds), *Thomas Middleton: The Collected Works* (Oxford: Clarendon, 2007).
29. Paul Slack, *The Impact of Plague in Tudor and Stuart England* (London: Routledge and Kegan Paul, 1985), 213–15.
30. Thomas Dekker, *The Wonderfull Yeare*, in F. P. Wilson (ed.), *The Plague Pamphlets of Thomas Dekker* (Oxford: Clarendon, 1925), 27.
31. Michel Foucault, *Discipline and Punish*, trans. A. Sheridan (New York: Random House, 1977), 198.
32. Ibid., 197.
33. Slack, *The Impact of Plague*, 256–66.
34. Qtd in Gurr, *The Shakespearean Stage, 1574–1642*, 155.
35. Slack, *The Impact of Plague*, 230.
36. Robert Lerner, 'The Black Death and Western Eschatological Mentalities', *American Historical Review* 86.3 (1981), 551.
37. John Donne, 'After Our Dispersion, by the Sickness', in Lawrence Manly (ed.), *London in the Age of Shakespeare* (London: Pennsylvania State University Press, 1986), 115.
38. Cheryl Lynn Ross, 'The Plague of *The Alchemist*', *Renaissance Quarterly* 41.3 (1988), 443.
39. Alan Dessen, '*The Alchemist*: Jonson's "Estates" Play', *Renaissance Drama* 7 (1964), 49.
40. Dekker, *Wonderfull Yeare*, 37.
41. Jonathan Haynes, 'Representing the Underworld: *The Alchemist*', *Studies in Philology* 86.1 (1989), 35–6.
42. Ian Donaldson, *Jonson's Magic Houses: Essays in Interpretation* (Oxford: Clarendon Press, 1997), 77.

43. James Mardock, *Our Scene Is London: Ben Jonson's City and the Space of the Author* (New York and London: Routledge, 2008), 90.

44. See also Helen Ostovich (ed.), 'General Introduction: *The Alchemist*', in *Ben Jonson: Four Comedies* (New York: Longman, 997), 40–2.

45. R. L. Smallwood, '"Here in the Friars": Immediacy and Theatricality in *The Alchemist*', *Review of English Studies*, n.s. 32 (1980), 147.

5: New Directions: Staging Gender

1. Douglas Lanier, 'Masculine Silence: *Epicoene* and Jonsonian Stylistics', *College Literature* 21.2 (1994), 1.

2. Epigram 65: 'To My Muse', *Epigrams*, ed. Colin Burrow, in *CWBJ*, vol. 5, line 14.

3. Don E. Wayne, 'Drama and Society in the Age of Jonson: An Alternative View', *Renaissance Drama* 13 (1982), 107.

4. James Loxley, *The Complete Critical Guide to Ben Jonson* (London: Routledge, 2002), 164–5.

5. Ibid., 165.

6. Lanier, 'Masculine Silence', 3.

7. For an entertaining tour of Jonson's 'mental geography' which stresses the importance of male competition, see Ronald Huebert, 'A Shrew Yet Honest: Manliness in Jonson', *Renaissance Drama* 15 (1984), 31–68.

8. Sara van den Berg, 'True Relation: The Life and Career of Ben Jonson', in Richard Harp and Stanley Stewart (eds), *The Cambridge Companion to Ben Jonson* (Cambridge: Cambridge University Press, 2000), 3.

9. Mathew Martin, 'Wasting Time in Ben Jonson's *Epicoene*', *Studies in Philology* 105 (2008), 83, 87.

10. *Volpone*, ed. Richard Dutton, in *CWBJ*, vol. 3, Epistle.15–17.

11. See also Ben Jonson, *The Alchemist*, ed. Elizabeth Cook (London: A & C Black, 1991), for a similar but more inclusive note on sexual equivocation.

12. Ian McAdam, 'The Repudiation of the Marvelous: Jonson's *The Alchemist* and the Limits of Satire', *Quidditas* 21 (2000), 66.

13. The Austrian royal family, the Hapsburgs, were noted for protruding jaws and hanging lips.

14. Whether Jonson regarded all alchemical endeavour as the equivalent of the confidence games practised by Subtle, Doll and Face has been the subject of some critical debate. See 'Repudiation of the Marvelous', 59–61, for a brief overview.

15. John S. Mebane, *Renaissance Magic and the Return of the Golden Age* (Lincoln: University of Nebraska Press, 1989), 140.

16. Robert M. Schuler, 'Jonson's Alchemists, Epicures, and Puritans', *Medieval and Renaissance Drama in England* 2 (1985), 171.

17. For the cultural origins of the two images of Puritanism, see Kristen Poole, 'Saints Alive! Falstaff, Martin Marprelate, and the Staging of Puritanism', *Shakespeare Quarterly* 46 (1995), 47–75.

18. *Informations to William Drummond of Hawthornden*, ed. Ian Donaldson, in *CWBJ*, vol. 5, line 242. Robert Miola, 'Ben Jonson, Catholic Poet', *Renaissance and Reformation* 25 (2001), 103, sees 'mockery implicit in [this] gesture', and 'refractory' resistance to protestant doctrine whereas I see willing commitment, if also self-satirizing indulgence, in such celebratory 'reconciliation'. While I cannot presume she would agree with my suggestion of Jonson's renewed affinity for Protestantism, Julie Maxwell nevertheless makes a related observation concerning 'Jonson's self-irony: his comic ability to treat even his most intense personal experiences (in this case religious ones) with amused, intelligent detachment'; see 'Religion' in *Ben Jonson in Context*, ed. Julie Sanders (Cambridge: Cambridge University Press, 2010), 231.

19. In a recent study of Marlowe's radical politics, Patrick Cheney observes, 'Perhaps we are so used to thinking of Marlowe as struggling amidst the English Reformation, with its deadly opposition of Protestant and Catholic alike, that we sometimes forget the political form that the Reformation took. Not just in Italy but all around Europe the conflict emerged between a Catholic monarchy and a Protestant republic'; see *Marlowe's Republican Authorship: Lucan, Liberty, and the Sublime* (Basingstoke: Palgrave Macmillan, 2009), 28.

20. Cook (ed.), *The Alchemist*, 44, n. [2.2.]97–9.

21. For a treatment of the parallels between alchemical and apocalyptic writings in the early seventeenth century, see Richard Harp, 'Ben Jonson's Comic Apocalypse', *Cithara* 43 (1994), 34–43.

22. But see Julie Sanders (139–49) for a counter-argument.

23. McAdam, 'Repudiation of the Marvelous', 65.

24. Ibid., 71.

25. William Perkins, *A Discourse of the Damned Art of Witchcraft* (Cambridge: Cantrel Legge, 1608), 128; STC 19697; and Agrippa, *Three Books of Occult Philosophy*, trans. James Freake (St. Paul: Llewellyn, 1997), 123.

26. See, for example, 'A Womb of His Own: Male Renaissance Poets in the Female Body', chapter 6 in Katharine Eisaman Maus, *Inwardness and Theater in the English Renaissance* (Chicago: University of Chicago Press, 1995), 182–209.

27. Stanton J. Linden, *Darke Hierogliphicks: Alchemy in English Literature from Chaucer to the Restoration* (Lexington: University Press of Kentucky, 1996), 132.

28. Mathew Martin, 'Wasting Time in Ben Jonson's *Epicoene*', 83–4, 90. Martin's observations apply equally well to *The Alchemist*.

29. As Lanier observes, 'Jonson stresses that manly souls disdain representation, for their manliness in no way depends on any outward show of word or deed' ('Masculine Silence', 4).

30. Anne Barton, *Ben Jonson, Dramatist* (Cambridge: Cambridge University Press, 1984), 148.

31. Andrew Gurr provocatively suggests that Lovewit represents the 'landlords' of the Blackfriars Theatre, including Shakespeare, who take financial advantage of the players; see 'Who Is Lovewit? What Is He?' in Cave, Schafer and Woolland, *Ben Jonson and Theatre*, 5–19.

32. Jonson's dedication of *The Alchemist* to Lady Mary Wroth, which he writes in 'conscience of [her] virtue', appears to offer a parallel case within the life of the playwright.

33. Julie Sanders' metatheatrical argument below concerning the way identities are forged through such interaction – often specifically cross-gender in *The Alchemist* – is I think relevant here.

34. Ibid., 8.

35. The seminal article in this respect remains Robert Smallwood's '"Here in the Friars": Immediacy and Theatricality in *The Alchemist*', *Review of English Studies* 32 (1981), 142–60.

36. Fiona Shaw, 'Acting in the Swan', in J. R. Mulryne and Shewring (eds), *This Golden Round: The Royal Shakespeare Company at the Swan* (Stratford-upon-Avon; Mulryne and Shewring, 1989), 132–3.

37. William Shakespeare, *As You Like It*, ed. Alan Brissenden (Oxford: Oxford University Press, 1993), Epilogue.1–2.

38. Poem 2: 'To Penshurst', *The Forest*, in *CWBJ*, ed. Colin Burrow, vol. 5, lines 51–5.

39. Helen Ostovich notes this statistical fact about Pliant's part in the 'General Introduction' to her edition of the play in *Ben Jonson: Four Comedies* (London: Longman, 1997), 40.

40. Cf. Kate Chedgzoy, 'Households', in Julie Sanders (ed.), *Ben Jonson in Context* (Cambridge: Cambridge University Press, 2010), 254–62.

41. Gurr, 'Who is Lovewit?', 7.

42. Peter Holland, 'The Resources of Characterization in *Othello*', *Shakespeare Survey* 41 (1989), 119.

43. See, for example, Helen Ostovich, 'Patrons', in Julie Sanders (ed.), *Ben Jonson in Context* (Cambridge: Cambridge University Press, 2010), 296–302 and Clare McManus, *Women and the Renaissance Stage: Anna of Denmark and Theatrical Masquing in the Stuart Court (1590–1619)* (Manchester: Manchester University Press, 2002).

44. See Poem 28: 'A Sonnet, to the Noble Lady, the Lady Mary Wroth', *The Underwood*, ed. Colin Burrow, in *CWBJ*, vol. 5.

45. Ostovich, 'General Introduction', 37.

46. Simon Palfrey and Tiffany Stern, *Shakespeare in Parts* (Oxford: Oxford University Press, 2007).

47. Simon Palfrey, *Doing Shakespeare* (London: Arden/Thomson Learning, 2011), 10.

48. See also Ian Donaldson, 'Clockwork Comedy', in his *Jonson's Magic Houses: Essays in Interpretation* (Oxford: Clarendon, 1997), 89–105, on the clockwork precision of this play; and Julie Sanders, *Ben Jonson's Theatrical Republics* (Basingstoke: Macmillan, 1998), 78–9, on the 'double act' of Subtle and Face.

49. Palfrey, *Doing Shakespeare*, 135.

50. Ibid., 136.

51. Ostovich, 'General Introduction', 40.

6: New Directions: *The Alchemist* and the Lower Bodily Stratum

1. For a recent account of Ludlow's fart and its literary *Nachleben*, see Michelle O'Callaghan, 'Performing Politics: The Circulation of "The Parliament Fart"', *Huntington Library Quarterly* 69.1 (2006), 121–38.

2. Robert Bowyer, *The Parliamentary Diary of Robert Bowyer, 1606–1607* (New York: Octagon, 1971), 213 n. 1.

3. Ibid.

4. Gail Paster, *The Body Embarrassed: Drama and the Disciplines of Shame in Early Modern England* (Ithaca: Cornell University Press, 1993), 151.

5. William Shakespeare, *Troilus and Cressida*, ed. David Bevington (Walton-on-Thames: Arden, 1998), 5.11.47–8.

6. Juliet Fleming, *Graffiti and the Writing Arts of Early Modern England* (Philadelphia: University of Pennsylvania Press, 2001), 53–4.

7. Ibid., 54.

8. See Thomas Nashe, 'The Choise of Valentines', in H. R. Woudhuysen (ed.), *The Penguin Book of Renaissance Verse 1509–1659* (London: Penguin, 1992), 253–63.

9. For Jonson's reading and marginalia in general, see Robert Evans, *Habits of Mind: Evidence and Effects of Ben Jonson's Reading* (Lewisburg: Bucknell University Press, 1995). For the annotations to Martial, see David McPherson, 'Ben Jonson's Library and Marginalia: An Annotated Catalogue', *Studies in Philology* 71.5 (December 1974), 67–70; Bruce Thomas Boehrer, 'Renaissance Classicism and Roman Sexuality: Ben Jonson's Marginalia and the Trope

of *Os Impurum*, *International Journal of the Classical Tradition* 4.3 (Winter 1998), 364–80.

10. Amy Richlin, *The Garden of Priapus: Sexuality and Aggression in Roman Humor* (New York: Oxford University Press, 1992), 26.

11. Edmund Wilson, *The Triple Thinkers: Twelve Essays on Literary Subjects* (New York: Oxford University Press, 1948), 217.

12. Sigmund Freud, 'Character and Anal Erotism', in *The Standard Edition of the Complete Psychological Works of Sigmund Freud*, trans. James Strachey, 24 vols (London: Hogarth Press, 1959), 9.169–70.

13. Wilson, *The Triple Thinkers*, 215, 218–19, 228, 220–1.

14. Mikhail Bakhtin, *Rabelais and His World*, trans. Hélène Iswolsky (Bloomington: Indiana University Press, 1984), 10, 281, 353.

15. Ibid., 28–9.

16. See Anne Lake Prescott, *Imagining Rabelais in Renaissance England* (New Haven: Yale University Press, 1998), 116–28 and passim.

17. Peter Stallybrass and Allon White, *The Politics and Poetics of Transgression* (Ithaca: Cornell University Press, 1986).

18. Paster, *The Body Embarrassed*, 23–39, 143–62 and passim.

19. Bruce Thomas Boehrer, *The Fury of Men's Gullets: Ben Jonson and the Digestive Canal* (Philadelphia; University of Pennsylvania Press, 1997).

20. Jonathan Gil Harris, *Foreign Bodies and the Body Politic: Discourses of Social Pathology in Early Modern England* (Cambridge, UK: Cambridge University Press, 1998); *Sick Economies: Drama, Mercantilism, and Disease in Shakespeare's England* (Philadelphia: University of Pennsylvania Press, 2004).

21. Roger Finlay, *Population and Metropolis: The Demography of London 1580–1650* (Cambridge, UK: Cambridge University Press, 1981), 51, Table 3.1, gives the following estimates for London's population in the early modern period: c.50,000 in 1500, c.70,000 in 1550, c.200,000 in 1600, c.400,000 in 1650, c.575,000 in 1700. Roger Finlay and Beatrice Shearer suggest that the population was closer to 120,000 in 1550, 375,000 in 1650, and 490,000 in 1700; see 'Population Growth and Suburban Expansion', in A. L. Beier and Roger Finlay (eds), *London 1500–1700: The Making of the Metropolis* (London: Longman, 1986), Table 1, p. 39.

22. John Stow, *A Survey of London by John Stow, Reprinted from the Text of 1603*, ed. Charles Lethbridge Kingsford, 2 vols (Oxford: Clarendon, 1908), 1.19, 2.21, 2.52. For easy access, see the Kingsford edn of Stow on *British History Online*, www.british-history.ac.uk/source.aspx?pubid=593

23. Christopher Trent, *Greater London: Its Growth and Development Through Two Thousand Years* (London: Phoenix House, 1965), 83.

24. David Riggs, *Ben Jonson: A Life* (Cambridge, MA: Harvard University Press, 1989), 10.

25. Ibid., 10.
26. Nicholas Barton, *The Lost Rivers of London* (London: Leicester University Press, 1962), 29.
27. Epigram 133: 'On the Famous Voyage', *Epigrams*, ed. Colin Burrows, *CWBJ*, vol. 5, lines 124–6, 136–8.
28. William Slights, *Ben Jonson and the Art of Secrecy* (Toronto: University of Toronto Press, 1994), 114.
29. *Volpone*, ed. Richard Dutton, *CWBJ*, vol. 3, Epistle.111.
30. Ian Donaldson, *Jonson's Magic Houses: Essays in Interpretation* (Oxford: Clarendon: 1997), 62. See also Riggs, *Ben Jonson*, 191–2.
31. John Schofield, 'The Topography and Buildings of London, ca. 1600', in Lena Cowen Orlin (ed.), *Material London, ca. 1600* (Philadelphia: University of Pennsylvania Press, 2000), 300–1.
32. Stow, *Survey*, 1.18; Schofield, 'Topography and Buildings of London', 303.
33. For this project's history, see Robert Ward, *London's New River* (London: Historical Publications, 2003).
34. For Moryce's and Bulmar's water-works, see Stow 1.18. Jonson's great twentieth-century editors, C. H. Herford and Percy and Evelyn Simpson, identify the reference at *Alchemist* 3.5 with the New River project, while they associate the earlier water-works reference at 2.3 with Moryce's wheel and Bulmar's pump. See C. H. Herford and Percy and Evelyn Simpson (eds), *Ben Jonson*, 11 vols (Oxford: Clarendon, 1925–52), 10.70–1, n. 76 and 10.97, n. 124.
35. See, for example, Luc Ferry, *The New Ecological Order*, trans. Carol Volk (Chicago: University of Chicago Press, 1995), 76; Bruno Latour, *We Have Never Been Modern*, trans. Catherine Porter (Chicago: University of Chicago Press, 1993), 9.

7: New Directions: Waiting for the End? Alchemy and Apocalypse in *The Alchemist*

1. William Empson, 'Just a Smack at Auden', *Collected Poems* (London: Chatto & Windus, 1956), 62.
2. Ben Jonson, *The Workes* (London, 1616), 609. In her edition of the play, Helen Ostovich repeats this stage direction. See *Ben Jonson: Four Comedies* (London: Addison Wesley Longman, 1997), 1.1.116. All subsequent references to the play are to *CWBJ* (unless otherwise noted), and cited parenthetically.
3. Jonson, *Workes*, 659.
4. I regularly teach the play myself in a core paper for English and Theatre Studies majors.
5. Terence Hawkes, *Metaphor: The Critical Idiom* 25 (London: Routledge, 1989), 61.

6. Qtd in Stanton J. Linden, *Darke Hieroglyphicks: Alchemy in English Literature from Chaucer to the Restoration* (Lexington: University Press of Kentucky, 1996), 11.

7. *The Mirrour of Alchimie, Composed by the Famous Freyer, Roger Bacon* (London: 1597), A3r.

8. Stanton J. Linden, 'Introduction', *The Alchemy Reader from Hermes Trismegistus to Isaac Newton*, ed. Stanton J. Linden (Cambridge: Cambridge University Press, 2003), 7.

9. Keith Thomas, *Religion and the Decline of Magic: Studies in Popular Beliefs in Sixteenth and Seventeenth Century England* (London: Weidenfeld and Nicolson, 1971; reprint, 1997), 227.

10. For Dee's library and its influence, see William Sherman, *John Dee: The Politics of Reading and Writing in the English Renaissance* (Amherst: University of Massachusetts Press, 1995).

11. William Shakespeare, *The Tragedy of Hamlet, Prince of Denmark*, ed. Barbara A. Mowat and Paul Werstine (New York and London: Washington Square Press, 1992), 2.2.26.

12. C. G. Petter, 'Introduction', *Eastward Ho!*, ed. C.G. Petter (London: Ernest Benn, 1973), 3.

13. Stanton J. Linden, *Darke Hieroglyphicks*, passim; see especially chapter 5, '"Abstract Riddles of Our *Stone*": Ben Jonson and the Drama of Alchemy', 118–54.

14. See Charles B. Strozier and Michael Flynn (eds), *The Year 2000: Essays on the End* (New York: New York University Press, 1997), especially Sandra Schanzer, 'The Impending Computer Crisis of the Year 2000', 263–73.

15. For good summaries of the vast history of apocalyptic thought, see the first two sections of C. A. Patrides and Joseph Wittreich (eds), *The Apocalypse in English Renaissance Thought and Literature* (Ithaca, NY: Cornell University Press, 1984), 2–148. For a scathing account of the ongoing corrupting influence of apocalyptic and millennial thinking on global politics, see John Gray, *Black Mass: Apocalyptic Religion and the Death of Utopia* (London: Penguin, 2008).

16. See Norman Cohn, *Cosmos, Chaos, and the World to Come: The Ancient Roots of Apocalyptic Faith* (New Haven: Yale University Press, 1993).

17. John Foxe, *Actes and Monuments of Matters Most Speciall and Memorable, Happenyng in the Church* (London: John Day, 1583), t.p. The book was republished in 1732 as *The Book of Martyrs*, the title by which it is still colloquially known.

18. *The Book of Daniel and the Book of the Revelation of Jesus Christ, With Personal Commentary by Oral Roberts* (Tulsa, OK: Oral Roberts Evangelistic Association, 1968), 106. Hal Lindsey's *The Late Great Planet Earth*, first published in 1970, is a classic, best-selling application of Christian prophecy

to twentieth-century politics; Lindsey yokes the fate of contemporary Israel to the codes the book of Revelation provides.

19. *OED*, apocalypse, s.v. 2b.
20. Anne Barton, *The Names of Comedy* (Toronto: University of Toronto Press, 1990), 78–9.
21. Anne Barton, *Ben Jonson, Dramatist* (Cambridge: Cambridge University Press, 1984), 136–54.
22. Just so Midas:

> broke a twig
> From a low branch of oak. The leaves
> Turned to heavy gold as he stared at them
> . . .
> He picked up a stone and weighed it in his hand
> As it doubled its weight, then doubled it again,
> And became bright yellow
> . . .
> A ripe ear of corn
> Was crisp and dry and light as he plucked it
> But a heavy slug of gold, intricately braided
> As he rolled it between his palm.

Ted Hughes, *Tales from Ovid* (London: Faber & Faber, 1997), 202. Mammon alludes to the 'boon of Midas' (2.1.102), but shows no awareness of the warning against overwheening greed which Ovid's tale suggests.

23. 'Introduction', *Every Man Out of His Humour*, The Revels Plays (Manchester: Manchester University Press, 2001), 59.

8: Pedagogical Strategies and Web Resources

1. Despite the popularity of Shakespeare on film, films based on Jonson are few and far between. Perhaps the only example of *The Alchemist* on film is *Shooting Fish* (1997), described on IMDb: 'Two con artists' plans to steal enough for a house are twisted when a pretty girl enters the picture. Directed by Stefan Schwartz. Starring Dan Futterman, Stuart Townsend, Kate Beckinsale.' The film is amusing, but so loosely based on Jonson's play that it barely qualifies as a source. Acknowledgement lies in the name of the computer used for scamming their eager victims: 'Jonson'. Otherwise, the film is more romantic comedy than satiric comedy, and it has very little bite.

2. See Ostovich, '"Our sport shall be to take what they mistake": Classroom Performance and Learning', in Karen Bamford and Alexander Leggatt (eds), *Approaches to Teaching English Renaissance Drama* (New York: MLA, 2002), 87–94.

3. Diarmaid MacCulloch, Charlotte Methuen and Lucy Wooding, 'The Siege of Münster', Melvyn Bragg (interviewer), *In Our Time*, podcast audio, 5 November 2009, www.bbc.co.uk/programmes/b00nkqrv

4. Barbara Rosen includes a transcription of this story in *Witchcraft in England 1558–1618* (Amherst: University of Massachusetts Press, 1991), 213–18.

5. Ibid., 218.

6. 'History', Royal Exchange, www.theroyalexchange.co.uk

7. And see the note to this line.

8. Many of these accounts are accessible in PDF format from the Bryn College website.

9. Arthur Vincent, *Lives of Twelve Bad Women: Illustrations and Reviews of Feminine Turpitude Set Forth by Impartial Hands* (Boston: L. C. Page and Company, 1897), 54. Reprinted in pdf on the Bryn Mawr website.

10. 'Mary Frith Otherwise Moll Cutpurse, a Famous Master-Thief and an Ugly, Who Dressed Like a Man, and Died in 1663', in the *Ex-Classics's* version of the *Newgate Calendar* (www.exclassics.com/newgate/ng25.htm). This account of Moll is a transcribed open-access excerpt from the popular 'auto-biography' of Mary Frith: *The Life and Death of Mrs. Mary Frith Commonly Called Mal Cutpurse Exactly Collected and Now Published for the Delight and Recreation of All Merry Disposed Persons* (London, 1662). Students wishing to read and cite the text in its original context can find it on *EEBO*. A transcribed version is also available through *Literature Online* (*LION*).

11. www.nationalgallery.org.uk/paintings/adriaen-van-ostade-an-alchemist

SELECTED BIBLIOGRAPHY

Aaron, Melissa D., '"Beware at What Hands Thou Receiv'st Thy Commodity": *The Alchemist* and the King's Men Fleece the Customers, 1610', in Paul Menzer (ed.), *Inside Shakespeare: Essays on the Blackfriars Stage* (Selinsgrove, PA: Susquehanna University Press, 2006), 72–9.

Alwes, Derek B., 'Service as Mastery in *The Alchemist*', *Ben Jonson Journal* 17.1 (2010), 38–59.

Armstrong, William, 'Ben Jonson and Jacobean Stagecraft', in John Russell Brown and Bernard Harris (eds), *Jacobean Theatre*, Stratford-upon-Avon Studies 9 (London: Arnold, 1966), 43–61.

Barbour, Richmond, '"When I Acted Young Antinous": Boy Actors and the Erotics of Jonsonian Theater', *Publications of the Modern Language Association* 110.5 (1995), 1006–22.

Barish, Jonas, *Ben Jonson and the Language of Prose Comedy* (Cambridge, MA: Harvard University Press, 1960).

— 'Feasting and Judging in Jonsonian Comedy', *Renaissance Drama* n.s. 5 (1972), 3–35.

Barton, Anne, '*The Alchemist*', in *Ben Jonson: Dramatist* (Cambridge and New York: Cambridge University Press, 1984), 136–53.

Beaurline, L. A., 'Ben Jonson and the Illusion of Completeness', *Publications of the Modern Language Association* 84.1 (1969), 51–9.

— *Jonson and Elizabethan Comedy: Essays in Dramatic Rhetoric* (San Marino, CA: Huntington Library, 1978).

Beecher, Donald, 'Suspense Is Believing: The Reality of Ben Jonson's *The Alchemist*', *Theta* 8 (2009), 3–14, www.cesr.univ-tours.fr/Publications/Theta8

Bellanta, Melissa, 'The Larrikin Girl', *Journal of Australian Studies* 34.4 (2010), 499–512.

Bevington, David, 'The Major Comedies', in Richard Harp and Stanley Stewart (eds), *The Cambridge Companion to Ben Jonson* (Cambridge: Cambridge University Press, 2000), 72–89.

Blissett, William, 'The Venter Tripartite in *The Alchemist*', *Studies in English Literature* 8.2 (1968), 323–34.

Boehrer, Bruce Thomas, *The Fury of Men's Gullets: Ben Jonson and the Digestive Canal* (Philadelphia: University of Pennsylvania Press, 1997).

— 'Renaissance Classicism and Roman Sexuality: Ben Jonson's Marginalia and the Trope of *Os Impurum*', *International Journal of the Classical Tradition* 4.3 (1998), 364–80.

Boluk, Stephanie and Wylie Lenz, 'Infection, Media, and Capitalism: From Early Modern Plagues to Postmodern Zombies', *Journal for Early Modern Cultural Studies* 10.2 (June 2010), 126–47.

Bowers, Rick, *Radical Comedy in Early Modern England* (Aldershot: Ashgate, 2008).

Buccola, Regina, 'The Fairy Quean: Fairyland Meets the Fifth Monarchy in Ben Jonson's *The Alchemist*', in *Fairies, Fractious Women, and the Old Faith; Fairy Lore in Early Modern British Drama and Culture* (Selinsgrove, PA: Susquehanna University Press, 2006), 109–33.

Cave, Richard, *Ben Jonson* (Houndmills: Macmillan, 1991).

Cave, Richard, Elizabeth Schafer, and Brian Woolland (eds), *Ben Jonson and Theatre: Performance, Practice and Theory* (London: Routledge, 1999).

Craig, D. H. (ed.), *Ben Jonson: The Critical Heritage, 1599–1798* (London and New York: Routledge, 1990).

Crane, Mary Thomas, 'What Was Performance?' *Criticism: A Quarterly for Literature and the Arts* 43.2 (2001), 169–87.

Davies, Robertson, 'Ben Jonson and Alchemy', in B. A. W. Jackson (ed.), *Stratford Papers 1968–9* (Hamilton, ON: McMaster University Press, 1972), 40–60.

Dessen, Alan, '*The Alchemist*: Jonson's "Estates" Play', *Renaissance Drama* 7 (1964), 35–54.

— *Jonson's Moral Comedy* (Evanston, IL: Northwestern University Press, 1971).

Dick, Aliki Lafkidou, *Paedeia through Laughter: Jonson's Aristophanic Appeal to Human Intelligence*, Studies in English Literature 76 (The Hague: Mouton, 1974).

Donaldson, Ian, *Ben Jonson: A Life* (Oxford: Clarendon Press, 2012).

— *Jonson's Magic Houses: Essays in Interpretation* (Oxford: Oxford University Press, 1997).

— 'Language, Noise and Nonsense: *The Alchemist*', in Earl Miner (ed.), *Seventeenth-Century Imagery: Essays on Uses of Figurative Language from Donne to Farquhar* (Berkeley: University of California Press, 1971), 69–82.

Duncan, Douglas, *Ben Jonson and the Lucianic Tradition* (Cambridge and New York: Cambridge University Press, 1979).

Dutton, Richard, '*Volpone* and *The Alchemist*: A Comparison in Satiric Techniques', *Renaissance and Modern Studies* 18 (1974), 36–62.

Dynes, William R., 'The Trickster Figure in Jacobean City Comedy', *Studies in English Literature* 33.2 (1993), 365–84.

Eggert, Katherine, '*The Alchemist* and Science', in Garrett A. Sullivan, Patrick Cheney and Andrew Hadfield (eds), *Early Modern English Drama: A Critical Companion* (Oxford: Oxford University Press, 2006), 200–12.

Ellis, Anthony, *Old Age, Masculinity, and Early Modern Drama: Comic Elders on the Italian and Shakespearean Stage* (Aldershot: Ashgate, 2009).

— 'Senescence in Jonson's *Alchemist*: Magic, Mortality, and the Debasement of (the Golden) Age', *Ben Jonson Journal* 12 (2005), 23–44.

Empson, William, '*The Alchemist*', *Hudson Review* 22.4 (1969–70), 595–608.

Evans, Robert, *Habits of Mind: Evidence and Effects of Ben Jonson's Reading* (Lewisburg: Bucknell University Press, 1995).

Farrell, Mary, 'The Alchemy of Rabelais's Marrow Bone', *Modern Language Studies* 13.2 (1983), 97–104.

Flachmann, Michael, 'Ben Jonson and the Alchemy of Satire', *Studies in English Literature* 17.2 (1977), 259–80.

Gertmenian, Donald, 'Comic Experience in *Volpone* and *The Alchemist*', *Studies in English Literature* 17.2 (1977), 247–58.

Gibbons, Brian, *Jacobean City Comedy: A Study of Satiric Plays by Jonson, Marston, and Middleton* (Cambridge, MA: Harvard University Press, 1968).

Greene, Thomas M., 'Ben Jonson and the Centered Self', *Studies in English Literature* 10.2 (1970), 325–48.

Gurr, Andrew, 'Prologue: Who Is Lovewit: What Is He?', in Richard Cave, Elizabeth Schafer and Brian Woolland (eds), *Ben Jonson and Theatre: Performance, Practice, and Theory* (London and New York: Routledge, 1999), 5–19.

Harp, Richard, 'Ben Jonson's Comic Apocalypse', *Cithara* 34.1 (1994), 34–43.

Harris, Jonathan Gil, *Foreign Bodies and the Body Politic: Discourses of Social Pathology in Early Modern England* (Cambridge, UK: Cambridge University Press, 1998).

Harris, Jonathan Gil. *Sick Economies: Drama, Mercantilism, and Disease in Shakespeare's England* (Philadelphia: University of Pennsylvania Press, 2004).

Haynes, Jonathan, 'Representing the Underworld: *The Alchemist*', *Studies in Philology* 86.1 (1989), 18–41.

Hirsch, James (ed.), *New Perspectives on Ben Jonson* (Madison, NJ: Farleigh Dickinson University Press; London: Associated University Presses, 1997).

Hiscock, Andrew, *The Uses of This World: Thinking Space in Shakespeare, Marlowe, Cary and Jonson* (Cardiff: University of Wales Press, 2004).

Jackson, Gabriele Bernhard, *Vision and Judgment in Ben Jonson's Drama* (New Haven: Yale University Press, 1968).

Jensen, Ejner J., *Ben Jonson's Comedies on the Modern Stage* (Ann Arbor: UMI Research Press, 1985).

Johnston, Mark Albert. 'Prosthetic Absence in Ben Jonson's *Epicoene, The Alchemist*, and *Bartholomew Fair*', *English Literary Renaissance* 37.3 (2007), 401–28.

Jones, Myrddin, 'Sir Epicure Mammon: A Study in "Spiritual Fornication"', *Renaissance Quarterly* 22.3 (1969), 233–42.

Judd, Arnold, 'Lovewit's Triumph and Jonsonian Morality: A Reading of *The Alchemist*', *Criticism* 11.2 (1969), 151–66.

Kay, W. David, *Ben Jonson: A Literary Life* (Houndmills, Basingstoke: Macmillan; New York: St Martin's Press, 1995).

Kernan, Alvin, 'Alchemy and Acting: The Major Plays of Ben Jonson', *Studies in the Literary Imagination* 6.1 (1973), 1–22.

Knapp, Peggy A., 'The Work of Alchemy', *Journal of Medieval and Early Modern Studies* 30.3 (2000), 575–99.

Knights, L. C. 'Ben Jonson: Public Attitudes and Social Poetry', in William Blissett, Julian Patrick and R. W. Van Fossen (eds), *A Celebration of Ben Jonson* (Toronto: University of Toronto Press, 1973), 167–87.

— *Drama and Society in the Age of Jonson* (London: Chatto & Windus, 1937).

Knoll, Robert, *Ben Jonson's Plays: An Introduction* (Lincoln: University of Nebraska Press, 1964).

Knowles, James, 'Jonson's *Entertainment at Britain's Burse*', in Martin Butler (ed.), *Re-Presenting Ben Jonson: Text, History, Performance* (Houndmills, Basingstoke: Macmillan, 1999), 114–51.

Lanier, Douglas, 'Masculine Silence: *Epicoene* and Jonsonian Stylistics', *College Literature* 21.2 (1994), 1–18.

Levin, Richard, 'Another "Source" for *The Alchemist* and Another Look at Source Studies', *English Literary Renaissance* 28.2 (1998), 210–30.

— '"No Laughing Matter": Some New Readings of *The Alchemist*', *Studies in the Literary Imagination* 6.1 (1973), 85–99.

— 'Occult Interior Design in Jonson's Day and Ours, and a New Source for *The Alchemist*', *Research Opportunities in Renaissance Drama* 46 (2007), 116–18.

Linden, Stanton J., *Darke Hierogliphicks: Alchemy in English Literature from Chaucer to the Restoration* (Lexington: University Press of Kentucky, 1996).

Low, Jennifer A., *Manhood and the Duel: Masculinity in Early Modern Drama and Culture* (London: Palgrave Macmillan, 2003).

Loxley, James, *The Complete Critical Guide to Ben Jonson* (London: Routledge, 2002).

Lucking, David, 'Carrying Tempest in His Hand and Voice: The Figure of the Magician in Jonson and Shakespeare', *English Studies: A Journal of English Language and Literature* 85.4 (2004), 297–310.

McAdam, Ian, 'The Repudiation of the Marvelous: Jonson's *The Alchemist* and the Limits of Satire', *Quidditas* 21 (2000), 59–77.

McEvoy, Sean, *Ben Jonson, Renaissance Dramatist* (Edinburgh: Edinburgh University Press, 2008).

— 'Hieronimo's Old Cloak: Theatricality and Representation in Ben Jonson's Middle Comedies', *Ben Jonson Journal* 11 (2004), 67–87.

McIntosh, Shona, 'Space, Place and Transformation in *Eastward Ho!* and *The Alchemist*', in Joan Fitzpatrick and John Martin (eds), *The Idea of the City: Early-Modern, Modern and Post-Modern Locations and Communities* (Newcastle upon Tyne: Cambridge Scholars, 2009), 65–77.

McManus, Caroline, 'Queen Elizabeth, Dol Common, and the Performance of the Royal Maundy', *English Literary Renaissance* 32.2 (2002), 189–213.

Marcus, Leah S., *The Politics of Mirth: Jonson, Herrick, Milton, Marvell, and the Defense of Old Holiday Pastimes* (Chicago: University of Chicago Press, 1986).

Mardock, James, *Our Scene Is London: Ben Jonson's City and the Space of the Author* (London: Routledge, 2008).

Martin, Mathew, 'Play and Plague in Ben Jonson's *The Alchemist*', *English Studies in Canada* 26.4 (2000), 393–408.

Maus, Katharine Eisaman, *Ben Jonson and the Roman Frame of Mind* (Princeton: Princeton University Press, 1984).

Mebane, John S., *Renaissance Magic and the Return of the Golden Age* (Lincoln: University of Nebraska Press, 1989).

Meskill, Lynn S., 'Jonson and the Alchemical Economy of Desire: Creation, Defacement and Castration in *The Alchemist*', *Cahiers élisabéthains* 62 (2002), 47–63.

Miller, Anthony, 'Ben Jonson and "the Proper Passion of Mettalls"', in Andrew Lynch and Anne M. Scott (eds), *Renaissance Poetry and Drama in Context: Essays for Christopher Wortham* (Newcastle upon Tyne: Cambridge Scholars, 2008), 145–57.

Miola, Robert, 'Ben Jonson, Catholic Poet', *Renaissance and Reformation* 25.4 (2001), 101–15.

Oseman, Arlene, 'Going Round in Circles with Jonson and Shakespeare', *Shakespeare in Southern Africa: Journal of the Shakespeare Society of Southern Africa* 15 (2003), 71–82.

Ouellette, Anthony J., '*The Alchemist* and the Emerging Adult Private Playhouse', *Studies in English Literature, 1500–1900* 45.2 (2005), 375–99.

Partridge, Edward B., *The Broken Compass: A Study of the Major Comedies of Ben Jonson* (New York: Columbia University Press; London: Chatto & Windus, 1958).

Phillips, Patrick, '"You Need Not Fear the House": The Absence of Plague in *The Alchemist*', *Ben Jonson Journal* 13 (2006), 43–62.

Potter, Lois, 'How Quick Was a Quick Change? *The Alchemist* and Blackfriars Staging', in Peter Kanelos and Matt Kozusko (eds), *Thunder at a Playhouse: Essaying Shakespeare and the Early Modern Stage* (Selinsgrove, PA: Susquehanna University Press, 2010), 200–11.

— 'The Swan Song of the Stage Historian', in Martin Butler (ed.), *Re-Presenting Ben Jonson: Text, History, Performance* (Houndmills: Macmillan, 1999), 193–209.

Raza, Amra, 'Dynamic Linguistic and Artistic Patterns in Jonson's *The Alchemist*', *Journal of Research (Humanities)* 42–5 (2006), 37–70.

Rebhorn, Wayne, 'Jonson's "Jovy Boy": Lovewit and the Dupes in *The Alchemist*', *Journal of English and German Philology* 79.3 (1980), 355–75.

Riggs, David, *Ben Jonson: A Life* (Cambridge, MA: Harvard University Press, 1989).

Rivlin, Elizabeth, 'The Rogues' Paradox: Redefining Work in *The Alchemist*', in Natasha Korda and Michelle Dowd (eds), *Working Subjects in Early Modern Drama* (Aldershot: Ashgate, 2011), 115–30.

Ross, Cheryl Lynn, 'The Plague of *The Alchemist*', *Renaissance Quarterly* 41.3 (1988), 439–58.

Sanders, Julie (ed.), *Ben Jonson in Context* (Cambridge: Cambridge University Press, 2010).

—— *Ben Jonson's Theatrical Republics* (Houndmills: Macmillan; New York: St Martin's Press, 1998).

Sanders, Julie, Kate Chedgzoy and Susan Wiseman (eds), *Refashioning Ben Jonson: Gender, Politics, and the Jonsonian Canon* (Basingstoke: Palgrave Macmillan, 1998).

Schafer, Elizabeth, 'Troublesome Histories: Performance and Early Modern Drama', in Ton Hoenslaars (ed.), *The Cambridge Companion to Shakespeare and Contemporary Dramatists* (Cambridge: Cambridge University Press, 2012).

Schuler, Robert M., 'Jonson's Alchemists, Epicures, and Puritans', *Medieval and Renaissance Drama in England* 2 (1985), 171–208.

Shanahan, John, 'Ben Jonson's *Alchemist* and Early Modern Laboratory Space', *Journal for Early Modern Cultural Studies* 8.1 (2008), 35–66.

Shapiro, James, *Rival Playwrights: Marlowe, Jonson, Shakespeare* (New York: Columbia University Press, 1991).

Shargel, Raphael, 'The Devolution of *The Alchemist*: Garrick, Gentleman, and "Genteel Comedy"', *Restoration and 18th Century Theatre Research* 19.2 (2004), 1–21.

Slights, William, *Ben Jonson and the Art of Secrecy* (Toronto: University of Toronto Press, 1984).

Smallwood, R.L., '"Here, in the Friars": Immediacy and Theatricality in *The Alchemist*', *Review of English Studies* 32.126 (1981), 142–60.

Smith, Melissa, 'The Playhouse as Plaguehouse in Early Modern Revenge Tragedy', *Journal of the Washington Academy of Science* 89.1/2 (2003), 77–86.

South, Malcolm H., 'The "Vncleane Birds, in Seuenty-Seuen": *The Alchemist*', *Studies in English Literature* 13.2 (1973), 331–43.

Stallybrass, Peter, and Allon White, *The Politics and Poetics of Transgression* (Ithaca: Cornell University Press, 1986).

Sullivan, Ceri, *The Rhetoric of Credit: Merchants in Early Modern Writing* (Teaneck: Farleigh Dickinson University Press, 2002).

Sweeney, Gordon, *Jonson and the Psychology of Public Theatre* (Princeton: Princeton University Press, 1985).

Thayer, C. G., *Ben Jonson: Studies in the Plays* (Norman: University of Oklahoma Press, 1963).

Turner, Henry S., *The English Renaissance Stage: Geometry, Poetics, and the Practical Spatial Arts 1580–1630* (Oxford: Oxford University Press, 2006).

Williams, B., Jr, 'Thomas Rogers as Ben Jonson's Dapper', *Yearbook of English Studies* 2 (1972), 73–7.

Wilson, Eric, 'Abel Drugger's Sign and the Fetishes of Material Culture', in Carla Mazzio and Douglas Trevor (eds), *Historicism, Psychoanalysis, and Early Modern Culture* (New York: Routledge, 2000), 110–34.

INDEX